To Sue

Catherine Rayner is a nurse and former English lecturer.
She is a life member of the Brontë Society and has served on its Council of Trustees. She is actively involved with the Brontë Society and has a life-long interest in the lives and works of many Victorian authors.
Catherine lives and works in the East Riding of Yorkshire and has two children, five grandchildren and two great-grandchildren.
Her hobbies are reading and studying a wide range of subjects, including history, crime, archaeology, and child psychology. She enjoys swimming and walking, when able, and visiting sites and buildings of historic interest.
Catherine was involved for many years in the care of adults with both learning difficulties and mental health issues which has led her to further research in social psychology, addiction and emotional trauma.
Catherine has written two books about the Brontës and is currently writing a literary handbook for walkers on Haworth and its surrounds, in partnership with her brother.

Love + Best Wishes
Catherine
2018.

Dedication

This book is dedicated to children everywhere who can learn to appreciate the social environment in which the Brontë children grew up and the effect that it had on their short and dramatic lives.

By contrasting the childhood of the Brontës with those of present-day children, one can appreciate that although the times and circumstances are different, sibling love and rivalry remain constant.

To John, Helen, David, Bryan, Heather, Aysha, Jay, Sasha, Saskia, Rowan, Aya and Ilyas and with special thanks to Mel for all of his support.

Catherine Rayner

WILD IMAGININGS: A BRONTË CHILDHOOD

AUSTIN MACAULEY PUBLISHERS™
LONDON • CAMBRIDGE • NEW YORK • SHARJAH

Copyright © Catherine Rayner (2018)

The right of Catherine Rayner to be identified as author of this work has been asserted by her in accordance with section 77 and 78 of the Copyright, Designs and Patents Act 1988.

All rights reserved. No part of this publication may be reproduced, stored in a retrieval system, or transmitted in any form or by any means, electronic, mechanical, photocopying, recording, or otherwise, without the prior permission of the publishers.

Any person who commits any unauthorised act in relation to this publication may be liable to criminal prosecution and civil claims for damages.

A CIP catalogue record for this title is available from the British Library.

ISBN 9781786937773 (Paperback)
ISBN 9781786937780 (Hardback)
ISBN 9781786937797 (E-Book)

www.austinmacauley.com

First Published (2018)
Austin Macauley Publishers Ltd.
25 Canada Square
Canary Wharf
London
E14 5LQ

Acknowledgements

This book was written over a long period of time with the help of my family and encouragement from members of the Brontë Society and the Brontë Parsonage Staff.

It was informed by a wealth of information provided by the thousands of books and papers written by authors who have diligently examined the Brontë family and their lives and works in the social context of Victorian England and the Industrial Revolution.

We wish to acknowledge the help and kind permission of the Brontë Society in supplying photographs of the Brontë Sisters' home to be reproduced in this book.

Special thanks go to the members of my family who have encouraged and supported my writing over many years, especially, Mel, John, David, Heather and Aysha. Thanks are also due to Dr Patsy Stoneman, Mrs Sarah Fermi and the late Virginia Rushton, who all saw the early manuscript and offered advice and assistance.

The dialogue is my own but based on many recorded incidents as well as what and where, I believe, things may have taken place and how the children and adults would have spoken and behaved.

Chapter One
April 19th, 1820

A child's scream rang out into the night. It was loud and shrill; a scream of nightmare.

In her crumpled bed, five-year-old Elizabeth Brontë had fought her way through the suffocating sheets, faced with solid darkness she cried out in terror. Somewhere, hovering at the back of her mind was a fading dream involving a large black house. Feeling scared, the little girl screamed again. This time, the welcoming sound of running footsteps; the relief of candle light; and the soothing sound of her mother's voice turned the little girl's cries into a single sob.

'Elizabeth, Lizzy, darling, whatever is the matter?' her mother called in alarm, as she set down the candle and gathered the little girl into her safe and welcoming arms.

'What is it darling, what has frightened you?'

Elizabeth could not answer. She clung to her mother's neck and cried. Two heads rose up from the other side of the bed as her sisters, Maria and Charlotte, woke up and rubbed their eyes.

'What is the matter, Mama, why is Lizzy crying?' asked Maria, the eldest child.

'Tell her to stop it, Mama, she is keeping me awake' yawned Charlotte, as she snuggled back under the covers.

'Go back to sleep both of you,' whispered their Mama, 'it was just a bad dream, she is all right now.'

Elizabeth's sobs gradually settled as she was rocked to and fro and the nursemaid, Sarah, arrived to see what all the noise was about.

'She's been quiet all day, ma'am. The others say that she doesn't want to move to the new house. She's scared about living in a new place and wants to stay here where she knows everyone. Must say, I know how she feels, if you'll pardon me saying so.'

'No, I will not pardon you, Sarah, and especially not now, in front of the children,' Mrs Brontë replied in an angry whisper. 'Go back to bed and on your way, check that she hasn't woken the little ones.'

Mrs Brontë continued to rock her daughter and smooth her hair and murmur soft words. Elizabeth's little face was hot and wet; she was trembling. Her mother sighed and held her close. This move to a new place, called Haworth, eight miles away from their nice home in the small Yorkshire village of Thornton, had become a problem to her and she had her doubts about moving away from this friendly environment. She also knew that her elder children were feeling unsettled and bewildered. She had tried to pass on to them the enthusiasm that her husband, the Reverend Patrick Brontë, had about the move; and, had explained how it would mean a bigger house next door to the church, in a busy, expanding town where there would be lots to do and new and interesting people to meet. The new house had gardens for them to play in; but, most of all, Mr Brontë had been especially pleased that the house backed on to open heathland for miles to the west. There were hills, streams and rough farmland: all a huge natural playground for their young family of six children.

'You will be able to run around and have lots of adventures and learn about the flowers, insects and all the natural life of the area,' Papa had informed his children. 'It reminds me of the hills in Ireland where I grew up and all the wonderful times I spent with my siblings dashing around and playing in the fresh air. You will love it up there and it will keep you all well and happy.'

The eldest three girls: Maria, Elizabeth and Charlotte, had seemed taken with the idea at first, but as the day of the move drew nearer, they had all expressed worries about leaving their home. The three youngest, Patrick Branwell, known as Branwell, and the two babies, Emily and Anne, were too young to really understand what was happening. Oblivious of the imminent changes, two-year-old Branwell had been charging around the house all day. Excited and full of energy, he tried to help Papa load the two carts standing outside in the road and he generally got in everyone's way. In the morning there would only be the beds to load and they would be off on their journey.

Mrs Brontë rocked her daughter. She knew by the change in her breathing that the little girl had finally gone back to sleep. For a while, she reflected on the last few years that they had spent in this house. She had made some good friends, especially the Firths. Mr Firth and his daughter, Elizabeth, were godparents to little Lizzy. Then, there were the Morgans, and Mrs Brontë's own relatives, the Fennells, nearby. These were all good Christian people whose help and support had been invaluable to the Brontë family.

Mrs Brontë was aware that they had the respect and affection of the villagers in Thornton and Patrick was doing well in his ministry. However, their growing family had been a driving force in his decision to look for a larger parish where his salary would increase, and they would find a bigger house to accommodate them all.

Maria Brontë had been visiting relatives in Yorkshire, from her birthplace in Penzance, Cornwall, when she had met, and soon married, Patrick Brontë. After the birth of their eldest two girls, they had moved to Thornton, where the youngest four children had all been born. Knowing that her husband was ambitious and determined, she had expected that they would eventually move on to a bigger and better locality; but with six children all aged under seven-years-old, Maria was tired and her days were overrun with the needs of her growing brood. The appointment of a nursemaid, Sarah Garrs, and then her sister, Nancy, as housekeeper, had helped but had also incurred more expense.

Suddenly, Elizabeth stirred and half woke. A tired sob escaped, as she lifted her head, and looked up at her mother.

'You must go to sleep now, Elizabeth, we have a long journey over the top moor tomorrow and we must be ready to leave by seven o'clock in the morning. Papa wants you all out of your beds by five so that they can be taken down and stacked on the carts. Hush now, think of nice things. Imagine the moors and hills with miles of heather and waterfalls and birds and flowers, like the scene of Paradise in your picture book. It will be lovely, I promise.'

Tip-toeing back to her own bed, with the candle now just a mere stub, Mrs Brontë slid under the covers trying not to wake her husband; yet, he turned over and enquired what the matter was.

'Elizabeth was crying. She had a nightmare and seems very unsettled. We are doing the right thing aren't we, dear husband? This is all such an upheaval whilst the children are all so small.'

'Now, now, Maria, we have discussed this move many times,' replied Patrick, drawing his wife, who was now shivering with the cold, into his arms. 'It is the fact that the children are so young that makes it the right time to move on. It means a much bigger and better house, a larger income and a better standard of living. You will soon make friends and continue a social life befitting the parson's wife and the children will have new opportunities and miles of open space to play amongst. I have seen the heathland Maria. It stretches for miles behind the Parsonage. Why, if we had six lads, I would throw open the back door and let them loose every day! That is where children learn, amongst nature, just like I did in Ireland when I was a boy.'

'But, Patrick, moorland can be quite wild and dangerous and full of rough people and strange customs. We have five little girls and a young boy to protect.'

'People called us rough when we were young, when in fact we were honest and hardworking,' replied her husband. 'It was the poverty that marked us out and labelled us, Maria, we weren't alone in that. What made us different was the drive that my parents planted in us. My mother, Alice, was a match for anyone. She worked hard and she encouraged us all to do the same. You and I are intelligent people and we will foster that in our children. We will make them study. Education is the way to rise in the world. They will have access to all manner of books and learning. We will also allow them to appreciate science and the natural world. Nature will reveal to them a true understanding of the Lord. This is a marvellous opportunity and I am convinced that it is the way forward.'

Despite her husband's reassurance, Mrs Brontë felt that she must say one last thing.

'It's just that,' she paused, 'I cannot help thinking about what happened to the last parson they tried to appoint a few weeks ago, that poor Mr Redhead. They hounded him out of the church and the town. What if they decide that they don't want or like us, Patrick, what will happen to us then? We shall be homeless.'

'Now, Maria, be calm,' her husband soothed, 'I have explained to you that that was all about the trustees not being consulted about their new minister. It is all sorted out now and I have been chosen and appointed. You are worrying unnecessarily. Hush now, before we wake the baby and she wants another feed. You must get some sleep my dear we have an early start in a few hours' time.'

'If you are sure, Patrick? I will always be guided by you but I am tired and a little scared at the thought of meeting new people and starting all over again, with friends and acquaintances. I so want us all to be well and happy. I so hope that this move is the right thing for us all.'

Patrick held his wife closer and kissed the top of her head,

'I am right my dear, I am sure of it. The Lord will guide us. Trust me, all will be well.'

Chapter Two
April 20th, 1820

By morning the house and children were in chaos and it was nearly eight o'clock before everyone and everything was loaded on to the two flat carts, hired by Mr Brontë. The horses stamped and tossed their heads, impatient to be off as the children milled around, excited but nervous. Elizabeth seemed happy and her Mama could see that she had no recall of her disturbed sleep. Although cloudy with a strong breeze it was not raining so their journey would be dry, though long and uncomfortable.

Finally, the family, servants, goods and carts, set off. By taking roads, tracks and pathways they would cover a distance of around ten miles; a full day's travel in these times of poor highways and reliance on horse power. Friends and parishioners lined the road waving and shouting their goodbyes. Reverend Brontë had been their minister for nearly five years and they would miss his sensible, intelligent help and advice. He had cared well for his flock and they were sorry to see him go.

Mr Brontë, tall and elegant in his frock coat and black hat, nodded and raised his walking cane in acknowledgement as he strode in front of the first cart. It contained a myriad of household possessions, his wife and the three youngest children; Branwell, not yet three years old and the only boy, his quiet sister Emily, a twenty-month-old toddler, and the baby, Anne, barely twelve weeks old. Every so often, along the way,

Mr Brontë would lift Branwell down and let him walk for a short distance as the little boy chatted excitedly.

The journey would take them on the narrow road that led high over the hill tops, firstly through the village of Denholme, then climbing higher still up on to moorland before dropping down into Oxenhope. Coming down to the valley bottom, they would travel on the road above yet alongside the River Worth until finally making the long climb up to the top of Haworth via a very steep hill that could not be avoided.

Haworth was known as a village but was, in effect, a small town spread over a wide area that included smaller villages and outlying farms and moorland. It was at the centre of a thriving textile industry that had ten spinning mills in and around it, where worsted cloth was prepared for sale in the large neighbouring towns of Bradford, Leeds and Halifax. As well as textiles, there was farming and quarrying to occupy the local people. There was, however, little or no education and few organised leisure activities.

Around six thousand people lived and worked in and around Haworth in the 1820's. This wide and sprawling area of many acres was where Mr Brontë would be expected to offer help and religious instruction to all of its inhabitants. The working population laboured hard six or even seven days a week and were often too tired by Sunday to do much but attend their local churches or rest their weary bones. It was a difficult life and often a short one. Over the centuries these tough Yorkshire folk had learned to be independent and self-regulated. Mr Brontë had a very difficult job ahead of him.

'Are we there yet, Papa?' Branwell asked over and over again, each time they reached the brow of a hill, or passed a farmhouse or an inn. 'Is it much further, Papa? My legs are tired.'

Ruffling his son's shock of red hair, his father laughed and told him to march like a soldier and he would be able to walk a lot further.

In the second cart, sat the three eldest girls: Maria, the eldest child at six years old; Elizabeth, five, sat with Nancy on one side of the cart; and the nearly four-year-old, Charlotte, was squashed on to the bench opposite with Sarah and an assortment of chairs, beds and bedding.

'I am uncomfortable,' Charlotte wailed to anyone who would listen, 'Sarah, I cannot move and my arm has gone into pins and needles, and I feel sick. Can I walk for a while?' The little girl pulled at the strings of her bonnet and fiddled with her pinafore. She did not like the way that the cart rocked, it made her feel dizzy and sickly, but no one took any notice of her complaints.

Time and again, the procession had to stop to let the children exercise their legs and to re-arrange furniture which was in constant danger of falling off and breaking. For an hour they rested at a wayside inn at Leeming Wells, above Oxenhope, and had some bread and cheese and water and everyone used the privy. They were high above the valley and a strong wind blew in their faces as they resumed their journey.

For a while, the younger ones slept. Branwell, who had exchanged carts at every stop and then clambered over everyone, much to their discomfort, finally fell asleep in the lap of his favourite sister, Maria. However, after half an hour, Maria developed pins and needles. She attempted to carefully shake and bend her arm without waking her brother, and accidently gave Elizabeth a sharp blow on the side of her face. Elizabeth cried out in pain and shock as Charlotte announced, once more, that she still felt very sick.

'My tummy is bumping into my heart,' Charlotte declared with lips trembling and a face as white as chalk. Elizabeth's screams had become the focus of Sarah's attention and, unfortunately, had disturbed Branwell. The little boy woke up disorientated and with a stiff neck and his cries added to the general melee. As Sarah lent across to comfort Elizabeth, and calm Branwell, Charlotte vomited down the front of her cloak.

'Maria, stop swinging your arm,' demanded Sarah, 'Hush. Hush, Elizabeth, you are all right. Nancy, pass me a cloth so that I can clean Charlotte up, she has brought back all that good food we had at the inn. Really Charlotte, you should have said that you felt unwell. Branwell, sit still or you will fall out, you silly boy. Now be quiet and do as you are told, all of you.'

'Is there a problem, Miss Garrs?' The tall figure of Mr Brontë appeared at the side of the cart.

'Sorry, sir,' Sarah replied, 'It's just that it's a bit crowded with Branwell in as well, they are all getting fractious and Charlotte has been sick.'

'Pass Branwell to me, Nurse,' Mr Brontë instructed. 'We will be arriving within the hour and he can stay with me for the rest of the way. Let us arrive with some decorum, please! Soon be there girls,' he called to the children as he strode off carrying a wriggling Branwell under one arm.

Charlotte tried not to cry as Sarah roughly dabbed her cloak and wiped her mouth and berated her for not telling anyone that she felt ill. Charlotte could only sit in mournful silence wishing that she could go to the other cart to be with Mama and not sit here with the awful smell on her clothes and the continuing swaying. There would be no point in reminding Sarah that she had said that she felt ill, she would be told not to be cheeky and that children should be seen and not heard! It was all very unfair. Charlotte clung to the side of the cart and scowled at the landscape as she wondered how much longer this awful journey was going to take?

Rain clouds were blowing in from the west when they finally reached Haworth. The foot of a long cobbled lane rose up the side of a hill, where at the top, stood the Church of St Michael and All Angels and their new Parsonage home.

The horses had a rest and a drink from a water trough before taking the strain of the weighty carts and tackling the steep incline.

'Giddy up, giddy up,' called the carter. 'Whoa, steady, you daft beast! Take it slow, take it careful Jess. Mind now. Careful, careful, not so fast.' The cobbles were shiny and slippery causing the carts to lurch from side to side. Mr Brontë watched in alarm. He decided that everyone should disembark and walk up the hill, for their safety and to lighten the load for the horses.

In this manner, the Brontë family arrived in Haworth. Tired after their long journey, all slowly walking behind the carts and holding hands or being carried, they reached the second half of the rising lane as it bent from west to north. Mrs Brontë carried the baby whilst Mr Brontë swung Branwell on to his broad shoulders. Sarah and Nancy struggled to carry Emily between them as Maria, Elizabeth and Charlotte held hands and walked with their heads down.

Many of the local folk were on the lookout for a first glimpse of the new parson and his family and stood around chatting. Some shouted a welcome, most just stared at this queer procession climbing up their main thoroughfare. Large stone built houses lined either side of the rising street and people leaned out of windows, stood in doorways or followed them up the road. Dogs barked, the horses neighed and the church clock struck four. More and more people began to appear. By the time the little convoy reached the small square, at the top of the street, a crowd had gathered. Most faces were smiling, some scowling and a few staring suspiciously. One or two lent forward to shake their new parson's hand.

'Welcome t'Aworth,' a young man shouted.

'Good luck, you're reet welcome,' called another.

'See you i' church on t'Sunday, parson sir,' called a woman surrounded by a bevy of children.

'Ope you're better than last 'un,' came another shout from an upstairs window.

'What's tha'names lasses?' an old woman demanded of the girls. They were too shy to answer.

The Brontë children had been brought up listening to their father's strong Irish brogue and their mother's soft Cornish lilt. They spoke a rare mixture of the two with some Yorkshire dialect added but the people around them had a much stronger accent. Many of their words seemed to run together, be cut short or be missing altogether.

A sudden pat on her head, by a young man leaning on the side of the Black Bull public house, brought Maria to a halt.

The man swept down in a low bow and took his hat off to the three girls.

'Tis a pleasure to si thee, yun ladies.' He grinned. The girls just blushed and hurried after their Papa.

Chapter Three
April 1820,
The Brontë's New Home

The Parsonage had been vacant and silent for nearly a year when the Brontë family climbed up the steep main street of Haworth in April 1820. With its empty rooms and dark passageways, it waited for people to arrive who would push open its doors and brighten its cold interiors with warmth and laughter.

The Reverend James Charnock had died the previous May and his family had had to leave as was the church custom following the demise of the vicar. Mrs Charnock had left in great fear for her future and that of her husband's four surviving children, to whom she was stepmother. However, she had no choice but to go and no idea what fate would befall both her and the young children.

During the winter of 1819, when the house had stood empty, howling winds, rain and snow had blown down from Haworth moor; a land of sweeping hills and desolate valleys, rushing streams and rocky outcrops, which stretched from the back door of the house and spread many miles to the west. Heavy mists and a wet winter had caused damp to seep in between the doors and window frames. Driving rain and snow had fallen into the chimneys. Gradually, the rooms had become colder and colder with no fires, no furniture and no people to warm them.

Over the stone flagged floors, field mice, rats and little voles had scampered around in the dark. Large house spiders built silken webs between walls and ceilings, catching flies, wasps and midges. They entered the empty house through broken and cracked spaces in the brickwork or down the dark chimneys. A dead sparrow lay on the parlour floor and a heap of black soot filled the empty fireplace, mingled with wet leaves and decaying feathers brought down during winter storms. A layer of dust covered all the surfaces and the large folding shutters rattled over the window panes when strong wild winds swept down from the moors. Outside, at night, owls hooted from the chimney stack and small rodents ran to their deaths in the undergrowth. Weeds and tangled bushes spread over the gardens and dead leaves carpeted the ground before gently rotting into the earth.

The house stood silent, solid and brooding during sunny days. Windows and chimneys rattled and creaked on stormy nights as the wind moaned in the chimney stacks. The strong winds blew the knocker on the front door, rapping persistently, as if a frantic traveller was desperate to gain admittance.

Nevertheless, and despite the neglect of the past year, the Brontë family would be more comfortable than most people in the town once they had moved into this rather elegant Georgian house. In the Parsonage, they would have their own nine-roomed house, as well as a surrounding garden. In the back garden, they would have their own well and toilet facilities. This was exceptional in a village where many people lived in small cramped rooms, including attics and cellars. Often a number of families shared one house, one kitchen and one lavatory, or privy, between them. The communal water supply in the town, which was the only supply for the majority of the townsfolk, had to be pumped up from two wells which often dried up in the summer months, or froze in the winter.

Untreated water sometimes carried deadly diseases like cholera and typhoid, but in these early years of the 19th century this was not known. People carried on drinking infected water and sharing toilet facilities, with no idea that it could be the cause of their sickness or even their deaths.

Everyone watching that spring afternoon, when the family arrived, would have noted the tall and elegant Reverend Brontë. He strode in front of the little procession holding on to the lead horse, which was pulling the heaviest cart, with his small son perched on his shoulders. The strange looking, red haired little boy waved at them followed by the thin, white-faced mother and the brood of five small girls. They would have stared at the family's belongings; some people marvelling at their possessions, whilst others, disappointed at the amount and the quality, would gossip afterwards with their neighbours.

As the procession of people and carts reached the top of the street a group of three young men stepped forward.

'We've bin asked to 'elp you unload, sir,' said the first young man.

'Aye, sir,' said another.

'Mr Taylor, at Stanbury said to give an 'and then take 'osses and carts back, after like.'

'Thank you very much,' acknowledged Mr Brontë, 'Mr Taylor very kindly arranged the carts for me and said he would have someone meet us here. I am very grateful for your help.'

Soon, willing hands helped to manoeuvre the vehicles and their heavy loads around the tight bend at the top of the main street and left into a narrow lane. This narrow cobbled track ran beside the church and church tower, beside the graveyard and then on between the Parsonage on the left and a huge barn to the right, before petering out on to the open moorland.

Walking up this lane, the older children stared in wonder at their new home. It was so big. The girls shouted in surprise and pleasure as they entered through a side gate and ran through a garden. In front of them was a large square stone house; they climbed the shallow steps that led to the front door, where a large iron door knocker with a lion's head was mounted. Taking an iron key from his pocket, Mr Brontë unlocked the heavy oak door. Beckoning to his wife, he took her hand and they walked into their new home, closely followed by their children.

The house felt very cold and the children's footsteps echoed on the flag-stoned floors as they stared around them. Mrs Brontë opened a door on the left and walked into the empty parlour.

'Come quickly, Nancy,' she called, 'you must get some fires lit immediately, it is far too cold for the baby. Children, you may have a run around and explore for a while, and Sarah will get some food ready shortly. Papa will be helping with the furniture. Come now Sarah, the children are tired and hungry. We have an awful lot to do before it gets too dark.'

Mr Brontë opened a door to the right of the passageway to a small comfortable room that he immediately earmarked for his study. Pulling his wife into the room; the baby asleep in her arms, he hugged them both. 'We are home at last, dear wife. This is to be our abode for a very long time, God willing, and I shall do my best to make you all very happy here. Please put aside your fears. You will realise that what we discussed last night has arrived, we are here and it is a wonderful place and the townspeople all seem delighted to welcome us.'

Mrs Brontë blushed and smiled. 'Come now, Patrick, you need to unload the carts and I need to organise the children.'

'I know, I know, Maria, I just wanted a moment alone to tell you that I am so happy to be here and that it will be a new and exciting start for us all. I am sure that God has brought us here to do His work and that He has a plan set out for each and every one of us. I am sure that we will all come to love this place. You are glad to be here, aren't you?'

'It is certainly a grand house, Patrick, but I haven't had time to even look around yet. Be off with you and let me get to work!' she playfully pushed him away and began her own tour of the house.

It did seem much bigger than the one they had just left. Maria had, already, noted the front and side gardens as safe places for the children to play. Still carrying the sleeping baby, she climbed the stairs and stepped into one of the back bedrooms. Opening a shutter with her free hand she beheld a small hill at the back of the house and then a far vista of wild open land stretching as far as the eye could see. Behind her, the excited shouts and cries of her children as they ran through rooms and explored the gardens, made her smile. She looked down at the sleeping baby and kissed her. Perhaps Patrick's delight at their new home and his enthusiasm for this place would spread and her doubts and fears would disappear. She so wished it to be and closed her eyes to pray to the God she believed was watching over them all, to give her strength and courage.

Within an hour, Nancy had lit fires in every hearth in the house, having discovered the wood and peat kindly left by Mr Sugden, one of the churchwardens, outside the back door. Her efforts had been mainly rewarded with smoke and soot from the un-swept chimneys. Sarah let the youngsters run around whilst she unloaded food and pans from the cart and helped Nancy to get the fire going in the kitchen range. It was a while before they could get enough heat to boil some water in the huge copper kettle.

Nancy jumped as a strange man put his head round the kitchen door.

'Good evening, miss, names Paslaw, Stephen Paslaw, parish clerk. Is Mr Brontë around? I have some messages for him. I did knock but everyone seems to be busy.'

'Oh, yes,' stammered Nancy, 'we only arrived an hour ago. I think the master is putting beds together upstairs, I will take you up.'

Men were still carrying furniture into the house and the children were running from room to room, front garden to back garden, upstairs to downstairs, cellars to bedrooms, outside steps to inside staircases, generally getting in everyone's way. Mr Brontë, with the help of the hired men, unloaded all of their belongings into the various rooms and by seven o' clock the carts, men and horses were on their way back to Stanbury.

As the elder children explored the house and garden they discovered the house had a small back kitchen, or scullery, as well as a kitchen and this was where the laundry and heavy housework would take place. In the back garden was the earth toilet, which had two wooden seats, a large one for adults and a small one for children. They each climbed up to see how they felt until they had to rescue Branwell, who had sat on the larger one and almost toppled in. They gathered around the well and noted the bucket and rope which would allow the adults to drag water up from the water shelf thirty feet below ground. The well was fed by streams running through the moorland rock and peat behind the house; and, in those early years, it was clean and clear.

Everything to do with the house came from or around the moors; the stone from which it was built and the large, heavy flagstones for the floors and the roof, the water in the well, the peat that was burnt to make the fires and the wood that was used for the doors, shutters and window frames. Gardens surrounded the house and were bordered by a low stone wall that separated it from the church lane on one side, the moors at the back and the graveyard on the remaining two sides.

Having thoroughly examined the house and garden late on that first afternoon, Maria and Elizabeth settled on a little shelf half way up the stairs where their papa had already decided to install a grandfather clock, once he had the means to purchase one. They chatted excitedly about how big the house and garden seemed and whether there would now be enough room to have the pets that they longed to keep. These had been denied them in the confines of the Thornton home.

'If we could have pets here, what animals would you most like to keep, Elizabeth?' Maria asked.

'Cats,' replied Elizabeth, 'they are lovely and soft and feel furry and I like it when they purr and snuggle up and keep you warm. I should like to live here much more if I had a cat. What do you wish for Maria?'

'I should like a big dog,' stated Maria, 'and I would train it so that it bit Branwell when he was naughty.'

Branwell and Charlotte, chasing each other down the staircase, overheard and stopped to join in their sisters' conversation.

'Papa will buy me a pony now that we have a garden and when I am older I shall have a great big huge horse and none of you girls will be allowed to ride on it,' interrupted the little boy, scowling at his elder sisters.

'If we are allowed to keep animals,' said Charlotte, 'I think that I should like some ducks and some chickens, and then we will have some pets but also something to eat when we are hungry.'

'Yes, and a big goose,' piped up Branwell, 'because they are like guard dogs and they make a lot of noise if people try to get into your house, like burglars.'

'It's burglars, silly,' laughed Maria 'and no-one would dare to break into a Parsonage. We are all safe, Branwell. A goose would be good for eggs and perhaps for Christmas dinner.'

'Is it nearly Christmas now?' asked Branwell.

'No,' replied Elizabeth crossly, 'now go away you silly boy, I shall tell Papa not to let you have a pony until we have all our pets first.' Branwell laughed and after pulling Charlotte's hair, he toddled off down the stairs to the safety of his Mama.

Chapter Four
The First Night

By eight o' clock that night, an hour past the children's bed time, after a simple supper of bread and jam and milk warmed up with hot water added, Mr Brontë called everyone into the front parlour. The fire was now burning quite well and giving out some warmth. It was dark outside and, after lighting a candle, he closed the shutters over the windows. The glow of the fire light and the candle made the room feel warmer and cosier. The downstairs floors were of the same large grey flagstones, with no carpets or coverings. The table, with a heavy cloth, and six of their eight dining chairs had been put into this room, along with: a long low settle , a few books and a large peat scuttle that stood in the hearth. It was enough for them all to feel more at home and now their father spoke quietly and firmly to his wife, servants and young children.

'God has brought us to our new home and we must thank Him,' he said. 'We must pray that we all work hard in His service and that we look after our new home and each other. We are blessed to be here and we must all work together and do our best. By His mercy, this will be our home for a very long time and I trust we will be worthy of it and pray that we will prosper and do well. Amen.'

After the long, exciting and tiring day, all the children, apart from the baby, were ushered off to bed. Their Mama and Sarah helped them to wash their hands and faces with cold water from jugs in two of the three front bedrooms. Maria,

Elizabeth and Charlotte snuggled down together in a double bed covered with rough cotton sheets and knitted blankets. The small fire that had been lit earlier had died down to warm ashes. The cold air in the recently empty room was hard and icy; the children huddled together for warmth. There was no question of having a light as it was too dangerous and wasteful, to leave these young children with the comfort of candlelight.

In the smaller of the two back bedrooms, Emily and Branwell were tucked into a narrow single bed, with Branwell's head at one end and Emily's at the other. Their room looked out on to the moors and a strong wind was blowing against the window pane and rattling the shutters. The little ones wrapped their legs around each other for warmth and security.

With the shutters closed, the children lay in complete darkness waiting for sleep to overcome them. Emily and Branwell fell asleep almost before their mother had kissed them goodnight and left the room. The three elder girls giggled and chatted, squirming and wriggling for another half an hour whispering about their new home and what it was going to be like living in Haworth. Gradually, one by one, they fell asleep to dream of horses, carts, steep hills, dogs and cats.

Elizabeth awoke to the sound of the baby crying to be fed. She could hear the murmur of her mother's voice as she hushed the crying infant. The wind had got up and was blowing hard around the house and suddenly the church bell began to toll the hour. Three times it rang out into the darkness. Elizabeth wondered how they would all sleep with that noise every hour of the night.

Feeling the need for the lavatory, she sat up and gently moved the arms and legs of her two sleeping sisters and clambered over their warm bodies. The room was very cold and Elizabeth could see nothing. She went to the window and quietly edged open one of the shutters. In the sky, dark clouds were scudding past as they were pushed along by the wind. The moon, high in the sky behind the house, cast a shadow which put the front garden into inky darkness. There was just enough reflected light to make out the top of the church tower and the graveyard area beside the church.

Elizabeth did not like graveyards and she especially disliked them in the dark. The graveyard went around the side as well as the front of the house and around three sides of the church. There seemed to be a lot of headstones as Elizabeth peered through the window in anxious excitement to see if anyone was about. She could see only shadows and closed the shutter again. Then, left in the darkness, she couldn't find the chamber pot which should have been somewhere under the bed. Climbing on to the covers she shook the nearest child. 'Wake up, wake up, I'm scared and it's too dark in here,' she moaned.

Maria's voice suddenly rang out in the darkness. 'Lizzie, what is the matter? Get into bed you silly girl you will catch your death of cold. What are you doing out of bed?'

'I'm scared. I want to go back to our old house, I don't like it here,' cried the little girl. 'There are dead people outside in the garden.'

Her voice rose and her cries got louder and louder, Charlotte sat up and asked what was happening. Suddenly, Sarah appeared at the door with a candle in her hand.

'What's going on?' she called in a loud whisper. 'Don't wake the baby; the mistress has just put her back down in her cradle. Why are you crying, Elizabeth? We had all this last night. Be quiet and go back to sleep.'

'She is scared of the dark and she doesn't like being so close to the graveyard,' explained Maria. 'Don't worry, Sarah, I'll take care of her.'

Sometimes, Maria quite enjoyed being the eldest child and felt a responsibility for her siblings. She pulled Elizabeth gently back into bed and wrapped her arms around her, soothing the frightened little girl and stroking her hair in the same way that she had seen Mama do the night before.

'It will be fine in the morning, Lizbeth. Please don't be scared. Nothing can hurt you. Close your eyes and think of nice things. Did you see all those hills and fields at the back of the house? Papa said that we can go exploring soon and he thinks that there are lots of flowers on the moors and that there is a waterfall a few miles away. We could go and see it and I think that there will be lots of streams and little becks to explore. It will be lovely in the summer. It will be our playground and we shall have picnics and run about in the sunshine. Please stop crying you will love it here when you get used to it, we all will.'

Maria felt that she was trying to convince herself as much as her sister. Moving from Thornton was a big change and she had left behind some nice friends and a home and bedroom where she felt safe and comfortable. Everything here was strange and different. That bell was chiming again, the quarter hour, and it sounded so loud and so near. Elizabeth was right, the graveyard was very close to the house and it was very dark. The house was higher and set apart from the main part of the village; the highest and last house before the town gave out onto the open heath. The moors may be lovely in the summer and in the daylight; but, would they be very wild and dangerous, especially in bad weather and in the darkness? Maria thought and fretted, agonised and worried as she continued to stroke Elizabeth's hair and murmur reassurances. That was until Elizabeth gave a little shudder and a sudden warm, wet feeling spread from the sheet beneath them all, adding to Maria's discomfort.

Chapter Five
April 1820

The next day dawned with the children feeling strange to be waking up in their new house. Charlotte sat up in bed, remembering that today was her fourth birthday; she pushed her sleeping sisters awake.

'It's my birthday, look at me, I am four years old,' she cried happily.

Maria pulled her down and kissed her.

'Happy birthday, big girl, you are now old enough to tie your own boots, brush your own hair and, let me think, do all the chores so that your sisters don't have to do any housework.'

The girls laughed and tumbled around the bed, they sang little songs and shouted happy birthday to Charlotte. Once they had arrived downstairs for breakfast, Papa picked Charlotte up and kissed her shouting out many happy returns for the day and ruffling her hair with his long fingers.

'You are now four years old and it is time that you grew taller!' he remarked as he placed her back on her feet, 'Emily is catching you up!'

Charlotte's face fell at the thought that her height displeased her Papa, but he smiled when he saw her frown and added in a whisper in her ear, 'The best things come in small packages.'

The children spent the morning playing until Mama took them all into the old church. This building was the focus of their Papa's work and the place where they would all worship.

The children stared around them and whispered to each other as Mama, carrying Anne and holding Emily by the hand, led them through the south door into its dim and gloomy interior.

A church to St Michael and All Angels had stood on this spot for more than 500 years; although it was very dark and cold inside, the children were full of wonder as they studied the high-roofed building. The church was divided in to two halves with a row of six columns down the middle. Against the west wall stood the grey church tower which housed three bells and had a spiral staircase which one could only enter by a tiny outside door in the south wall.

Standing against the inside south wall, the tall pulpit dominated the interior. It was constructed on three levels and Mama explained that the parish clerk would sit at the bottom level and their Papa would be seated in the middle. He would then climb the stairs to the top part to deliver his sermons. Here, the people could clearly see and hear their minister, with the help of a large sounding board which helped to echo the sound of the parson's voice and carry it throughout the building.

'There is something written on that board at the very top,' cried Maria, 'Can I climb up and read it, Mama?'

'Alright, dear, but be careful, read it out loud so that we can all hear you. Be careful on the steps. Just you go and the rest of you wait here,' admonished Mama as she saw Elizabeth and Charlotte make to follow their sister.

They all stared upwards as Maria climbed the three sets of stairs until she seemed very high up. She was nervous as she looked down on them all, but, looking up she could clearly see the inscription and read it out in her best reading voice.

'I deter-mined not to know anything among you, save Jesus Christ, and Him cru-cified. One Cor twenty-two. For to me, to live is Christ and to die is gain,' Maria called down. 'Then it says a P and an H and a one and twenty-one. William Grimshaw A B Minister 1742.'

'Well done, Maria, now come down and I will explain the text to you all,' Mama called back.

'What does it mean, to die is gain, Mama?' asked Elizabeth as Maria arrived back beside them. Mama tried to explain that it was a direction to everyone that they should believe in God through Jesus Christ who had died on the cross to save their souls and not be tempted by false gods and bad people. To die in the love of Jesus was to leave this world for Paradise. Branwell and Emily were not sure what Mama meant and lost interest and wandered away.

'What are the letters and numbers, Mama?' asked Charlotte.

'They refer to the books of the Bible, from which the quotations have been taken. Cor is Corinthians and Ph is Philistines, the numbers are those of the chapters and verses. That is how you find your way around the Bible, children, it is all lettered and numbered so that as you read and learn it you can instantly find the parts that you need. The Bible is full of many stories about the times and the people who lived before and after Christ our Lord,' Mama explained. The older ones were now eager to explore and set off on their own to have a good look at everything.

In the semi-darkness they all examined the old tombstones which formed part of the stone floor and the church aisles. The elder girls tried to read out the words engraved on the flat tombstones, which were carved in old English script. Covering most of the floor stood a variety of box pews, made of sturdy oak, elm and mahogany woods. These were large and small wooden boxes with seats inside and a door. During the services, they housed many of the congregation and some had been owned and used by the same family for generations. Many had their names carved or burnt into the wood, sometimes including passages from the Bible. Families would huddle inside for warmth and many children had to be poked awake during long dreary sermons in the semi-darkness. Those who were not rich enough to own their own pew would be squashed in to general pew boxes or left standing in the aisles.

Further seating was arranged in wooden galleries, built up around three sides of the church, halfway up the walls and covering part of the windows. Large church candles and rush lights were fastened to various walls and pews, to give light during services; today, it all seemed very cold and unwelcoming to the children. The stone floor echoed their footsteps as they tried to move quietly and reverently around in the gloom.

Maria and Elizabeth walked hand in hand as young Emily toddled around after them. Maria lifted her up to one of the memorials and traced her fingers over the inscription; reading the words out slowly to the little girl and letting her repeat the letters. Unseen, Charlotte had clambered into the high pulpit and was peeking over the edge of the very top deck.

'Look at me,' the little girl suddenly shouted down, 'Look how high up I am. Come up, it's wonderful. You can see all over the church from up here.'

'Charlotte,' Mama's voice rang out, 'Come down at once. Remember where you are. I have not brought you here to play. This is a church. You are here to look around and see all the beautiful things placed in this building for us and the people of Haworth. You do not shout in church Charlotte, come down at once and show some respect.'

'Whereabouts will we sit, Mama, when we come here for the Sunday service?' asked Maria, aware that her Mama was cross but knowing that she could be side tracked with questions.

'On Sunday, for our first visit in front of the townspeople, Papa thinks it best for just you and Elizabeth to attend with me and Nancy. Sarah will stay at home and look after the little ones. Charlotte will come the following week and we will see how you all behave. I think our pew is that square one next to the altar, according to your Papa. It is quite small and some of you will have to sit with your backs to the pulpit and congregation which cannot be helped. You will be on show to the whole town. The church will probably be full as people will want to see and hear your Papa. It will be a test of how we conduct ourselves as a family and I shall expect absolute perfect behaviour and your best attention. It is of the utmost importance that you all show that you are humble, obedient and part of God's grace.'

'Of course, Mama,' replied Maria nudging Elizabeth.

'Of course, Mama,' Elizabeth echoed.

Suddenly the sounding of the church clock striking the half hour above their heads made them all jump.

'Now that is something else you will all have to get used to,' Mama tried to speak over the noise without appearing to be shouting. 'There is the clock and there are the bells. The bells strike to call people to service or to make announcements. Your Papa informs me that there are actually three bells and on Sundays they ring once for each day of the month. They ring a different sequence of notes for christenings, weddings and funerals, and you will soon get to know the different sounds.'

'They wake me up in the night,' complained Charlotte.

'Me too,' chorused the others.

'No,' explained Mama, 'that is the sound of the clock chiming. That works differently from the church bells. You will all get used to them and the different sounds they make. The time will come when you will not even notice them, they will be so familiar.'

Charlotte could not imagine being unaware of these great booming noises every quarter of an hour for the rest of her life, but she did not dare to contradict her mother, she was already in her bad books.

Chapter Six
A Walk Around the Church

After a while, the children gradually split up and wandered on their own, in and out of pews, around the six columns, up and down the aisles, behind the old stone font where babies were christened and into the tiny Lady-chapel. Maria stood on tip toe to try and see inside the font, but it was covered over by a heavy wooden lid. She questioned Mama about it and was told that it was an old myth, stretching back in time; that fonts should be covered and sealed when not in use so that the holy water could not be seen and drunk by the devil! Maria asked her mother about her own christening and why babies were christened and where the water came from and what did it all mean. Mama, as usual, was patient and informative and explained and answered all her questions.

'Is there really a devil, Mama?' The little girl asked her mother.

'There is one over there hiding in that box pew and his name is Patrick Branwell Brontë!' Mama laughed.

'Come out, Branwell, we can all see you,' called Maria, although she had no idea where Branwell was hidden. He came out of the nearest pew clutching half a candle and a dead flower that he had found under the seats.

'Really, Mama,' Maria persisted, 'Is there an actual devil that takes children and makes them bad?'

'Well,' replied Mrs Brontë, whispering as not to frighten the younger children who were milling around, 'there is certainly good and bad in the world and we know that there is a God, who is good, so we can only presume that there is a Devil who is evil.'

'Oh, I see,' cried Maria, in surprise, 'God and the Devil, good and evil.'

Elizabeth shot off to haul her brother out from another pew where he was scrabbling around under the dusty seats looking for treasure. She resisted slapping him when he whacked her across the leg with his fist. 'You are a naughty boy, Branwell,' she hissed. 'God will punish you one day. He sees what you do even if no one else does,' and with that, she pushed him roughly into the aisle.

Mama continued to explain as her children now gathered around her. 'It is like light and dark, happiness and sorrow, life and death. Our lives are full of opposites and contradictions. We should live in a way that creates as much light and goodness as possible and try to keep away from the bad and the darkness. Unfortunately, sometimes our actions and our lives are not always under our control and sometimes people stray from the straight and narrow way that leads us to God. This is why your Papa is here. It is his job to help people who have strayed to come back into the light and find their way back to God. One has to read one's Bible and study the ways of Jesus and learn how to be good. I think that is enough for you to understand Maria, you will learn more as you get older, life is not as simple and straightforward as that. As you grow, your Papa and I want you all to be good and follow the path of righteousness and not go down the road to sorrow and evil.'

Maria took her mother's hand. 'I will always try to be good Mama. I think I understand the difference between good and bad. I will really try my best but sometimes it seems very hard to get everything right.' Her mother smiled down at her eldest daughter and felt a rush of love and pride for this clever little girl.

'I am sure that you, all of you, will make us very proud. Are you glad that we have come to Haworth? Do you think we will all settle here, children?'

Maria smiled up at her Mama, 'I think perhaps it will be easier to settle in and to be good if we had a few pets, like perhaps a dog and a cat and some chickens…possibly?' Maria smiled her sweetest smile and looked up at her mother through huge round eyes. 'Yes, Mama, I am sure that that would make living here especially nice.'

The others laughed and clapped on hearing Maria's words.

Mama just twitched her nose and gave a little smile. Oh yes, Maria was certainly a very clever little girl!

Chapter Seven
The First Sunday

Maria and Elizabeth spent an agonising Sunday morning being examined and stared at by a church full of worshippers, as their Papa preached a long sermon on the parable of the Good Samaritan. In the west gallery, stood a collection of musicians who played various instruments to accompany the hymn singing. There wasn't an organ in the church and the players often drowned out the voices of the congregation. The girls hated being scrutinised by the townsfolk; but they enjoyed the service and were careful to be quiet, attentive and well behaved as they shook hands with some of the church members after the service. Papa was pleased with them and proud to show off his eldest girls to everyone. Eventually, leaving Papa to finish off his parish duties and Mama to talk to various people in the congregation, the two girls wandered out into the graveyard.

It was a large area, crammed with old and new tombstones. Some lay directly on to the ground, some stood upright and others were arranged like table tops on piles of stones. Many graves were unmarked by a stone and were just mounds of grass-covered earth, others had little posies of spring flowers left by relatives. It was, to the girls, a large but solemn playground full of interesting plants and wildlife, little pathways and long grasses or sprawling ivy. There were no trees and only the occasional small bush. The graves were all crammed together with hardly any room to walk between them. Several gravestones were adorned with carved stone effigies of angels, urns, scrolls and trumpets and each was engraved with names and dates; some as far back as the sixteen hundreds whilst others were within the last few months.

They found it a fascinating place. Mama had warned them on their first day at the Parsonage to not spend time in the graveyard and not to scramble over the graves. If they needed to enter the area they must step carefully between the stone monuments and show silent respect for those buried beneath.

Suddenly, they heard a sharp tapping and realised that a stonemason was close by inscribing one of the tombstones. They turned to watch him, chiselling and hammering and noted the cloud of dust rising into the air.

'Na' then,' he called across. 'You mun be t'new parson's lasses, eh?'

The girls looked at each other unsure what to do or how to reply. Maria was frantically trying to work out what the man had said in his unfamiliar dialect, and knowing that she must not be rude or bad mannered, thought it best to just give their names and be polite.

'We are the daughters of the new parson. I am Maria and this is my sister Elizabeth,' she announced, adding, 'We are very pleased to meet you.'

The man laughed at her formality and said, 'Well now, in that case, mi' name's Jonas Murgatroyd an' a farm out at Stanb'ry but a cover for t' sexton on a sunda' while 'es at t'church like, an' I mun 'appy to meet thee too.'

Elizabeth felt inclined to giggle, Maria pushed her and said, 'Come along, Elizabeth, we have to go now. Good-bye, Mr Murgatroyd, it was nice to have made your acquaintance.' The two girls walked off leaving the stonemason smiling and rubbing the back of his head. What a queer little pair they were!

The girls continued to pick their way amongst the graves trying to retrace their steps back to the church. A large upright tombstone barred their way and Maria leaned forward to read its inscription. Tracing her fingers over the lettering she read out loud the words carved into the cold slab. The names of eight children and their parents were listed and it made the girls stand in awe, their lips trembling, as Maria solemnly spoke all of their names.

'Hannah, Joseph, Elizabeth, William, Sarah, Mary, Joshua and the last one Elijah, all died in infancy. Children of Roger and Martha Robinson, deceased. 1778,' she read.

'What does deceased mean?' whispered Elizabeth.

'I think it is another word for dead,' replied her sister. 'Let's go and find Mama, I don't like standing here amongst all these dead people and their babies.'

Mama had been watching them from the church door as she exchanged pleasantries with the sexton's wife. She saw their solemn faces as they came towards her.

'Come children,' encouraged Mama holding out her arms to her two girls, 'what on earth are you doing amongst the graves?' She took hold of their hands and began to walk them up the little path that led through the graveyard and into their front garden.

'Do not fret yourselves girls, everyone is born to die. God has people of all ages in his Heaven. The people buried here will all be in Paradise now, far away from the sufferings of this world. There is no need to dwell in the graveyard when we have our new house and gardens. Come now, Nancy has gone on ahead to prepare luncheon. Let us see if Sarah has managed to spend the last two hours keeping the four little ones amused.'

Aware that the graveyard had upset her girls, and concerned that Elizabeth might have more disturbed nights, Mama suggested that the following day Sarah and Nancy should take the four eldest children out on to the moors for a little while. Fresh air, exercise and sunshine would restore the children and help them to settle in and enjoy their new surroundings.

Mrs Brontë was well aware of the delicate nature of her children, and the necessity to raise them as educated gentlefolk. The family was stationed above the poor and the working classes yet did not have the wealth and prosperity of the middle classes, at a time when income and status were most important in society. When she had married Patrick, she had been aware of his humble beginnings in Ireland and his long, hard fight for an education and his drive to be a preacher. She knew that marrying him would mean their lives would be a constant struggle to maintain their position and that the larger their family grew the less money there would be to keep up a reasonable standard of living. She worried that the children kept arriving; six in six years! The thought of any more worried her deeply.

Mrs Brontë ushered the girls into the house with these thoughts crowding her mind. She was aware that some families had twice and three times as many children as she and Patrick and although they were currently in a big house and had an income, more children would be a struggle for everyone. Hearing the baby crying in the parlour, she acknowledged that everything was in God's hands and she determined to try and think positively about the future.

Chapter Eight
April 1820

Over the first few days, a variety of people called at the Parsonage, some on church business; others brought little gifts and came to introduce themselves to the new family. The Brontë children, though very young, had been taught good manners and were well spoken. They shook hands and smiled politely to the new adults who visited and although no children came by, they had each other for company and games.

On the Monday following their first church service, when lessons, play and chores were over, Mrs Brontë allowed Sarah and Nancy to take the four eldest children out on to the heathland for a walk. She gave strict instructions not to go beyond the stone quarry, which stood on the hill about a quarter of a mile away from the back door. It was a cold day with a strong wind blowing from the west and the children were wrapped up warmly in shawls, cloaks and boots.

Sarah and Nancy also had to adapt to their new home. The sisters enjoyed being together and Sarah was happy to care for the children and enjoyed her role as nanny and part-time housekeeper. Nancy, however, sometimes felt overwhelmed with the amount of cooking and cleaning she had to do, but knew that Mr Brontë was a good and fair man. She was pleased to be able to work in such a pleasant household. That windy afternoon, as Sarah ushered the four children out of the back door, Nancy grabbed the parcel of bread and butter she had prepared for their picnic treat.

'I don't know if young Branwell will make it to the hill top,' Sarah called out over the wind, 'and I do not fancy carrying him.' Nancy looked at the little boy marching forward over the uneven path, his little legs tripping up where the long grasses poked through and the wind nearly blowing him over.

'The wind will be behind us coming back, it will blow him back down again,' she replied.

The girls laughed, linking arms they watched the children running forward and being buffeted by the strong gusts. Their small faces lit up with the delight of running free in the open air. Birds swooped and there was the sound of sheep in the distance. The clouds raced across the sky and the spring sunshine lit up the hillside.

'I like this place much better than Thornton,' said Sarah. 'It seems fresher and cleaner up here and it will be lovely in the summer when we have sorted the gardens out. Mrs Brontë says that we will grow all manner of our own fruit and vegetables. Perhaps, we shall have a few livestock or chickens. I think that she intends to ask the sexton's son, John Brown, to give a hand with the heavy work. He seems a nice young man. I saw him bringing you some potatoes yesterday. What did you think of him?'

Sarah took a side-ways glance at her sister to see whether she blushed, which she instantly did. 'Stop that right now, Sarah, you are always match-making. I am too busy for a young man and I am sure that I do not know what you are talking about.' Sarah just smiled and gripped her sister's arm tighter as a strong gust threatened to blow them over.

The children were slowly separated and scattered as the force of the wind buffeted their little bodies. 'Anyway,' shouted Nancy above the noise and wishing to change the subject, 'Maria and Elizabeth want some pets so don't be surprised if they ask us to approach Mrs Brontë on their behalf. It would be nice to have a dog or a couple of cats around the place, but I don't want any more work right now and they can leave lots of hair and dirt. I don't know if Mrs Brontë would approve, especially with a baby in the house. Perhaps when little Anne is older, do you think?'

'I think that you are trying to change the subject and you fancy the sexton's son,' laughed Sarah. 'Now come on, we had better catch up and gather these little scamps before they all blow away.'

The children were approaching the top of Penistone Hill and the higher they got the more they could see of the surrounding countryside. To the north, they could make out a track running parallel to them on the other side of a deep valley. A small hamlet of houses could be seen and a couple of farmhouses clung to the steep hillside. To the east, behind them they could just see the roof of their new home and the church tower nestled behind it. The town of Haworth was hidden from view and could only be discerned by the many wisps of smoke being lifted on the wind in long, dancing spirals. To the south, as they gained the top of the hill, lay an expanse of moorland with a church spire in the distance, about two miles away.

It was looking out over to the west, however, that brought them all to a standstill and made them stare in sheer wonder at the scene. For miles and miles, as far as the eye could see, there were hills and fields, bathed in sunlight. A number of farmhouses dotted the landscape and small groups of sheep and larger ones of cattle could be seen grazing on some of the land in the distance. The sky seemed to reach down and touch the earth where the hills rose into its bright blue atmosphere. Birds fluttered and tumbled in the wind and the sounds of water could be heard nearby. In the far distance, along some path hidden from view, a drover's cart and horse could be seen winding its way towards the far hills. The whole scene was one of natural beauty.

Maria looked around her and decided that they would come here as often as possible to run through the grasses and heather, splash in the streams and sit and listen to the sounds of the animals and the wind blowing across the wide open spaces. She thought of the tales of Adam and Eve and the Garden of Eden, this place was Paradise, Paradise on Earth.

The higher the little party walked, the stronger the wind blew, making a booming and whistling above and around their heads. 'It is too noisy,' shouted Sarah, 'let us go down towards the valley on the right and see if it is more sheltered.'

As they descended the valley side, Branwell called out. 'Is all that noise cannon fire, Sarah? Is it soldiers on the moors fighting battles. I would like to see the soldiers. Is it Napilions's men? Let us go and chase them.'

Sarah picked Branwell up and whirled him round. 'Your head is full of soldiers and battles little man. Whatever has your Papa been telling you? There are no soldiers up here Branwell and Napoleon is in exile on the island of Saint Helena.'

'How do you know that?' asked Nancy, looking at her sister in surprise. 'You know nothing about Napoleon Bonaparte.'

'Well, actually, I heard Mr Brontë explaining to Branwell about the Battle of Waterloo, although I don't think Branwell understood very much. He just likes to hear about soldiers and fighting. Waterloo is a village in Belgium and it was where the Duke of Wellington fought the French, led by Napoleon, and defeated them in a huge battle. Isn't that right Master Branwell?'

She spun Branwell around once more then stood him back on the ground.

'I want to be a soldier and fight at Waterloo against the France people!' shouted Branwell as he fell over from dizziness and the gusting wind.

'Come on children,' Sarah cried, 'I will race you all down the hillside.' With the wind whipping around their arms and legs, running, falling and rolling, they arrived breathless and happy in a heap beside a small beck.

'What a lovely place!' remarked Maria leaning over to dangle her hands in the cold, clear water.

'This is beautiful,' whispered Elizabeth kneeling down beside her sister. 'Look, Maria, there are little fishes and plants in the stream.'

'Be careful girls,' called Nancy, 'it's boggy in places. Come and look at these flowers Charlotte, there are some primroses between these two stones.'

The children spent an hour playing by the stream, chasing insects and watching the moorland birds. The loudest of the birds were the curlews, wheeling and calling above their heads. Meadow pipits and wheatears were also flying around or searching through the rough grass. High above them a couple of early swifts darted around trying to catch the flying insects. Sphagnum mosses and young heather made up much of the soft peaty ground beside the water.

Branwell and Sarah spent a happy hour lifting up various stones and watching the spiders, wood lice, ants and worms, slither and scurry away back into the dark earth.

Sitting on top of a huge block of millstone grit, they ate their picnic and drank water from the gushing stream.

'I like this place very much,' said Maria to anyone who was listening. 'We must come here again.'

'We have this entire moor on our doorstep,' replied Sarah. 'When you are all older, and can walk further, we shall probably explore the whole area and visit the farms and meet the farmers and their families and see all their animals. You are all very lucky to live here. Where Nancy and I used to live it was very grey and there were no fields or gardens. We hardly ever went out into the country and we had no picnics or days out, did we Nancy?'

Nancy shook her head as she gazed at the water tumbling along between the stones in the stream. 'You are certainly very lucky children,' she commented, 'Very lucky indeed.'

As the happy group returned to the Parsonage later that afternoon, the tired children and their guardians were met by Mr Brontë who was in the church lane to greet the small party holding hands with Emily, who had cried when she was deemed too young to accompany them.

'Well, my dears, you look very happy and well. Did you enjoy your little walk?' Handing Emily over to Sarah, he swung Branwell up on to his shoulders and the little boy laughed.

'Have you been a good boy and looked after all these young ladies, Branwell?' Papa enquired.

'Yes,' nodded Branwell, 'and I made sure that they came home safely Papa, but I did hurt my leg, look!' Papa examined the little leg thrust out beside his face, which revealed a long raised scarlet scratch all the way down one side.

'I see,' his father said gravely, as he gently ran his figure along the jagged line. 'Was this wound made by a sword, a bayonet or a lance, Branwell? Did you win the fight and protect your sisters? Or did the soldier get away to fight another day?'

'Oh, I won,' replied his son, proudly, 'I fought all the bad soldiers and won the war, Papa. All the bad people have gone now, we heard their cannons, didn't we Sarah? I saw lots of them coming to attack.' The little boys face was red and his eyes wide with excitement as his Papa continued the fantasy.

'Were they Wellington's men or Napoleon's, Branwell?'

Branwell though for a moment and tried to remember what Papa had told him about The Duke of Wellington and what Sarah had said earlier. This Duke was his Papa's hero and was British, so the Emperor Napoleon must be the French leader who he had beaten in battle.

'Napilion's, Papa, that is why I fought them and scared them away.'

'Well done, my boy,' Papa exclaimed looking again at the red mark on his son's leg. 'All soldiers get battle scars Branwell, I think that this is just the first of many.'

His father laughed as they made their way back into the Parsonage, where Mama was seated with the baby, waiting to hear all about their afternoon's adventure.

Chapter Nine
April 1820

That night, after the children were all in bed, Mr Brontë took his wife's hand and sat her down beside him on the upholstered settle in the parlour. Anne was asleep in her cradle beside the fireplace and the house was quiet.

'I feel certain, Maria, that we have made the right decision,' he whispered to his wife. 'It was such a pleasure for me to see the children appear over the crest of the hill and come running down to the lane today after their afternoon walk. They were excited and full of life, happy and exhilarated with what they had seen. It is a beautiful area. We are very lucky to be here and we must thank God for bringing us to this special place.'

'I want to agree with you, Patrick. I am trying very hard to be positive,' his wife replied, conscious of how happy Patrick was to be here and how she had resolved to help ensure that they all prospered. 'It is just that we are somewhat isolated from the town with very little shelter from the elements. What will it be like here in the winter when the storms come rushing over the moors? Will we be able to keep warm and sheltered, Patrick? I am a little concerned. There seem to be no schools nearby and not even a Sunday school. Our children are bright and intelligent and we must make sure that they get a good education, especially Branwell.'

Patrick turned to her in surprise, his face clouding over as a stern scowl crossed his handsome features. 'You forget, my dear, that I have a degree from the University of Cambridge. I am more than capable of teaching my own children!'

'Oh, please, Patrick, I meant no offence.' Maria hastened to say, noting the rising tone in her husband's voice and laying her hand on his arm, in an attempt to placate him.

'You are more than qualified to supervise their education and I will, of course, do my best to ensure that the girls are well taught in all household matters as well as the feminine and cultural side of their upbringing. I am only concerned that this is a large parish and you will be so busy with all your church duties, that you may not have a lot of spare time to attend to their studies.'

'My family are second only to my commitment to the Lord,' replied Patrick. 'I will not only find time for their education, I shall supervise it myself!'

He rose from his seat and stalked across to the fire.

'The elder girls will continue to learn to read and write with supervised lessons every morning and the afternoons will be devoted to exercise, nature and the arts. I envisage them all learning to read and understand some of the world's greatest literature; Shakespeare, Bunyan, Milton, Scott and Pope, Johnson and Robbie Burns. Also, they will read newspapers and journals as well as books on nature, geography, history and science. The Bible and prayer books will of course be their bread and butter. My children will study French and German. Branwell will learn Greek and Latin and study ancient history. They will all become proficient in music and drawing, they will know of famous people and events, both now and throughout history and they will learn to hold political views and argument. Through all this they will grow into responsible and independent adults with intelligence and wisdom. I am determined that they will all do well and that Branwell will, one day, be a son we can be proud of – a man who will go far and excel in all areas whilst pursuing a noble profession. Do not doubt me, Maria! The education of my children is paramount!'

Patrick scowled down at his wife and waited whilst the content and conviction of his words were absorbed and understood. Eventually he said in a calmer and quieter tone,

'I have always known and said to you that the way to excel is through education. Education is the keystone to success, to understanding and to happiness. It is only through education that man can rise above the animals. If I can climb from the poverty of my Irish birth and reach the hallowed halls of the University of Cambridge, joining the very college attended by the great William Wilberforce, what great things can my children achieve? I am most surprised, Maria, that you should think that I would not devote myself to the welfare of our children's minds and souls. It is my duty as a Christian and as their father. I am more than a little hurt that you would think otherwise.'

Knowing that she had wounded her husband, no matter how unintentionally, Maria dropped to her knees in front of him and catching hold of his hands she stared anxiously into his stern face.

'My dear, dear Patrick, how could you think such a thing of me? You are the wisest man I know and I never doubted that you would be our children's' guide and mentor. I meant only that I would not want you to become overburdened and that I wish to do all I can to assist you in all your cares and duties. The children will follow whatever lessons you choose for them, and I too will be guided by your superior knowledge and experience.'

Mrs Brontë had known this proud and sometimes stubborn man for over ten years and knew how best to bolster his ego and soothe his hurt pride. He was not a man to be crossed and even she had to be careful at times so as not to upset him.

'I am sure that between us we shall raise six beautiful and highly intelligent children, Patrick,' she concluded with her sweetest smile.

'Only six!' cried Patrick extricating his hands from her grasp and frowning down on his wife as he began to pace the room. After a few minutes he stopped and turned towards her.

Seeing her knelt on the floor, her eyes wet with tears and her face thin and pale he became suddenly aware of how tired she looked. Experiencing a sudden surge of love for her, and a need to protect this vulnerable woman whom he had coaxed into coming here, he knelt back down in front of her. Wanting to make amends for his outburst, he took her hands in his.

'I appreciate that you are tired my darling, this has been a very busy time for us both. I do understand that the children are young and trying at times. That will soon pass, and we have Sarah and Nancy now to help out. I realise that you have given me six healthy babies, Maria. However, in time I am sure that the good Lord will bless us with a few more, perhaps another boy or two, as companions for Branwell. That would be nice, wouldn't it?'

Maria stared at her husband then looked across at the sleeping child in her cradle and thought back to the six pregnancies, the six labours and the six births. She loved all of her children dearly; yet, right now, the thought of more was too much for her tired body and worried mind. The resolve and confidence she had felt only yesterday began to ebb away as she looked in to Patrick's eager face, full of hope and reassurance. She knew that whatever happened she would have very little say in her future. She made another attempt to mollify the determined man kneeling before her.

'For now, Patrick, let us just be happy with what we have. We have been very blessed to have our little family and you have the son you have always wanted. Be content, my dear husband, let us look to those children that we have rather than to what might be in the future.'

'Yes, well,' replied Patrick, 'I wasn't suggesting that we add to our little brood immediately. It is something that we should be prepared for.' He stood up and again began to wander around the room. 'We have this beautiful house, Maria, a mansion compared to my first childhood home in Ireland. Remember that I was born into what was a mere shack in comparison and the eldest of ten children. Admittedly, my father did well over the years and moved and prospered, but when I was only a boy, we had very little. What we did have were fields and streams and valleys, with mountains in the distance, as our playground. That is where my love of nature developed and where I came to understand the bounty of the Lord. It is what spurred me to study and what drove me on to better my prospects and to discover the world of science and literature as an expression of God's gifts. This is what I wish for our offspring'.

Stopping and standing over the fireplace, Patrick continued his discourse. 'Unfortunately, as a child, my freedom was a freedom blighted by poverty. Whilst we loved the landscape around us, the land around our cottage gave little in return for all our digging and planting. We lived on meagre vegetables with milk from an old cow and meat from an occasional slaughtered pig. Water and potatoes were our staple diet. It was a case of the survival of the fittest. I was a thin and wiry youngster, but lucky to have been the first born.'

Returning once more on to his knees before his wife, Patrick again took her hands and looked into her anxious face. 'Our children have so much more, Maria. I know that my income is not huge, but we will manage. We have God to guide and protect us. What my mother would make of this huge house, with its many rooms, its own well, its gardens and modern furniture! My, my, how I wish she could see how her eldest son has risen in the world.'

'I know, Patrick, I know that your mother did a remarkable job with her large family in such dire circumstances,' Maria replied. 'You have worked and prospered despite enormous disadvantages. I also know that more children may well come along but for now I would just like us to enjoy our new home with its extra space and gardens and the surrounding area. I just feel that we must be careful not to try to fill it up so that we lose all the advantages of having more space. In your role as pastor, you will need to entertain and to accommodate visitors, curates and people of business. We must also provide our children with a quiet area where they can study. Let us not be too hasty to increase our family. So many parents lose their children in infancy, we are very lucky to have six healthy children, let us be satisfied, Patrick, at least for now.'

Patrick shook his head, in a kindly and placating manner. 'I am, my dear, I am...for now! Come, it is time we got some rest, another busy day tomorrow. I have two sermons to compose, a church council meeting and many letters to write. I would also like to begin making enquiries about the facilities around Haworth. Parishioners are already complaining about poor living conditions in some areas, pressure on jobs due to the threat of new mechanised equipment and a general absence of education and occupation. You are right, my dear, my work here will be long and hard. However, with you by my side and our growing family to keep us young at heart, we shall all do very well, I am sure of it.'

Patrick stood up and gently lifted the cradle to take the sleeping baby up to their bedroom and held out his hand to his wife, who still knelt on the floor.

'I will just sit a moment Patrick, whilst the fire still has a bit of warmth, if you don't mind. I have a few things to sort out and I need to make a list for Nancy for the shopping. You go on up, I will follow shortly.'

With instructions to be no longer that fifteen minutes. Maria moved across to the dying fire and stared into its embers. It was early days she knew, and yet Patrick was right. The children had chatted about the moors and their walk right up until bed time. They did seem to be settling in rather well, perhaps because they were young and excited and had no worries.

Maria, on the other hand, felt weary and unsettled. The enormity of having six children on the stipend that Patrick was earning worried her, as did the fact that they would always be living in houses owned by the Church. The payment of Patrick's wages depended on the church trustees. It was a voluntary arrangement paid out of the income produced from the church lands in rents and produce. Out of this money the parson had to pay many expenses including, to his horror, repairs to the fabric of the church and the Parsonage. Although the post was for life, if and when Patrick died, his family would lose his income and they would lose their home. She fleetingly wondered how the wife and family of the last vicar were faring. She wondered where Mrs Charnock had found herself and her children and if they were managing. What ever would she do if she lost Patrick? They would be homeless, with no income and she would have six children to look after. The thought made her shudder and she realised how cold the room had become.

Maria knew that she loved Patrick with a deep and abiding love, but he was master of his household and could be a forceful and demanding man on occasion. She had heard, many times, the story of his rough and difficult upbringing in Ireland in a large family with little money and poor shelter. She knew how he had fought every step of the way to improve his status in life by studying hard to better himself and, with the help of his old schoolmaster, had eventually been rewarded for his efforts. That a child from a peasant Irish family should eventually gain a place at one of the most famous universities in England, if not the world, was testament to Patrick's fortitude and intelligence and she was enormously proud of him.

However, right now, Maria was tired and anxious and felt that a rest and a little peace would be nice. Perhaps she could suggest a short trip to see her family in Cornwall, taking the baby with her? Or, would Patrick think that she was running away; overwhelmed with the enormity of their new circumstances just when he needed her company and support? Her head swam with all the problems and questions as she wearily stirred the ashes in the grate. Eventually, as the glow faded and the room grew even colder and too dark to see, she dragged herself up to bed.

Even as she began to undress, little Anne began the snuffling, wriggling and whimpering that meant that she was waking up ready for her next feed. Lifting her youngest child into her arms, Maria hugged the warm damp baby to her breast and tried not to think about the prospect of more babies in a never ending round of pain and weariness.

Chapter Ten
1820–1821

Settling in to their new home had been noisy and fun for the young Brontë children, and the now crowded and busy Parsonage rang out with laughter and tears from morning until night. Their papa was caught up in the relentless demands of his important job; seeing to the church and social matters, visiting members of the large and busy parish of all ages and circumstances. Mr Brontë had no means of transport and had to walk many miles to offer advice and comfort.

The church ministers taught their parishioners a way of trying to understand and deal with the hardships of life; teaching them that however difficult their lives on Earth, if they believed in the Lord and followed His teaching, then one day they would enter an everlasting Heaven. For many, that day came sooner rather than later as the churchyard was filled with victims of childhood ailments like whooping cough and measles, for which there was no cure. People died in their dozens from cholera and typhoid, bronchitis and tuberculosis, accidents at work or fires and accidents in their homes. Some simply died from the effects of a poor diet and overwork.

With little knowledge of the cause and treatment of disease, every day it seemed that the passing bell rang out to announce another funeral. The chipping of the stonemason's tools and the scraping of the gravedigger's spade were a constant background noise in Haworth, especially to those at the Parsonage, living so close to the church and its graveyards.

Life at the Parsonage was organised and almost regimental to accommodate the growing children and busy adults. The younger children were cared for by Mama and Sarah who washed and fed, nursed and played with them. The older children had more freedom to play amongst themselves and usually had short lessons, where they continued learning to read and write in the mornings with more leisurely activities in the afternoons. Learning through play and interaction with each other was an important part of their development and included a lot of made-up games in the garden, the cellar or in their bedrooms. Hide and seek was a particular favourite. The girls also enjoyed gentle ball games and skipping whilst Branwell preferred to play at soldiers and battles.

Maria, Elizabeth and Charlotte loved to play together; pretending to be grown-ups and dressing up and playing with their few toys. Maria used their dolls as people around whom she could enact stories or create fantasies to amuse the younger ones. The children were happy in those first few months, gradually gaining skills and getting used to their environment. They soon forgot their old home and settled in to the Parsonage. They loved the moors and playing in the garden, they enjoyed sitting in the warm kitchen with the smell of baking and they enjoyed their lessons with the eagerness of quick and intelligent children. Maria's reading skills improved and she was soon able to read to the younger ones. She was like a little mother as she chased them, tickled them and made them all laugh. Her parents saw and treated her as the eldest and expected a very grown up and sensible girl who would take the lead when Mama was tired, and help to organise and amuse her five younger siblings. Maria never minded this role and the young ones loved her for it.

However, these months of carefree happiness came to a sudden and frightening end one cold day towards the end of January 1821. Maria walked into the parlour to fetch some crayons and found her Mama collapsed on the floor and the toddler, Emily, sitting crying by her side.

Maria rushed to fetch Papa. His study across the hallway was empty. Shouting for help she ran upstairs, bursting into the nursery where Sarah was rocking Anne to sleep.

'Sarah, come quickly, Mama is lying on the floor and she is very white and I cannot wake her up,' the girl cried as she rushed back down to the parlour.

'Go and fetch Mr Brontë, he is in the church vestry,' Sarah shouted as she ran down the stairs.

Elizabeth and Charlotte were in the hallway, disturbed by the commotion and anxious as to all the shouting and rushing around. Maria fled down the garden path, through the churchyard and flung herself into the vestry where her father was saying prayers following a small church meeting. He started in alarm as his eldest daughter suddenly appeared breathless and frightened.

'Come at once Papa, please hurry, Mama is ill,' the girl pleaded. Her father instantly slammed his prayer book shut and ran from the room.

Mr Brontë had felt for some time that his wife was unwell; she seemed tired and listless, sometimes holding her stomach or having difficulty walking and lifting up the children. Finding his wife stretched out on the parlour floor, white and moaning quietly with pain, his heart clenched in his chest. He had seen too much illness amongst his parishioners not to realise that his wife was gravely ill. He half dragged and half carried her up to their bedroom and, laying her gently on the bed, sent immediately for the doctor.

As Sarah gathered all the children into the parlour she tried to calm their fears and answer their anxious questions. She too had felt that Mrs Brontë had not seemed well or strong for some time. She had lately taken on a bigger share of the work. Nothing had been said and Sarah had resented it a little at first, but now her only feelings were of alarm and fear for Mrs Brontë's health. She gazed over the heads of the six small children and began to worry about what would happen if their mother did not recover.

The next days and weeks proved a dark and anxious time. By April, with their mother still very ill, all six children had succumbed to scarlet fever. As Sarah, Nancy, a hired nurse called Martha Wright and Mr Brontë all struggled to cope with the illness in the house, the situation became overwhelming. Patrick tried daily to fulfil all his church duties but was usually alone at night to care for his dear wife. In his deep anxiety, Patrick wrote to his sister-in-law for help. Eventually, to the relief of everyone, Mrs Brontë's sister Elizabeth Branwell, the children's aunt, arrived from Cornwall to help.

Chapter Eleven
The First Loss

The arrival of Aunt Branwell, as she was known, was a great comfort to everyone. The nurse, who was quite unpopular, was dismissed. It was a reassurance to Mrs Brontë to have her sister to take care of her and for Mr Brontë to know that his wife was in good hands when he was occupied with his church duties. The children all liked and responded well to their Aunt and were glad that this nice, but rather stern lady, had arrived to help to look after them.

One day, when Mrs Brontë was feeling a little better, she was able to sit up by the bedroom window. Wrapped in a green coverlet from the bed, she gazed out to where Maria and Elizabeth were passing a ball to each other. Loud running footsteps on the stairs caused her to look round.

Patrick burst into the room, his face full of smiles and with a general air of good health and good news.

'My darling wife,' he exclaimed. 'Look what I have received in the post today. It is my poem, *The Maid of Killarney*. It has been published in the Cottage Magazine and they have sent me a copy. Look how well it looks in print. Can you see it? Here look!'

Mrs Brontë took the magazine and read her husband's poem as he strutted around the bedroom beaming in delight. It wasn't the first time that Patrick had found his prose and poetry in print and he thoroughly enjoyed it. This was a nice story set to verse and, once again, Patrick had gained acknowledgement and credit for his writing abilities.

'You are such a clever man, Patrick,' she smiled at him. 'I am so very proud of you. I wish you had more time to write, perhaps venture to produce more poetry and religious tracts, a book even. You are so talented.'

Patrick smiled at his wife, happy to see her sitting up and pleased to hear her words of praise and encouragement. Patrick knew his writing was above average and felt that he had a gift for it. It was a great pleasure to see his words in print and it made him want to write more.

'I shall take it downstairs now to show the children. Would you like me to send your sister up with some food or are you alright for now? We just need you to recover and all will be well again, my dear.'

Giving his wife a quick kiss on the cheek, Patrick bounced out of the room calling out the children's names so that they could come and marvel at their Papa's achievement.

Patrick's pleasure and optimism were not to last. During the summer, the children slowly recovered from their illnesses but their nights were often disturbed by the low moans and cries of pain coming from their parents' bedroom. The days were long and anxious ones, where the six small children crept around on tip toe so as not to disturb their poor Mama, who was now permanently assigned to bed.

It was hard for the energetic children to stay quiet or to move around a house without making a noise, impossible even. Playing in the garden carried their innocent chatter up into the air and could be heard in the bedroom where their poor Mama lay sick with pain. It wasn't that she did not want to hear her children; it was the sound of their voices distressing her enormously as she wondered what would happen to her children if she did not survive this awful illness that was eating away at her insides.

This meant that the children were often sent away on to the moors, with Sarah or Nancy, to a place where they could be noisy and active without upsetting anyone. They could run and shout, laugh and cry, squabble and make up, like any normal youngsters. On wet and miserable days, they would often take themselves off into the cellar and play quiet games. There was enough room for skipping, ninepins and playing with their dolls. Maria could sit by the grate where enough light came through for her to read stories to everyone; or, better still she would make them up. Huddled in this gloomy, icy room, the children whispered amongst themselves, making up all sorts of games and fantasies until they became too cold to stay any longer and would burst into the kitchen for food and to get warm again.

By September, the whole household was aware that there was no hope for Mrs Brontë. Mr Brontë had handed over his parish duties to another vicar, Mr Anderton, who would see to all the parish business for him whilst Patrick and Aunt Branwell nursed Mrs Brontë day and night. Maria and Elizabeth were sent to stay with their godmother, Elizabeth Firth, back in Thornton; yet their anxiety and fear for their mother overwhelmed them and they wanted to go back home.

The dreadful day arrived on the 15th September. With her six children gathered, and her husband and sister by her side, Mrs Brontë finally died after months of suffering. Years later, when the children were older, the younger ones could remember little or nothing of their Mama. Charlotte could only recall her mother playing with Branwell one day in the parlour. Branwell and Anne had no memory of her, but Emily, who was three at the time, could recall the night before her mother's death, when she had been allowed into the bedroom, as they all were, to kiss her mother good-night.

One image of that awful night would remain with Emily. She had knelt beside the bed and seen the thin and wasted hand of her mother on the green coverlet reaching out to touch her. Burying her face into the cover Emily had felt the light pressure of her mother's fingers amongst the fair curls of her hair. Somehow, a broken fingernail had caught in the fine strands. As Emily had attempted to stand, her hair had pulled painfully and as she had twisted, the nail had become more entangled.

The pain was sharp and intense, which was probably why it had stayed in her memory.

Emily had not cried out. If her mother's hand had wrenched every hair from her head she would not have uttered a single sound. She had felt a terrible fear, a fear that she could not explain. She knew that Mama was very ill but Emily was a child who, at that tender age, knew nothing of death or what it meant. It was only as she grew older that Emily became aware that this was the last and only memory of her Mama that she had or would ever have. It was a memory that stayed with her, one that hurt and pained her to remember. Gradually the grief would subside but, as in all deaths, there would always remain in the background a silent anguish that would never go away.

The toddler, Anne, now eighteen months old, seemed unaffected by Mama's disappearance. She was aware that someone was missing but had seen little of her mother over the past six months. She continued to play, chatter and toddle around seemingly unaware of the effect this death was having on the rest of the family.

The older children, however, were heartbroken and fully aware that their mother was dead. With Patrick and Aunt Branwell utterly distraught, the children again huddled together for comfort as they wept day and night, calling for their dear Mama, unable to understand where she had gone or why she had left them.

Sarah and Nancy did their best to distract the little ones with walks, picnics, cuddles and treats; but the children remained tearful and quiet. It took an effort of will from Patrick to try and cope with the constant questions that his children asked. Where was Mama? Was she coming back? Where was she living now? Having lost one parent, the children were naturally fearful that they might lose another and took to following their father around like ducklings whenever he was home.

This both comforted and irritated Patrick, who needed their closeness but was worn down by his grief and the constant noise from their childish prattle. He wanted peace to mourn his wife, and for his God to give him the strength to carry on his work, both as a father and as a minister. There were times when his burden seemed too heavy and he prayed hard for the Lord to help him.

Sometimes, he wondered whether Maria would have lived if they had stayed in Thornton. where she had been well and happy. He cursed himself for his ambition to come here to better his prospects. Mostly, he wept alone but tried to remain strong amidst his deep sorrow. In his heart, he knew that he must provide for his children, to tend to their needs and nurture them just as he would have done if Maria had lived; but, for some time he had neither the strength nor the inclination. The servants and his sister-in-law saw to everything, his grief was overwhelming.

Chapter Twelve
Dec 1821 and Early 1822

Patrick Brontë's heartbreak and despair could not be allowed to continue for long. He had a parish to organise and a family to raise. He knew that he had to get back into his routines. His church and congregation needed him and so did his children. Patrick was a practical, hardworking man who had strong views and opinions and this fall into sentiment and grief could not be indulged.

After conducting a funeral one day, walking from the graveside, he paused by the same tombstone that his daughters had found on their arrival at Haworth. He read the long list of children's names and those of their unhappy parents. He thought of the young lady and her newly born baby, whom he had just buried, and the heartbroken husband currently knelt weeping over her grave. Grief and hardship were part of everyday life and for Patrick to lose his wife was no different from the lot of many of his parishioners. Many lost their partners and it was a rare family whose children all survived to adulthood. Patrick ran his hand over the gravestone and let out a long sigh. It might only be a couple of months since Maria's death, but he must move on. He must seek a solution.

A few days later, needing to conduct some business in Bradford, Patrick stayed with his friends the Firths at Kipping House, in Thornton. Here, he had lived with his family and he now worried that they should have remained. Elizabeth Firth had been a close friend to Mrs Brontë and showed Patrick affection and concern in his widowhood. Misunderstanding this warmth for something more meaningful, Patrick returned home and such was his state of mind, he saw a sudden and perfect answer to his dilemma. He would ask Elizabeth Firth to marry him. Her wealth, her regard for his children and her affection for him and his former wife, plus her gentle nature and educated mind, were exactly what was needed to restore him and his children and solve all their problems.

Therefore, one day barely two months after his wife's death, Mr Brontë sat down with Aunt Branwell and explained his thoughts and feelings.

'My children need a mother, Elizabeth. They are almost as lost and bereft as I am. They need routine and discipline back into their lives and I must provide it. I have thought a lot about the future and what would be best for all of us. I have decided to approach an old friend of mine to see if she will consider me as a husband and to be a mother to my children. She is a lady, and a wealthy one at that, and has all the intelligence and sensitivity of the fair sex. You will know and remember her, it is Elizabeth Firth. I intend to write to her very soon with my proposal. Meanwhile, I should be grateful if you would continue to stay and help me to take care of the children. The time is coming when they need to start their lessons in earnest and move on from this terrible event in their lives. Do you agree?'

Although rather shocked at Patrick's rather insensitive and sudden answer to his grief, Aunt Branwell understood that he needed a helpmate and the children needed a mother. It was not unusual for men to marry hastily after they had lost their wives, especially busy, important men like Mr Brontë, who had so much parish work and needed a companion to assist him. The children would benefit from a young step-mother who could supervise and play with them; someone who had compassion but also energy and motivation. There was no doubt that money would be needed, now and in the future, if all six children were to receive the education and refinements that their father wished them all to have. Perhaps Miss Firth would prove a very good choice and it would mean that, at last, Aunt Branwell could return home to the rest of her family.

It was agreed that Aunt Branwell would stay on in Haworth to help her brother-in-law until such time as he found a new wife. She would then return to Penzance and continue the life that she had left behind; a prospect that she was greatly looking forward to.

However, when Mr Brontë tried to propose to Elizabeth Firth, he received a very stern refusal. The young lady had been a firm young friend to Mrs Brontë, and had admired and respected Patrick, to whom she had turned during her father's last illness and death. She was godmother to two of his daughters, but friendship and marriage were two very different issues. Miss Firth was appalled at the thought of marriage to Patrick or the prospect of raising his children. She had a refined and wealthy life in Thornton and had no intention of throwing herself away on this poor parson, who was almost twice her age, despite their past, close friendship. Angry at his audacity and his assumption that she would consider him as her husband, she refused to have anything to do with him or her god-daughters for the next two years.

With little realisation that he was not an attractive proposition to young ladies as he had perhaps presumed, Mr Brontë tried for the next two years to gain a new wife. He proposed to the daughter of a clergyman friend and also to Mary Burder, a lady friend to whom he had been engaged some fifteen years previously. Both ladies were horrified to receive a marriage offer from Patrick, now in his late forties, and with little money. The thought of having to mother to his six young children was extremely distasteful to them and they rejected him immediately.

Eventually, Mr Brontë began to appreciate that he might need the help and support of his sister-in-law, in the long-term and, gradually, she too came to realise the same thing.

Her sister's death had, in effect set the course for the rest of Elizabeth Branwell's life. Despite her longing to return to her former home, she would for ever more be the companion and helpmate to her brother-in-law and a surrogate mother to her five young nieces and nephew. The law, at that time prevented a man marrying his dead wife's sister. Therefore, Elizabeth and Patrick could never be more than close friends. She took on the role of mistress of the household, organising the housekeeping, the servants and the general running of the home. She would supervise the children in their learning and their play whilst also playing hostess to visitors and the local gentry, as necessary. She would, be a sister to her brother-in-law, but could never be his wife. Any hopes of returning to the carefree and happy years she had spent in her home town had come swiftly and sadly to an end. She would never return to that much loved place.

Chapter Thirteen
February 1822

The permanent installation of Aunt Branwell, as a mother substitute, was becoming accepted by the beginning of 1822. This genteel, rather independent lady was quite different from her sister. Elizabeth Branwell was a year older than Mr Brontë and was therefore old and wise enough in some ways to use her experience of life to assist her young charges. She, like their father, realised that the six youngsters needed organisation and discipline if they were to grow and develop into sensible and intelligent adults. Hugs and kisses did not come as readily to Aunt as they had to Mama for she had had little or no contact with small children. She had had a strict but pleasant upbringing in a world where children were seen rather than heard and she had rather old-fashioned views about many things.

'If I am to stay on here, Patrick,' she stated one day, 'I will need a permanent room of my own and privacy when I need it. We need to review the bedrooms. If you no longer need the larger of the two front ones, I should rather like to have it. Perhaps you would prefer the one above your study?'

Mr Brontë was a little taken aback at this suggestion, but he had resigned himself to the fact that a wife might not be forthcoming for some time, if at all. He needed his sister-in-law more than he cared to admit and was willing to ensure that she had all the comfort and support that she needed in order to persuade her to stay.

'Of course, Elizabeth,' he replied, 'You must choose whichever room you wish and we will re-arrange the children's rooms and mine, accordingly.'

'Well,' replied Aunt Branwell, 'I am not saying that I will not allow for the children's needs. They will be able to use my room as necessary, if they are ill for instance, but it would be nice to have somewhere of my own. Much as I am willing to help you in any way I can, brother-in-law, this is not my home town and I do find Haworth disagreeable at times. Furthermore, I am not fully suited to this northern climate.'

If there was one thing that Aunt Branwell particularly disliked about Haworth, it was the cold and damp, so different from the warm and sunny aspect of Penzance. She hated the driving rains, the fog and the biting winds that blew throughout the year. She was to be found often huddled up in her old fashioned clothes and bonnets, with shawls around her shoulders and patterns on her feet to guard from the cold of the Parsonage flagstones. In this first year, following her sister's death, she spent a lot of her time by the fire in her room, sending orders down to the servants and allowing the children to visit her, one by one, rather than engaging herself in their lives and occupations.

The children turned in on themselves for love and affection, then they went to Sarah and Nancy for comfort and failing that they gradually re-engaged their Papa as he eventually turned his attention once more to their health and welfare.

Like children everywhere, the young Brontë's gradually adapted to life without their mother. They had no choice, although the loss in their lives was permanent and would affect them all for as long as they lived. Papa and Aunt Branwell recognised that the children all had talents and abilities and they were determined to educate and instruct them. The adults agreed that a happy but disciplined day spent working and learning was what the children most needed. They set out in earnest to provide it.

Days, became rather structured, the children had a routine they could work with and would help to focus their attention away from their sadness. Mornings were spent in the parlour or Aunt's bedroom with Aunt supervising the elder children with their reading or letters, writing and numbers. The younger children had Sarah's help, they played with simple counting games, building blocks and picture books. Prayers and sermons were heard every Sunday in the church, and prayers were held every morning and night when the family gathered in Papa's study. Bible stories and readings were part of their everyday lives and as they grew, their Papa introduced more books and widened their knowledge through journals, newspapers and discussion.

Afternoons were spent learning new skills. These often took the shape of nature walks, music, singing or efforts at drawing and painting. The girls were taught to sew and to perform light household duties. Sewing was a necessity in a household where nearly all the clothing was hand-made at home from cloth bought at the drapers' shop. Good plain sewing was a vital skill for young girls of the Brontë family's income and position in life. They would have to constantly provide the linen and clothing for themselves, their families and their households, throughout their lives. They had started very young making samplers, which were squares of linen on which they practised the various types of stitching. All the young Brontë girls would sit for hours perfecting the art of sewing. They all produced samplers with their letters, numbers, names and bible verses sewn in different coloured threads.

Branwell had his education especially supervised by his father. Mr Brontë was determined that the boy would one day lead the family to fame and fortune. As a very small boy, Branwell was coached and influenced by his father who tutored him in reading, writing, numbers and geography, history, science and literature, as soon as he could read.

The six children, growing up together; living, sleeping, playing, studying and eating, became a close-knit and concentrated unit. The absence of other children as playmates, and their own tendency to remain either in the Parsonage or on the moors together, made them inter-dependent at all times.

Close in age, looks and taste, they fought and argued, laughed and cried together, creating bonds of love and friendship between each child and of the family as a whole. Eventually, even their ideas and imaginations, became inter-linked and inter-woven.

This closeness was further enhanced as it also included natural pairings; the two oldest, the two youngest and the two middle children. This created an extra bond between them which saw Maria and Elizabeth arm in arm and finishing each other's sentences; Charlotte and Branwell could be found deep in conversation, making up stories and discussing things that they heard or read about in the newspapers; Emily and Anne also gradually formed an unbreakable bond as the two youngest girls, alike in looks and manner though different in size and outlook.

The children were lively and intelligent, constantly seeking out new things to learn, new games to play, and new places to explore. The wild moorland provided a huge and rich source of education with all its natural colours, sounds and smells. The children watched every day, the changes in the weather, the light, the temperature and the seasons. The moors taught them about plants, animals, science and physical properties, colour, climate, and beauty. It was their natural classroom.

At night, when they were sleeping in the bedrooms at the back of the house facing westward out across the moors, the children would often gaze out at the night sky. Emily loved to sit at the window with one of the shutters open and stare at the stars. The utter blackness of the landscape with its total lack of light from any earthly source meant the stars shone out in a kaleidoscope of patterns and mystery. The children gradually learnt how to recognise the different constellations, the planets and the brightest stars. Throughout the year, they marvelled at the movements of the stars and the phases of the moon as the seasons passed and the nights grew lighter and darker. Watching out for shooting stars as they suddenly exploded across the sky and as swiftly burnt themselves out was a special treat. Each child would make a wish whenever they were lucky enough to see one. The night sky was a whole new area of entertainment and delight.

By day, the children were encouraged to read everything that was on the book shelves or any magazines, papers or books that came into the house. Mr Driver, a local vicar, passed on his copy of Blackwood's Magazine to Mr Brontë and this journal was read cover to cover by the older children and its articles and features discussed and argued over. On the book shelves were copies of Pilgrims Progress, Aesop's Fables and The Arabian Night's Entertainment, which were all either read to them or read by them, as each child grew more able to read and understand. As well as the Bible they had geography books, books on birds and nature, and copies of their own father's writings. Any written material that came into the Parsonage was quickly read, analysed and discussed with or by the children, often with the added help and wisdom of their Papa.

A routine was established and the children behaved the same way as most young people of their class although, their circumstances meant that they lived either within the confines of the Parsonage or out on the heathland. They had few trips into Haworth or beyond, due to the logistics of taking them in an age with little or no transport. The weather, too, influenced a lot of their movements. Set high up on the edge of the Yorkshire moors, with little or no protection from the elements, the Parsonage was battered by the winds and the rains. The children had neither the extra footwear nor the clothing to protect them in bad weather. The winter of 1822 was harsh. Snow lay on the ground for weeks, confining the children to the house for days on end. It had to be dry and sunny or dry and windy to enable them to get out even in to the garden.

There was a separateness that existed between the Brontë's and their neighbours. The clergyman's family could not be seen associating or mixing with the working class poor who lived in Haworth town. Many children of their own age were working in mills or helping out at home. There were no local schools providing mixed education or offering social interaction. The

Brontës' status in Haworth was wedged somewhere between the upper working and lower middle classes. Their Papa was relatively poor from a middle class perspective, but infinitely richer than many of his working parishioners. Behind this separation was the fear socialisation could carry the danger of disease and infection to vulnerable and delicate children.

Chapter Fourteen
May 1823

One day, about eighteen months after the death of their mother. when the children were all past the baby stage and showing their own personalities and characteristics, Mr Brontë decided to test his children's thoughts and knowledge. He suspected that they knew far more than he realised, and he decided that if the children could speak under cover they would give him an idea of their abilities. There was a mask in the house, that had accidently been left by some visiting mummers; players who went around the village acting, singing and playing instruments for entertainment. Bringing it into the parlour one morning, Papa decided to put his children to the test.

'Now children, are you all here? Go and find Branwell please Maria, we are going to play a game.'

As Maria rushed away, Papa led the children into the hallway and organised them into a line according to their ages. When the other two arrived, they too were placed in the sequence. Maria stood behind the front door and Anne, now three years old, sat on the bottom step of the staircase. Walking down the line and starting with the youngest, Papa told Anne to hold the mask over her face. The little girl struggled with the ribbons and tapes and Charlotte moved over to help her.

'Now children,' announced Papa, 'I am going to ask each of you a question and because you are masked you can give any answer that you wish. Are you ready, Anne? This is your question. What does a child like you want most in the entire world? Can you tell us that Anne?'

The little girl sat for a while with her hands behind her back and rocked from one side to the other, but stayed silent. 'Come, Anne, tell us all about something that you would really like,' coaxed Papa.

'I think I would like to read books and be grown up like Maria,' was the answer when it was finally whispered.

'That is excellent, Anne,' replied Papa kneeling down beside her. 'You are saying that you want age and experience and that is a very good answer. Is that what you meant, my dear?'

'Well, Papa, I would like a fluffy kitten as well!' Anne replied and everyone laughed as Papa began to unfasten the ribbons to put the mask on Emily's face. Emily tried to help and got all tangled up. Eventually, Papa stood back and asked her in a solemn voice what she thought should be done with her brother Branwell, when he was naughty. Branwell immediately began to giggle and Elizabeth pushed him in his ribs with a loud shhh!

Emily looked warily towards Branwell. 'Can we really say anything that we wish, Papa?' she asked tentatively. When Papa had reassured them all that this was indeed the case, Emily replied. 'I think that you must reason with him and show him his faults, because he is often a naughty boy.' Branwell pulled a face and shook his fist at his sister, but Papa laughed.

'And what if he is too stubborn and naughty to listen to reason?' Papa continued.

Emily stood for a while wondering what to say. She was a little worried that Branwell would be mean to her if she said anything too horrible. 'Can we really say what we want behind the mask, Papa?' Emily asked again.

'Now, now, Emily, Come on dear. Just say what you think, it is quite all right.'

'In that case, then I think that he should be whipped until he learns to be good and to behave himself and be nice to his sisters.'

Branwell let out a howl and made to run towards Emily, but Papa stepped in.

'No, Branwell, you all have immunity; that is you can say whatever you wish whilst you are wearing the mask and there must be no reprisals, no punishments. Now my boy it is your turn. Give him the mask, Emily, and let us see what this young man has to say.'

Branwell snatched the mask from Emily's hand and spent a while trying to tie the ribbons. No-one offered to help him.

'Just hold it in place, Branwell,' said Papa beginning to get a little impatient. 'Now then, this is your question. How does one tell the difference between the intelligence of men and that of women?'

Branwell looked at his sisters and then looked down at himself and laughed. 'By the difference in their bodies,' replied the little boy, 'and the clothes that they wear and boys have better brains,' he declared.

Papa smiled as his five daughters all shouted in unison and broke out of their line to pat Branwell hard on his head.

'You must be neither man nor woman then Branwell, as you have no brains at all!' shouted Maria.

'Now, now children, calm down. Come now, let us get back into line. Give the mask to Charlotte, Branwell.'

Branwell was cross and deliberately dropped the mask on the floor. Papa scowled at him, picked it up himself and placed the mask over Charlotte's face and asked her to name the best book in the world.

'That is an easy question, Papa, it is the Bible. Ask me something harder.'

'Alright, alright, Charlotte, are you ready? What is the second best book?'

Charlotte was silent as she quickly ran a list through her head of all the books she had seen or read. Should she say the Book of Common Prayers? The book of hymns? Or, Papa's favourite, the long book of blank verse called "Paradise Lost", from which he often quoted? Perhaps she should choose one of

Papa's own publications? She was at a loss and frightened to give the wrong answer.

'Charlotte, just tell us what book you like second best, not what you think I might like to hear,' coaxed her father as he realised his daughters' dilemma.

'In that case, my favourite is the *Book of Nature*,' was Charlotte's swift reply. This was a book that she had begun to study in depth, despite her tender years. She liked to try and identify the birds, flowers and animals that she saw on the moors and match them to those in the book.

'An excellent choice,' beamed her father, 'clever girl Charlotte, I can see that you love your books and you are learning fast.'

'Now, Elizabeth, put on the mask and answer me what is the best way to educate women?'

Elizabeth insisted on tying all of the ribbons and getting the mask in place before she answered as this gave her time to think of a good reply. She thought for quite a long time and wanted Maria to prompt her but the mask prevented any eye contact.

'Well, I know that it is good to be educated but I think that women also need to know how to run their house, to cook and to sew and to do their household chores.'

'A most worthy answer, Elizabeth,' beamed her Papa. 'One of you girls may well be the mistress of this house one day, when I am old or infirm. Or you bonny girls may all have rich and handsome husbands and you will need to know all about household accounts, organisation and proper housekeeping.' He winked at the girls and laughed at their expressions.

Finally it was Maria's turn and when the mask was once again in place Papa asked her what she thought was the best way for people to spend their time. Maria had studied her Bible and listened well to her father's sermons. She felt that this life was to be led in service and obedience to God's will and that, after death, one would go to Heaven and live forever in Paradise just like Mama had done. She replied seriously, 'By living your life in a way that prepares you for a long and happy eternity, Papa, just like Mama did.'

Mr Brontë, smiled sadly and patted Maria's arm. 'Well done, Maria, well done my dear!' he murmured, then stepped back in front of them all.

'Enough children, return to your studies, the game is over. Branwell! Leave Emily alone and go and start your numbers. I shall be through into the study shortly and I expect you to have your seven times table written out in full.'

Mr Brontë was well satisfied with the answers his children had produced. These questions and answers helped him to make up his mind about some of his concerns for their future. His children were, he felt, ready for a much broader education and it was time for them to begin their training for the years ahead. The answers from his two eldest girls settled Papa's mind as to their future education. Maria would be schooled for teaching and Elizabeth in housekeeping.

It was tradition in those days for a less able female child, or one that had low marriage prospects or an infirmity, to stay at home and dedicate her life to looking after the house and her aging parents. Elizabeth appeared to be already thinking along those lines. Charlotte, like Maria, seemed especially bright and would probably make a worthy teacher or governess. Emily and Anne were still young but were learning to read and were articulate and industrious; they, too, would probably make able governesses or ladies' companions, if they did not have marriage as an option. All his girls would need to be schooled at a young ladies' academy where they would be taught a variety of female occupations as they got older. Needlework, French, English, music and art were all seen as suitable subjects for genteel young ladies and having mastered these skills, they would pass them on to their pupils in their roles as governesses or be well set up to make a good marriage.

Branwell, whilst young and hot headed at the moment, could read and write very well and his father was determined that he would follow in his own footsteps and become a scholar. For the time being however, and especially with his highly-strung nature, Branwell would continue to be taught at home, at least until his teenage years. Once he had taught him a wide range of subjects, Patrick would send his son to university and help him into one of the noble professions, possibly the church, the military or medicine.

Mr Brontë recognised that all his children had literary and artistic abilities, which must also be encouraged. However, they were not a rich family and his wages were not a lot to live on and feed and clothe everyone. He must be careful and economical if they were all to flourish. He decided to seek Aunt Branwell's thoughts on the matter and see whether she agreed with his assessment of the children's needs.

Chapter Fifteen
July 1823

Following the scene with the mask and having thought for a few days about how his children were progressing, Mr Brontë walked into the parlour one evening after the children were all in bed and invited Aunt Branwell into a discussion about their future.

'I have six healthy and happy children, Elizabeth, and they are growing and learning every day. Maria is nine years old and we must start to think about the future. What are we to prepare them for and how are they to make their way in the world? Branwell will do well of course, of that I have no doubt and for the time being I will continue to educate him to the highest standard. As to the girls, I am thinking of asking my old friend and the girls' godmother, Elizabeth Firth, for her advice about possible schooling, but I wanted to hear your views first.'

Aunt Branwell thought for a moment on what she had just heard. She knew that Patrick could be insensitive and a little thoughtless on occasion, but did he really need to seek Miss Firth's opinion? Elizabeth Firth had only just deigned to speak to him again following his disastrous marriage proposal. Was not their own Aunt and substitute mother the person who knew them and their needs best? Had she not nursed, fed and cared for them all? Had she not taught all the girls how to sew and helped the youngest to learn their letters and numbers? Hurt by her brother-in-law's remarks she delivered a stern reply.

'Well now Patrick, it depends what you have in mind and your financial situation. Are you asking me because you want financial assistance from me or do you just want my thoughts on the matter? I am sure that your friend Miss Firth must be far better placed to give an opinion, than someone who has spent every day with your children for the last two years!'

For once, Mr Brontë realised his mistake and recognised that by mentioning that he was to ask another woman's opinion, he had greatly upset his sister-in-law.

'Please, Elizabeth, I do not wish to offend. I only mentioned Miss Firth as she has some knowledge of girls' schools. I would not ever presume to look to you financially after all you have done for me and my motherless children. It is your opinion, which I hold in the highest regard, which brings me here tonight to seek your help and advice. I would greatly value your thoughts and feelings on the matter.'

Aunt Branwell, shuffled in her seat, coughed, blew her nose on her beautifully embroidered handkerchief and blinked the tears away that had suddenly sprung into her eyes.

'Well, brother-in-law, if you really want my opinion then you shall have it but it may not be exactly what you wish to hear.' She paused again for effect and then continued.

'With regard to my dear nephew, I agree that you are his best educator, but I have observed his behaviour and suggest that the boy lacks male company, yourself excluded. With your connections at Woodhouse Grove School, at Rawdon, I wonder if that would not be a better environment for him? He would be amongst lads his own age, rather than this dull female abode, he would learn all the rough and tumble of life that all boys need to suffer and he would gradually acquire manly ideas and manly pursuits.'

Before Mr Brontë could lift his hand in protest, Aunt Branwell continued.

'As to the girls, Maria and Charlotte are the brightest, but you need to be practical Patrick. They need to be self-sufficient, all of them. Even if one of the girls stays at home in later years to care for you and me. What if they all wish to marry? In which case they will need good housekeeping skills, rather than too much book learning. I know you hold education and study in the highest regard, but they need, first and foremost, to be refined young ladies, with the skills and virtues of their fair sex. I don't need to remind you that this house goes with your work and should you become ill or, God forbid, follow my poor dear sister to the grave, these children would be orphaned and them with no skills whatsoever.'

Again, Patrick began to speak but Aunt Branwell raised her hand.

'Furthermore, the girls are limited as to what employment they could reasonably accept as befits their class and station in life. It would be as teachers or governesses they would have to look, neither of which is a particularly happy occupation and nor is it well paid. Anne is the least robust, though none of them are particularly strong, Emily is very odd at times. I wonder how she will fare in adulthood. She seems quite different from the others, very self-contained, almost distant. She is the one that worries me the most. What about their sight, Patrick? Branwell is almost squinting and poor Charlotte can see nothing a yard away from her eyes and all this reading and writing can only do further damage—'

'Elizabeth, stop! Stop please!' Mr Brontë rose and held up his hands. 'Elizabeth, you are getting overwrought. I only wanted some thoughts on what you feel about the future; the girl's education and whether I should invest in schools, carry on as we are or perhaps consider a tutor to come here to help with them. It is your opinion on the training for the girls that I am seeking. I do not need a lecture on their health nor their personalities, Elizabeth. As to Branwell, his education will remain with me for as long as I choose, it is not up for discussion, by you or by anyone else!'

Aunt Branwell rose from her chair and faced her brother-in-law across the parlour.

'Well, I have had my say, Patrick, and if you think that I am not doing a good enough job and you would rather pay for some other woman to come here and educate the girls then so be it. If you did not want to hear my views then you should not have asked for them. I shall bid you Good night and retire to my room.'

She swept from the parlour; Patrick was left standing by the window, angry and upset. He knew that not only had he deeply offended the only woman who had stood by him these last few years, but also that his clumsiness and lack of sensitivity might well have her travelling back to Cornwall on the next available coach!

Chapter Sixteen
Aunt Branwell

In her bedroom, Aunt Branwell sat at her dressing table, tears rolling down her face. After all she had done for her sister's husband and the effort she had put into her nieces and nephew, Patrick was planning to consult other people who knew little or nothing of their situation and would, very likely, take the children's future completely out of her hands. She felt used and humiliated. Never had the prospect of returning to Cornwall seemed so inviting as it did at that moment.

Downstairs, Patrick paced the floor, angry with himself and frustrated with the way he had handled Elizabeth. He genuinely wanted and respected her opinion. He valued her knowledge and intelligence, yet she seemed to hint that Branwell would be better away from home, the girls would only be fit for marriage, if they were less educated and more flippant and feminine, that Emily was odd, that Charlotte was nearly blind! Oh no, this would not do, it had all gone wrong. He should never have consulted her. He should have made up his own mind. They were his children, his responsibility, no-one else needed to have a say.

Patrick flung open the parlour door and grabbing his coat he marched out of the house, banging the front door behind him. He knew what he would do, he would try again to take a wife and that would solve the problem once and for all. Elizabeth could go back to Penzance and he would be master in his own house again. He strode off into the darkness his face red and his mouth set in fury.

Upstairs, Anne jumped as the loud banging of the front door broke her dream and woke her with a start. She had been sleeping in Aunt Branwell's room for a while. She had had a nasty cold and Aunt wanted to keep a close eye on her. A candle glowed on the dressing table and she could see Aunt sitting on the stool, the candlelight reflecting the glistening of tears as she wiped them from her cheeks. The little girl hesitated, unsure of what to do. when suddenly Aunt let out an enormous sob and shook her head in despair. In seconds Anne flung herself across the room and into her arms. Without knowing what was wrong Anne clung to her Aunt as this kind woman who was a mother to her, cried in long broken sobs and buried her face into Anne's soft hair.

After a few minutes, the comfort of the little girl and her wide-eyed look of fear brought Aunt's tears to a halt. She blew her nose long and hard in to her handkerchief.

'Are you alright, Aunt?' whispered Anne, 'Have you hurt yourself?'

Aunt smiled down at this lovely little girl. Off all the children, Anne was so near to being her own child. In that moment, she realised and knew that she loved her. How could she ever think to leave her in the care of any other woman, and how could she ever be separated from these six beautiful children to whose mother she had sworn to keep and protect, in her place. Hugging her niece and rocking her in her arms she whispered.

'It is alright, my little darling, I tripped and hit my knee on the stairs and the pain made me cry. It is better now.'

It was a long time before she finally laid the sleeping child back down on her little bed. and some time later that she finally dried her tears and drifted off to sleep herself.

Chapter Seventeen
August–December 1823

Two years after the death of his wife, when Maria and Elizabeth were nine and eight years old, respectively. Mr Brontë sent them to Crofton Hall School near Wakefield with the help and encouragement of their godmother, Elizabeth Firth. The girls were very excited as they set out early one morning with their Papa. Everyone waved them off from the front door and seven-year-old Charlotte was rather sorry that she was not going with them but knew that her turn would come soon. She was determined to do well at school, already studying as much as she could and enjoyed reading and writing immensely.

For the next few days, the weather was fine and in the afternoons Sarah and Nancy took the remaining children out on to the moors. Their walks had got further and further as the children grew and a walk of three or four miles was commonplace. On the moors the children's joy and energy knew no bounds. They ran and played amongst the grasses, heather and the streams that ran throughout the moorland. The sight, sounds and smells of the moor were pure joy to the children. They were able to collect the wild blue berries that grew in abundance in July and August for Nancy and Aunt to turn into pies, jams and flavoured drinks. The children observed the wild flowers, watched the many moorland birds and learnt to recognise the habits and songs of the lapwings, meadow pipits, plovers, skylarks and curlews. They chased flies and beetles, butterflies and dragonflies, they splashed in the waterfall running down opposite Virginia Water; a working farm built on the sloping sides of the Sladen valley. They played amongst the huge boulders and rocky outcrops that had been created eons before by the movement of ice and earthquake and scoured and shaped by water, wind and frost.

Drawn to this world of nature the children imagined fairies and elves, wood nymphs and water sprites amongst the rocks and heather, as they walked, ran and skipped over it. Even if it rained and they were confined to the house, the children watched with excitement and wonder from the back bedroom windows as the huge clouds rolled across the sky and the darkness engulfed the land and emptied gallons of water on to the fields and into the streams.

The happiness and freedom that the four youngest children experienced that spring and summer was short-lived. Maria and Elizabeth were back home in the autumn; the school proving too expensive for their father's limited income, and by Christmas all six children had succumbed to three of the most dangerous childhood ailments of the time; whooping cough, chicken pox and measles.

All the adults at the Parsonage knew the dangers of these illnesses from which many children died and they all worked very hard to help the children recover. The work involved at the Parsonage where six children, all under the age of ten, were ill with coughs, sickness, diarrhoea and general fatigue was enormous. The children lost their appetites and became thin and weak, they vomited or felt sickly, and they were listless and fractious and sometimes too ill to get out of bed. They had fevers, night terrors and hallucinations and cried and clung to their Aunt and each other for comfort. Aunt Branwell and the two servant girls worked night and day to keep the children as well and comfortable as they could.

Mr Brontë went about his parish work, pale and worried, constantly frightened that one or all of his children would become dangerously sick, or even die. He prayed to God to spare them as he offered comfort in the homes where others were suffering and dying of the same diseases that afflicted his own children. It was months before all the children finally recovered and even then they remained weak and delicate for weeks afterwards.

However, their long months of sickness had been fruitful, the children had spent many hours in bed or propped up on the settle, in each other's company, and it fell on them to amuse themselves as best they could. As Maria and Elizabeth recovered, they spent happy hours reading stories to the younger ones when they felt too ill to play, or making up stories to cheer them all up.

The children had access to some magazines and a few books that Mama had brought with her from Cornwall. although many of her belongings had been lost when the ship carrying her possessions had been wrecked. Papa had books from his days at Cambridge University and the children had been given various little books and religious articles to help them to read. The weekly arrival of Blackwoods' Edinburgh Magazine which abounded in tales of current affairs, social gatherings, adventures and political dealings, was now a major event and a huge source of interest and entertainment to them.

Papa introduced them to more of his own writing and revealed that he had in fact, had other stories and poetry published. His "Cottage Poems" were read and learnt by heart by the family, who were very proud of their Papa's achievements. They all liked to read and listen to poetry and as they grew older and more able to understand the language and content, poems by Byron, Shelley, Wordsworth and Milton became favourites.

On special occasions when the adults were not too weary from the burden of their work, the children would beg them to read to them or tell them stories. Papa would talk about his childhood in Ireland, and Aunt had tales of her girlhood in Cornwall and stories of their mother when she was a child, which they never tired of hearing. In addition to their reading, the older children continued to make up stories of their own to amuse themselves and the younger ones.

Although there was little spare paper or writing materials in the house, the older girls sometimes wrote a few lines for the younger ones to read, or perhaps a few lines of verse or a tiny picture to treasure. Occasionally, when no one was looking, the bedroom walls were used to illustrate a point or to draw a picture to amuse each other!

The house was in a kind of organised chaos with Aunt Branwell orchestrating the movement of children and furniture according to everyone's needs. As each child succumbed to one illness or recovered from another, they were moved around from bedroom to bedroom and bed to bed; those with measles in one bed and those with whooping cough in another, those needing a warm fire in one room and those needing fresh air somewhere else.

Illness caused the children to have disturbed nights; sometimes, from the sound of others coughing or being sick, at others from the strange dreams or hallucinations that came with fever and restlessness. It was a very hard and trying time for everyone and some days, when Sarah and Nancy stared in horror at the mountain of wet and dirty bedding and the slop buckets and chamber pots, they felt very depressed and exhausted.

Chapter Eighteen
January 1824

Late one night, five-year-old Emily lay in the little room upstairs, ill with whooping cough, sweating and shaking as the rigours of fever wracked her thin body. Alone and unsure whether she was awake or asleep, she began to dream or imagine strange events happening around her bed. She had coughed so much that evening that she had been very sick. Aunt moved her into this little room to cool her down, leaving the window and shutters slightly open.

Tossing and turning, Emily was thirsty with dehydration and had pain and nausea, yet felt too ill and tired, to summon help. In her feverish state she became aware of Mama's voice calling for her and strained her eyes to see through the darkness. The thought of her mother being with her made Emily so happy for a few seconds, but, turning her head she 'saw' a woman in black, bent over like a hooded witch in the corner of the room; a woman so horrible and different from her Mama, that the little girl cried out in horror. Emily struggled to sit up, but she felt a strange heaviness in her limbs which seemed to hold her down on to the bed. Blinking hard, she peered into the dark corner. The apparition disappeared but was replaced by a sudden and urgent tapping at the window.

The heaviness seemed to disappear and Emily felt herself rise from the bed and go to the window which was now wide open with the wind rushing in. It was dark outside and the church clock was striking two o'clock. Or, at least, she thought it was the church clock, it sounded louder and closer. Perhaps it was the new grandfather clock that now stood on the shelf halfway up the stairs, or perhaps it was a rushing and banging inside her own head.

The tapping noise began again and Emily felt sure that it was coming from outside as if a branch or a twig was banging against the other side of the glass pane. Knowing that there was nothing in the garden tall enough to be knocking against the window Emily wondered if someone was actually knocking at the front door. Perhaps it was someone from the village needing Papa's help. Emily had heard her father report each day that sickness in the village was raging like a fire out of control, not just children but adults too were dying of an epidemic of diseases.

Emily had become very scared when she heard her father talk of death and sickness. She knew that being in Heaven would be nice but that getting there might involve a long and painful journey. It was being ill and in pain for a long time that frightened the little girl.

The tapping suddenly started up again and made Emily jump. Could it be Mama, knocking at the window come to fetch her and take her away to her grave in the cold church crypt? For a few minutes Emily was so scared that she could neither move nor call out for help.

Gradually, she became aware of other sounds: the low moaning of the wind somewhere down one of the chimneys, the rustling of the bushes in the garden, an owl hooting as it flew over the graveyard and the church clock tolling again, now the quarter hour. The window rattled and the shutters, which had been fastened back by Aunt, were shaking and banging noisily against the wall, as if trying to break loose from the catch. Suddenly a loud gust of wind blew hard against the window and Emily was sure she heard the voice of a child calling out into the night.

'Let me in. Let me in,' the voice pleaded, 'let me in, I cannot get in.'

Emily's eyes opened wide in horror, she held her breath and stared through the darkness towards the window. 'Let me in, Let me in, Emily,' the voice repeated.

Frightened out of her wits, Emily seemed to float across the room and found herself under the bed covers fighting for air. As they tangled around her body she felt their weight and an awful strangling sensation as the sheet became wrapped firmly around her neck and head. Terrified, she cried out, not knowing who or what was calling her name or coming to carry her off into the night.

It was only a minute later that Maria finally managed to open the door of Emily's room, which Aunt had fastened with the catch; high up at the top to stop it rattling from the window and to keep the other children away so that they did not disturb their poorly sister. The wind had risen and the window was shaking noisily as Maria entered the room. She moved forward in the darkness and closed it firmly allowing stillness and silence to return. Reaching out with her hand she felt for Emily under the covers.

At the feel of her hand Emily let out a terrified scream and Maria jumped back in alarm.

'Emmi, it's alright, Emmi, it's me, Maria, come to see if you are alright. I heard your window rattling and you were calling out in your sleep. I was knocking at the door. Didn't you hear me calling your name?' Untangling Emily from the wet and dishevelled bedding, Maria drew her out from under the bed clothes. The little girl was hot and coughing and was crying as Maria gently held her.

Suddenly, the door flung open and the light from a candle lit up the blackness as Aunt came forward to see what all the noise was about and check on her sick patient.

'What are you doing in here, Maria?' she demanded in a loud whisper, 'get back to your bed at once, I will see to your sister.'

But she screamed, 'Aunt, she was calling out and I thought that I would come and comfort her.'

'Don't worry child. It's alright,' Aunt replied, her voice weary but softening, 'she has a fever, that's all. You were the same when you had it. It makes you see and hear things that are not there. She is frightened poor child. Don't worry now. I will sit with her a while, you go back to bed there's a good girl.'

Maria left the room reluctantly. Aunt turned her attention to Emily. The poor child looked very distressed. Taking her in her arms and rocking her against her chest she spoke softly to the whimpering girl and gently stroked her hot face and damp hair.

How many more nights of this would they all have to endure before the children were well again? Aunt fretted. Would they all recover?

These six children, whom she never dreamed she would have the responsibility of rearing, were all becoming more and more precious to their Aunt, although she would not let them know it. Each one was very different but in many ways were so like their mother.

Aunt Branwell sat and hugged the now quietened Emily to her, and her own tears began to fall on the child's warm head; tears not only for the sadness of their mother's death, but the loss of her own life in Cornwall, to which she now knew she could never return. She wept for the loss of her own youth and chance to marry and have children of her own, the loss of her social life, the loss of her freedom and most of all, the fear that one of her sister's precious children, might be taken from her.

It was a very sad and worried Aunt Branwell who returned to her own bed in the cold small hours to snatch a few hours' sleep before another day of sickness and uncertainty.

Chapter Nineteen
May 1824

Winter turned to spring and the children slowly began to recover. One warm and sunny afternoon in May 1824, Aunt had taken Branwell off on a short errand to visit the Greenwood family at their large and lovely house in the valley at the bottom of the town. The Greenwoods were important and wealthy mill owners in Haworth. Papa had walked over to Stanbury to arrange a funeral. The five girls, under the care of Sarah and Nancy, were bored and restless.

'If we help you and Nancy with washing up and tidying the bedrooms, Sarah, will you play some games with us?' asked Maria innocently.

'As long as it's nothing that will get us into trouble with your Aunt and Mr Brontë,' came the reply. 'You do have a habit of getting into trouble when your Aunt's not around and she did 'specially say to keep a close eye on you all. Are you sure you can't just play on your own or do a bit in the garden?'

'Oh. No,' Elizabeth interrupted, 'we love playing when you are in charge, Sarah, you are so kind to us and we like you to join in our games.'

Sarah scowled at Maria and Elizabeth, unsure whether this was genuine flattery or if the girls were up to something. She suspected the latter, but was curious to know what they wanted and she could certainly do with a hand upstairs, three of the beds needed the sheets changing and the bedrooms all needed a good brushing.

'I'll be glad when you're well enough to go back to school. It's time Mr Brontë found a new place for you two girls. It was better when you two were at school, there was a bit less work for us to do,' called Sarah as she set off upstairs.

'I'm playing nothing 'til the bedrooms are all done mind,' added Nancy. 'nothing until all the work's done and then I will want a cup o' tea afore I start your daft games, think on'

The five girls set about helping. The three eldest went up to see to the beds and Anne and Emily helped with the washing-up. Upstairs, Elizabeth was hanging out of the bedroom window, looking at the cherry tree which grew in front of Papa's study. It was a sturdy tree that Mama had bought in their first spring at Haworth as a present for their father on his birthday. The top branches were nearly as high as the bedroom window and it was the only tree in the garden, the rest of which supported some fruit brushes and flowering shrubs. Trees did not grow easily in the moorland soil but this tree had thrived and Papa was very fond of it, not least because it was a constant reminder of his dear wife.

'Do you think it will take our weight?' asked Elizabeth. 'Not from up here,' gasped Charlotte. 'If we are going to act out the story, you must climb it from ground level.'

The previous night, the girls had discussed in bed an idea to act out an imaginary play using a real historic event. Today, 29th May, was known as Oak Apple Day and was a national holiday in England. It celebrated the birthday of Charles II, who had been restored to the English throne in 1660 after the Civil War. The King of England had hidden in an oak tree to escape from Oliver Cromwell's army in 1651, after the battle of Worcester. Hidden in the huge, leafy tree in the grounds of Boscobel House in Shropshire, the Parliamentarians, (or Roundheads) led by Oliver Cromwell, had failed to find the king and kill him. To celebrate Charles's deliverance and eventual return to the throne, a national holiday was held every year and people often wore sprigs of oak leaves as protection from anti-royalists!

The Brontë girls had decided as Branwell was away, they could enjoy themselves without him taking the lead role. If Branwell had been there, he would have insisted on playing the king. Today, Elizabeth would play the part of King Charles; Maria would be Oliver Cromwell; Charlotte, Emily and Anne would be roundhead soldiers searching for the monarch. Sarah could also be a soldier but they would stand her by the garden gate to watch out for the return of Aunt or Papa.

Once the house work was over, Elizabeth wrapped a bedspread around her shoulders and put a tea pot lid on her head, fastened with a shawl, to represent a crown.

'Right, I am ready,' she stated. 'I shall go out into the garden now, come looking for me after a couple of minutes and pretend that you don't know where I am. Don't let Sarah know that I am in the tree, she is bound to complain,' she whispered to Maria and Charlotte.

Elizabeth looked at the tree from all angles. Its lower branches were fairly thick and grew together in close clumps. The branches still had some pink blossom which would help to conceal her from the ground. Hitching her skirts up to her knees and grabbing a lower branch, Elizabeth made a couple of attempts to climb up but got tangled in twigs and leaves and dislodged clumps of blossom, which floated to the ground like pink rain. Finally, with one foot on a lower branch and the other dangling in mid-air, she lunged for an overhanging branch and hauled herself up about a metre into the tree. Her cloak caught on the shiny red leaves and the new shoots. Blossom continued to break off and fall to the ground. She must hurry before the others came out of the house, Sarah must not suspect where she was. Pushing branches and twigs out of the way, despite scratches and slipping on the damp branches, Elizabeth managed to fight her way into the middle of the tree, almost level with the top of the study window. Hearing voices from the hallway, she put her foot on the next branch up and partly disappeared under the canopy as Maria, Charlotte, Emily and Sarah came out of the front door.

Maria was carrying one of Branwell's toy swords and was also wrapped in a cloak.

'Search for him, men!' she cried. 'He must be caught and taken to the Tower of London to be executed.' Sarah stood looking bewildered. 'What do you want me to do?' she demanded, 'I'm not sure what's happening.'

'Go and guard the gate,' cried Charlotte pushing Sarah down the path, 'stand by the gate and keep checking the lane to make sure that none of the king's army, the royalist Cavaliers, come to rescue him. We know he is around here somewhere and his men cannot be far away.'

'Sir Antony Brontë!' demanded Charlotte, looking at Anne, who had just emerged from the side of the house, 'You must help me search for the king, our lives are at stake and he is a traitor to our cause. Search the undergrowth and root him out!'

'At once, my Lord,' cried Anne as she ran off around the garden slashing at the bushes and jumping amongst the plants.

'I will check around the walls,' shouted Charlotte, 'He must not escape.'

The four girls thrashed their way around the garden whilst Elizabeth watched from her precarious perch in the cherry tree. Her right foot was in the crook of two small branches which were digging in to her ankle. She was unsure of how much longer she could remain still and hidden.

After five minutes of searching, Maria shouted to her troops. 'We need more men, the king is very cunning, he must have found a very good hiding place or else someone is sheltering him. Let us spread our search into this old house, perhaps he is hiding in a cupboard or a cellar. Come with me, Sir Edward.' She called across to Sarah, 'Stay at your post Master Sarawitch you must stay on guard and let us know if the Royalists arrive.'

'Well I'm sure I don't rightly know what's going on,' Sarah called back. 'I have tea to prepare soon with Nancy and I suspect your Aunt won't be long.'

The four girls disappeared into the house running and shouting to flush out the king from his hiding place. Finding Nancy busy in the kitchen, they promptly arrested her and sat her in a chair where Anne attempted to tie her up with old washing line.

'Give it to me, Anne,' said Nancy laughing, 'I'll tie myself up. You go and do whatever it is you are supposed to be doing. I promise not to run away.'

Elizabeth stayed in her tree watching Sarah, who soon left her post by the gate muttering to herself about these 'daft tykes'. She walked slowly back up the path and disappeared into the house.

With everyone gone, Elizabeth decided to get down from the tree and really hide somewhere, then her sisters could do a proper search. She quickly dislodged her foot, but it was numb and as she tried to place it on the next branch down, her leg and foot seemed to turn to jelly. She had to cling to a branch above to stop herself from falling. A loud creaking and squeaking noise arose as the branch began to peel away from the bark, bending over and heading towards the ground, taking Elizabeth with it in a most unladylike fashion.

Elizabeth tumbled to the earth and rolled from the tree. She looked up in horror to see that the branch had split in a long yellow slice from the main trunk. Rubbing her numb leg and foot she hobbled inside, all thoughts of hiding banished from her mind.

'Quick, help!' she called out, 'Maria, Sarah, come and help, a branch has broken off Papa's tree, what ever shall we do?'

Charlotte and Anne came rushing down the stairs and Charlotte promptly tried to 'arrest' her sister taking no notice of her pleas.

'I arrest you. Charles the Second of England and we are going to take you to the tower to be executed. Grab her arms, Sir Antony, and let's get her tied up and taken to London.' Charlotte's face lit up with excitement and she busied herself with trying to overcome Elizabeth, as if the game was real.

'Stop it,' cried Elizabeth, 'stop playing, Charlotte, this is serious. I have broken Papa's tree, come outside and see for yourself.'

Charlotte calmed down and realised what Elizabeth was saying. The girls, Sarah and now Nancy, all ran outside to examine the damage. They stood, with their mouths wide open, as they saw the huge bright split standing out against the deep purple bark of the trunk.

'Papa will be so angry,' Elizabeth sobbed in despair. 'What can we do?'

It was Sarah who came up with a solution.

'We must be quick now else everyone will be back, including the master. Best thing is to break off the branch completely at the trunk and then we'll cover the mark with soot. The branch can go on the fire and your Papa will be none the wiser, not for a while any way. Be quick and fetch the axe and I'll see if I can get a clean break. Nancy, you go and fetch some soot and a bit of water and fat. Elizabeth, stop your matherin' and get ready to catch the branch with Maria and take it round the back and put it on the wood pile, or better still hide it. Emily and Anne, you get all them twigs and blossoms gathered up, before your Papa sees the mess. What were you thinking of, Elizabeth, you know how much your Papa loves that tree, you stupid child.'

Sarah did what she could. The girls ran nervously back and forth to check both ends of the lane for Papa or Aunt. In what seemed like an hour, but was only about ten minutes, the branch was fully detached and hidden in the back garden amongst the bushes. Sarah daubed the sticky soot mixture on to the yellow scar as best she could and moved a few leaves over it. Standing back she thought it wasn't too bad a job, although it was obvious to anyone who knew what had happened. Luckily, it would be a while until Mr Brontë or Miss Branwell took a particular notice and by then she hoped it would have healed naturally.

'Now girls, you must get in and calm down and stop all this nonsense,' chastised Sarah. 'Get yourselves washed and sit quietly in the parlour with a book or two before the grown-ups get back and think you've all gone mad. Don't be asking me to play in your daft games anymore, you'll get me the sack and I'll end up in the workhouse.'

'Sorry Sarah,' the girls all replied, 'thank you for helping us. We are really sorry Sarah, we won't make you play again. We will be good, we promise.'

Later that evening, as they whispered to Branwell the events of the afternoon, Branwell put forward an idea. 'We always seem to end up in trouble when we play out and Aunt really doesn't think we should be out in the graveyard or even in the garden, unless we are doing some gardening. Why don't we act out stories when we are on the moors or when we go down into the cellar where the grown-ups cannot see or hear us?'

'You are right, Branwell,' cried Maria.

'Yes,' added Elizabeth, 'we could just imagine to be anyone we liked and let them have adventures all over the world'.

'Or, we could make up our own world,' added Charlotte, 'like an imaginary world that is like our own but different, where we could make magic things happen.'

The more excited the children got the louder they raised their voices until, with the clock striking the dreaded 7 o'clock, Aunt arrived to pack them all off to bed.

Maria and Elizabeth lay together in the double bed in the back bedroom. They continued the conversation. They had been performing secret 'bed plays' for a while now, each pretending to be a famous person and acting out scenes from their lives.

'I think that we should keep our bed plays secret, just between you and me,' whispered Maria. 'I like to play during the day with the others, but we are the eldest and we know far more than they do. Let's just keep our bed plays to ourselves. When we play with Branwell, there always has to be soldiers and Emily and Anne get a bit confused when we try to act out historical stories from our history books.'

Elizabeth laughed, 'Playing at being a king didn't turn out very well for me today did it? I do hope that the cherry tree soon recovers. I would hate Papa to be upset because of what I did, although it was an accident.'

'I think that tonight I will be Princess Caroline and you can be a queen instead of a king. You might make a better job of it,' laughed Maria as they both snuggled down in the warmth of the big bed.

Chapter Twenty
July–August 1824

In December 1823, Mr Brontë had been delighted to read in the 'Leeds Intelligencer' newspaper, that a new and less expensive school would be opening in April 1824 in the neighbouring county. The school was intended for the sound education of daughters of the clergy, which, of course, included Patrick Brontë's girls. There was a long list of patrons including the famous MP and campaigner against slavery, William Wilberforce, who had also sponsored Patrick at Cambridge University. With five daughters to educate, this was exactly what Mr Brontë needed for his family and he was delighted to hear of it. Unfortunately, the children were currently ill but as soon as they were better he would arrange to start sending them off to the school, which lay about forty-five miles away near Kirby Lonsdale in Lancashire.

It was, on the 21st of July 1824, that Mr Brontë again accompanied his two eldest daughters to a new school. This time it would be the Clergy Daughters' School at Cowan Bridge. Catching the Leeds to Kendal carriage at Keighley, they took the long ride over the moorland roads and empty landscape. It was a difficult journey which took all day and saw them arrive tired and hungry late in the evening. Mr Brontë stayed overnight and, before catching the returning coach the following morning, was able to look around the buildings and meet some of the staff.

The school consisted of a long row of stone cottages and an old bobbin mill, which had all been converted into teaching rooms and dormitories. There was also a covered walkway, garden plots and dining and kitchen areas. The school stood beside the main road that led from west Yorkshire over in to Lancashire and eventually to the Lake District. It was a wild and isolated place set on the lower slopes of Leck Fell in the tiny hamlet of Cowan Bridge.

This was a place that knuckled down to the excesses of weather and was exposed to rain and snow, high winds and damp for much of the year. It suffered from the mists floating down from the neighbouring mountains of Ingleborough, Penyghent and Whernside, some miles to the north east. Added to this was the low-lying and moist air of the green river valley running below the school. The place had a cold beauty where there was little protection from the harsh conditions and it was difficult to stay warm and sheltered.

At the close of the lovely July day when Mr Brontë arrived with Maria and Elizabeth, the school was fairly new and everyone was on their best behaviour to make the children and parents feel relaxed and welcome. On this warm evening there was no indication of how the school would appear in the depths of winter or during the cold and wet of spring and autumn.

Mr Brontë was happy and thankful that he had found a place to suit his income, where his daughters could be properly educated for the specific tasks and occupations he had chosen for them as they grew to maturity. The school seemed like an answer to his prayers and he left feeling a great joy that God had provided well for him and his family.

It was not long before Mr Brontë travelled again to Cowan Bridge, in fact it was only a couple of weeks later on the 10th August, that he brought eight-year-old Charlotte to join her sisters.

Having arrived with her father towards evening time, Charlotte did not see her sisters until the following morning. Even then, she hardly had chance for more than a quick hello and a hug during the short morning break. Charlotte was quite shocked at how different everything was from her home and was more than a little afraid. She was amongst the youngest of the girls, whose ages ranged from six to twenty two. That first day she saw Elizabeth under the covered walkway just before luncheon. She was sheltering from a strong summer breeze and Charlotte ran over to talk to her.

'Oh, Elizabeth! It is so good to see you. They said that you were busy in lessons last night. Where is Maria? Isn't it a big school? How windy it is. Wasn't the prayers and Bible study long this morning? Does that happen every morning before breakfast? I didn't like the porridge much. I do not know where I am supposed to go for meals or where to keep my books. Can you help?'

Elizabeth smiled at her younger sister. 'It is not easy here Charlotte and some of the teachers and bigger girls can be quite horrid. You have to keep your books in the classroom and you cannot go into the room except during lessons. There are lots of rules and regulations and the staff can be very hard on us girls. Be careful to avoid upsetting the Superintendent, or any of the staff. Check your food as the housekeeper is quite dirty and the cook is nothing like Nancy. The milk is often sour and the porridge is sometimes burnt, oh and—'

'Elizabeth Brontë!' a voice shouted from the dining room door, 'What are you doing you wretched girl? You are late again. Come to the dining room at once or you will go hungry. Who is that you have there? A new girl? Stop spreading your slovenly habits and both of you come here immediately.'

Elizabeth grabbed Charlotte's hand and pulled them both towards the dining room. As she walked past the teacher, she received a sharp slap across her cheek.

'I expect an apology, Miss Brontë, at once,' shouted the teacher as Elizabeth hung her head and, fighting back tears, whispered that she was sorry.

Charlotte stared in horror at the red line across her sister's pale face. Where on earth had she come to? What was this dreadful place that smelt of burnt porridge and sour milk? Where was Maria and what would she do if she saw what was happening here? She looked around her and was gently pushed by Elizabeth towards a small table with a group of younger girls, Charlotte caught sight of Maria sitting some way off slowly shaking her head with her index finger held over her mouth, in a gesture to Charlotte to stay quiet and obedient.

Charlotte quickly sat down at the table with tears stinging her eyes. None of the girls had been spoken to like this at home, although they had all had the occasional spanking or slap from Aunt Branwell for being rude or naughty, but that had been deserved. This seemed so wrong and so unfair. Charlotte sat in her chair, confused with indignation. She felt lost and homesick. All the joy of coming to school and being with her older sisters melted away. She had hoped to work hard, learn all her lessons, do well and spend happy hours with her sisters and with new friends. She had assumed that the teaching staff would be kind and thoughtful and that the other girls would be friendly and helpful.

Charlotte looked around her. No one spoke and no one asked who she was or whether she was all right. Every girl sat in silence with their heads bowed as prayers were said. Afterwards a meagre meal of hot pot, containing fatty meat and gristle along with a few potatoes, was placed in front of them. One teacher wandered between the tables watching the girls and making sure they ate their food and did not chatter, whilst Miss Andrews, sat on a high stool and read a chapter from the Bible; the parable of the loaves and fishes.

Charlotte attempted to eat the plate of food in front of her. She was very hungry and had only had a spoonful of oatmeal for breakfast as the other girls had snatched up the porridge before she could get to it. The food tasted soapy but she ate it all and although it did not resemble anything like the food at home, it stopped her tummy from rumbling and she felt slightly better. There followed a baked rice pudding which was solid and cut into portions, one for each of the five girls sitting around the table. Charlotte's portion fitted into her hand and she ate it in two mouthfuls. She looked about her at the other girls and strained her eyes to find Maria and Elizabeth.

Catching Maria's eye, her sister gave another soft shake of her head and placed her finger over her mouth. Elizabeth too stared at Charlotte with a look that held a warning. 'Stay quiet, do as you are told and we will try and talk later. School is hard and you have to keep your head down and not upset anyone.'

Charlotte sat very still. There was turmoil in her brain. This was not what she had expected and nor was it what Papa had reported and promised. He had spoken of neat buildings, garden plots; kindly staff and a healthy fresh air feel to the school. He had praised the senior teachers and the superintendent. He had described how well and smart the girls had looked in their school uniforms. He had explained and accepted the need for discipline and for a structured day of study and learning based around religious principles and he had no concerns at sending his daughters to this school for long months at a time. He believed that they would be well cared for, well-educated and would benefit hugely from their experience.

Charlotte looked slowly around at the pale faces of her fellow pupils. She noted the lack of laughter, or smiles or noise of any kind, except the droning voice of Miss Andrews reading from the Bible. She observed the anxious and furtive looks of the older girls, the basic uniforms and the identical haircuts that allowed no personalisation; no fancy curls, or pretty length. Everyone's hair was cut short and hidden beneath tight-fitting bonnets which, to Charlotte, seemed to expose sad, thin faces and hollow eyes. The girls looked tired and their faces appeared empty of expression. Charlotte looked down at the table, at the meagre remains of an awful lunch and the smell of grease and burnt food that hung in the air. She noted the cuts and bruises some of the girls displayed on their hands and faces, the coughing and wheezing that some girls tried to muffle and the general demeanour of the downtrodden.

Charlotte felt that she had arrived in a place that was different from her home in every possible way. This place was so cold, austere, unfriendly and frightening that when the bell rang to end the meal and summon everyone into line to walk silently back to the schoolroom, her little legs barely supported her.

That first day was torture to Charlotte and the thought of having to stay there for at least the next nine months, until there was a holiday, appalled the little girl. Contact with her adored sisters was limited to a secret hug or kiss and the occasional furtive smile across the schoolroom. She had to watch in silence as Maria and Elizabeth, along with the rest of the girls, were regularly shouted at and even hit. A few of the teachers were cruel and showed no compassion or interest in the physical or emotional welfare of the pupils, during the long gruelling days of lessons and prayers. Other staff members seemed not to notice that the girls were suffering and just turned a blind eye to the fate of their pupils.

Homesickness made Charlotte feel physically sick and disturbed both her waking and sleeping. She dreamt often of home, and in a recurring dream just when Mama appeared beside her to gather her up in her arms and shower her with love and care, Charlotte would wake up crying into her pillow.

Chapter Twenty-One
September 1824

Three weeks after Charlotte had left for school, Branwell, Emily and Anne woke up to a beautiful early September morning with sunshine, light winds and late summer warmth in the air. After their morning lessons, Papa came into the parlour and looked at his three children. They were still pale and thin from the months of illness they had endured throughout the spring and summer and he was also aware that they were missing their three older siblings.

'Children,' he urged, 'it is a lovely sunny day and this afternoon I will arrange for you all to go for a nice long walk over the moors. Run and play as much as you wish and get lots of fresh air into your lungs. You need sunshine and exercise. Be ready as soon as you have had lunch and Nancy and Sarah will take you off to play.'

The three excited children rushed through their meal and had their cloaks and bonnets on as they waited impatiently for their nurses to get ready.

'I shall be a general when we are out and I will march to the very top of the moors and shoot any enemies I find hiding in the heather,' announced Branwell, to anyone who would listen. 'You and Anne can be two of my soldiers, but you have to do exactly as I say and carry out all of my orders,' Branwell instructed Emily as she walked past him to the back door.

'Anne and I are going to see if we can find any white heather amongst all the purple, so we will be too busy to play soldiers, Branwell. You will just have to make up your army in your head,' replied Emily, who felt that Branwell had become obsessed with soldiers since Papa had bought him some tin ones for his seventh birthday in June.

'You girls are such sissies,' moaned Branwell, 'we need more boys in this family!' He ran out of the back garden and away on to the moors with his stick sword held high in his hand and his red hair blowing in the breeze. As Nancy chased after him, begging him to slow down, Sarah, Emily and Anne set off running and laughing behind them.

For the next two hours the three children and the two young servants ran and chased each other amongst the heather. They walked over rough heathland, crossed tiny streams, strode up high hills and climbed over warm dry stone walls in the sunshine. The air was still and the further they walked on to the moor the hotter it became. They were glad to reach an area where there was a large rocky outcrop and a wide valley with a fast stream running through it.

They settled beside the stream and were dangling their hands in the water, watching leaves floating and bobbing in the fast flow when, suddenly, the whole earth began to shake. They all looked up in alarm. The very ground on which they were sitting appeared to move in a most alarming way. Everyone stopped what they were doing and held their breath as the earth continued to tremble beneath their feet.

Above them, the sky seemed to have darkened and all the sounds of the moors; the birds, the wind and the animal sounds of the sheep and cattle, appeared to have stopped. A strange and complete silence descended and the air around was still. Nothing moved. Suddenly a loud booming sound rang out and echoed around the hills. The children clung to their nurses in alarm.

'What was that?' gasped Emily, clutching hold of Sarah and starting to cry.

'Why is the earth moving?' asked Branwell, his voice trembling. 'I don't like it!'

Nancy and Sarah swapped horrified looks and could only gather up the three children and hold their hands. They, too, were frightened and had no idea what was happening.

Next, a flash of lightening, almost instantly followed by a crash of thunder, lit the sky and they all let out a cry of terror. Nancy shrieked in alarm which made all the children panic. Anne began screaming and Branwell lost all his bravery and curled up on the ground. 'I'm scared!' he wailed as Sarah put her arms around him and tried to comfort them all.

'It alright, stay calm, all of you,' Sarah demanded. 'Pull yourself together Nancy, you are scaring the children. Whatever it is we are all alright. It is just a violent thunderstorm. Now listen all of you. Let's just move out of this valley and back towards Haworth. We will be home in about an hour if we walk really fast. Now, come on, all of you, as quickly as you can.'

Despite being scared herself, Sarah realised that whatever had happened they needed to get off the moor and find some shelter. The sky was darker now and huge drops of rain were falling. She urged them all back up the path, almost pushing Anne and Emily and shouting encouragement to Nancy and Branwell to keep up. Below them, the water in the beck seemed to have risen and its speed increased. It was rushing through the valley at an alarming rate. A strong wind had arisen and with it the sudden cries of distressed animals could be heard throughout the valley.

For the next half an hour Sarah shouted, pushed and shoved the little party forward until they reached Ponden Hall, about two miles from Haworth Parsonage and the home of the wealthy Heaton family. The rain was now pouring down and they were all soaked through. The wind was howling and the children were all crying and were covered in mud and out of breath. They arrived at the Hall a very sorry sight. Mrs Heaton ushered them in to the long hallway and removed their sodden cloaks, boots and bonnets.

'Whatever are you all doing out in this weather so far from home?' she demanded. 'Mr Heaton is down at the mill checking to see if there is any damage. What a going on. I don't think I have witnessed conditions like this in years and did you feel the ground shake about an hour ago? I thought the house would topple. Do come through into the kitchen and warm yourselves by the fire. Cook will get you a warm drink. Come children, you can stop crying now you are all safe.'

Mrs Heaton chatted on nervously as she led them through to the kitchen. She had been frightened by the storm and worried when her husband had dashed out down to their mill, half a mile away.

'Get some more logs on t'fire,' the Heaton's cook shouted at the maid. 'Now then, how about some warm milk to settle you all? Little 'uns are fair shaking their teeth out.'

The children were all shivering from cold and shock after their awful journey in the driving rain. Everyone was very glad to be in the Hall, where the thick walls deadened the noise of the howling wind. Gradually they all relaxed with their drinks and the comfort of the fire light. Mrs Heaton knew the Brontë family well and her husband was a good friend of their father. She was delighted to be sheltering the Parson's young family.

'It's a pleasure to have you here,' she told the children. 'Your Papa is a good man and we all enjoy his sermons. There are many folk out here who think very highly of him and my dear husband is one of them,' she beamed.

After half an hour and with the rain still heavy, Sarah began to gather the children and their wet clothing.

'You have been so kind,' she explained, 'but I think that we really must get back to the Parsonage. Mr Brontë is bound to be very worried.'

With great reluctance, the party put their sodden garments back on and headed out once more. The wind and rain has lessened slightly but it was still a cold and miserable tramp back to Haworth. As they were sheltering for a few minutes to get their breath back under an overhang of rock by Penistone Hill the familiar figure of Mr Brontë could be seen coming towards them from the parson's field. He held out his arms as he ran forward and hugged his children to him as they all burst into tears at once.

Later that evening, after the children had been thoroughly dried, warmed, fed and put to bed, Mr Brontë and Aunt Branwell invited Nancy and Sarah into the study for an account of their experience. Sarah described how they had all been playing happily when the ground suddenly began to move beneath their feet. She described the loud explosion and the sudden storm.

'We were all very frightened, sir,' said Nancy, 'but our Sarah was very good and it was she who got us all back safely like. I am sure I was all a tremble and had no idea what to do.'

'I am very grateful to you both,' said Mr Brontë, 'I was watching from the upstairs windows just after the storm hit and I must admit I feared greatly for each and every one of you. People are saying that part of the moor has shifted or that a wall of water has erupted somewhere above Ponden. We shall find out the details lately. I think we must all remember that the Lord giveth and the Lord taketh away and that this may well be a sign from Him. I shall be preparing a sermon for this Sunday warning people of God's wrath. It is His way of telling us to follow His path and a reminder of how, on the Day of Judgement, the whole world will tremble and end in terror and destruction, as is written in the Revelations of St John. This time, He has spared you and my small children. However, remember that this is a warning and we must all take heed. Let us pray and thank Him for your deliverance.'

It was later learnt that a huge eruption of mud and water had taken place on the moor at a place called Crow Hill, possibly the result of a small earthquake. Mr Brontë went up the following day to view the area, where he found that large parts of moorland had been swept away in a tide of mud and water that had been building up for days under the peat. Bridges, dry stone walls, fields and animals had all been destroyed or swept down the valleys. The streams and rivers were contaminated for days with mud and undergrowth that had disgorged into the water. His children and servants had had a lucky escape. Mr Brontë was very keen to warn his parishioners that, in his opinion, this was an act of God that had been sent to remind people of their need to follow in the ways of Jesus.

Despite the soaking they had received the day before, all three children and servants were well and there were no nasty repercussions from their ordeal. They chatted for weeks about the storm and the bog burst. None of the children realised how close they had come to disaster. Papa was loathe to let them roam far whilst the memory of that fateful day was still in everyone's mind. Aunt Branwell was keen to keep them all close to the house for a while. The weather remained mild and sunny and the children craved the outdoors.

'Papa wishes you to play only in the garden for a while, until everything settles down,' warned Aunt Branwell. So each afternoon, after their lessons and their mid-day meal, the children played in the gardens, the field and the side lane. They watched as the sexton and stonemason worked in the churchyard, they played tag and hide and seek amongst the bushes and in the old barn across the lane and they brought out their few toys and played in the sunshine with their dolls, soldiers and skipping ropes. They picked posies of flowers, read their simple books and drew pictures on scraps of paper. They ran short errands into the village and ventured into the church to hide amongst the old pews and pulpit. This time of sunshine and happiness was fading as summer turned to autumn and Mr Brontë decided that it was Emily's turn to go to school.

By November, the nights had drawn in and Cowan Bridge was bracing itself for a long cold winter. Mr Brontë escorted his fourth daughter on the long journey over the moors into Lancashire, unaware that his elder three girls were suffering a harsh and punishing regime at his chosen school.

Happy to leave Emily in their care and assured by the Superintendent, Miss Andrews, that it was best not to disturb his elder children, who were hard at their evening lessons when he arrived, Mr Brontë went straight to bed after a nice warm supper. The coach came past very early in the morning and though he longed to see his daughters, Mr Brontë felt that a sudden visit might unsettle them and was inclined to agree with Miss Andrews that seeing a parent on the premises may make both his own and the other girls a little homesick and distract them from their studies.

'They are here to work hard and to learn to grow in God's grace,' explained Miss Andrews as she shook Mr Brontë's hand at five thirty the following morning. 'They are all doing well and it will only remind them of home if they see you. Best that you get straight back to your busy ministry as soon as possible. Your daughters are all in safe hands here and we will look after them. Please do not concern yourself, sir. Is there another child that you may wish to bring?'

'Ah, yes,' Mr Brontë replied, 'My daughter Anne will be coming next year, she is only four years old and I think she should be at least five. She is being taught the rudiments at home by her Aunt, whom we are very fortunate to have living with us. I have also a boy, but as a graduate of Cambridge, I see to his schooling myself.'

Mr Brontë rose to his full height and nodded to Miss Andrews, aware that he had made an impression on this young woman whom he did not much care for. Her manner seemed a little coarse and he had found her rather uninterested on the previous occasions when they had met. His daughters might be here as charity girls, but he was at pains to let the staff know that they came from very well-educated stock.

Chapter Twenty-Two
End of 1824 – Feb 1825

The days and weeks passed, Charlotte saw and experienced many things at school. Some things appalled her and others warmed her heart. An older girl called Mellaney Hane took a liking to Charlotte and became her friend and champion, sheltering her from some of the older, nastier girls who made fun of the Brontë children. The Brontë sisters were all charity pupils; part of their fees being payable by the church and part from their father's wages. Mellaney was also a charity girl and as such, like the Brontë girls, had to wear a slightly different uniform which marked them out from the others. Seventeen-year-old Mellaney had different lessons and sat at a separate part of the classroom from Maria and Elizabeth, but was better able to talk to Charlotte and watch out for her.

Charlotte became increasingly aware of what she saw as a strict and harsh regime. The girls were ordered and controlled by the teaching staff and threatened by the omnipotent presence of the school's main benefactor, Reverend William Carus Wilson.

However, despite the hardships of school, Charlotte wanted to learn and she worked diligently at her lessons. She kept an eager eye open for her sisters and was often filled with anger and hurt when they were reprimanded for various minor misdemeanours. Maria, especially, was a particular target for one teacher who appeared to watch her acutely in order to find fault and seemed to delight in choosing her for harsh and unwarranted criticism and punishment.

One day, Maria had arrived at breakfast with her hair sticking out from under her bonnet. The duty teacher immediately pounced and Maria was made to stand for the entire morning on a chair, with a placard around her neck with the one word, SLATTERN emblazoned for all to see. The girls were instructed not to speak to her or even acknowledge her presence. Charlotte put her head down to her books with tears in her eyes when she saw the shame and humiliation on Maria's face. Desperate to go forward and comfort her sister, Charlotte could only sit in anguish and misery knowing that any attempt to interfere would only bring double the retribution, on both of them.

As Charlotte's anger and sense of injustice grew, she became more and more aware of the poor conditions and the amount of pain and suffering that all the girls had to endure. Many of them showed signs of illness but this was often met with more punishment rather than care and consideration. Lessons covered six days of the week and were long and hard with constant reference to religion and the fate of the wicked in hell and the reward of Heaven for those who were good and hardworking.

Sundays were devoted to church services and had become more of a trial to the children as the wet autumn changed into icy winter. This was partly due to them having to take the long walk each week to the church in the parish of Tunstall, two miles away, where the Reverend Wilson held his Sunday sermons. As the walk turned from a mildly pleasant exercise in the weak autumn sunshine to a gruelling trudge through harsh wintry conditions, it became a weekly trial of strength and endurance.

Having reached the church, the girls were expected to stay throughout the long day in the unheated building so that they could attend all three services. A packed lunch of bread, and occasionally cheese, was consumed in the freezing cold vestry above the porch. The girls stamped their feet and swung their arms to try and stay warm. The Brontë girls, like many others, developed sore throats and coughs, chilblains, head colds, shivering and, after a while, a low fever that came and went and made them feel tired and ill.

To Charlotte's intense pleasure but secret concern, she awoke one morning in late November to find her little sister Emily asleep in a small bed that had been placed at the end of the long row in her dormitory. Along with another new six-year-old, they were sleeping end to end in the narrow iron bedstead pushed up against the grey wall. How had Emily arrived? Surely Papa must have brought her? Was he still here?

With a rush of excitement and hope Charlotte shot out of bed and ran to the teachers' quarters knowing that she might well be punished but not caring as long as she could catch her father and explain to him how awful the school was and how he must not keep sending his children here. Better still, her mind filled with ideas about begging him to take them all home. With eager expectation Charlotte hammered on the door of the headmistress's chambers. The door was opened by Miss Andrews who looked shocked and angry to see the young Charlotte, breathless and flushed on her doorstep.

'Whatever is the matter Miss Brontë? Is the school on fire?' she enquired.

'My father, Miss Andrews, is he here? Can I speak with him? Please, I must see him. It is terribly urgent.' Charlotte stood on the doorstep trembling but defiant. 'Please, I really must see him, at once. Please tell me where he is!'

'Where he is? Why he is travelling back to his parish of course. He is certainly not here. He left very early this morning after delivering your sister safely into our care yesterday evening. Your father is a very busy man Charlotte and knowing that his children are all safe and happy here, he had no wish to disturb you in your dormitory. Thankfully, he was able to return immediately to his important business at home. You are aware that you may write home once each term, so you will have to correspond with your father in the usual way. You know that we do not allow special privileges and I am sure that there is nothing so urgent that he needs to be disturbed. Now return at once to your dormitory and get dressed. You cannot run around the school in such an unladylike manner. Go now, before you are seen. You will learn by heart the 15th Psalm and recite it in class on Monday as punishment for your unseemly outburst.'

Charlotte stood with her mouth open and her heart thundering in her chest. The shock of knowing that her Papa had been so close, perhaps only one room away, as they slept, hurt Charlotte beyond measure. The fact that no-one had informed his daughters or invited them to a reunion with their beloved parent stung Charlotte to the core. She knew what had happened. She knew that her Papa would have asked to see them all and that the staff would have made excuses as to why he should not; falsely reporting that they were all well and happy, already asleep and best not to be disturbed or distracted with a mid-term visit from home which would only unsettle them. Charlotte could hear it all as if she had been there and she felt sure that her father, safe in the misguided knowledge that his children were thriving and needed all the education and discipline that they could get, was assured that they should be left to their studies and their sleep, in the school that was doing its very best for them.

Charlotte's whole body drooped as her heart seemed to contract and her breath stuck in her throat. All her earlier excitement disappeared and gave way to despair. Tears sprang unbidden as she turned away from the closing door and she became overwhelmed by a sense of profound loss. Whatever was happening here was wrong. This regime was unjust and unfair. Charlotte's feelings of impotence increased as she dragged herself back to her dormitory in time to see the other girls filing out to go down to prayers in the schoolroom. Emily was standing patiently at the end of the line and Charlotte ran to her and engulfed her in a huge hug, as tears streamed down her face.

'Oh, Emily, Emily,' she whispered, 'what will become of us? How will we all endure this place? How will it all end?'

Emily, enormously happy to see her sister but totally bemused by Charlotte's hug and strange questions, stood patiently basking in the nearness of her sister and returned her hugs and kisses. A sharp shout from one of the teachers and a command for Charlotte to get dressed and report for punishment for her tardiness, broke up their bitter-sweet reunion. A bewildered Emily followed the older girls, Charlotte, unheeding of any punishment that could possibly be worse than her current anguish, flung herself on to her bed and sobbed.

Charlotte would never forget the lesson she learned that day. It was the deep conviction that life was not fair, justice was not automatic and that people, even those with good intentions, could hurt and upset you. That the staff had deliberately kept the girls from the pleasure of seeing their father festered in Charlotte's mind and heart.

For days afterwards, Charlotte felt not just sad but abandoned. In her mind she felt that had she been allowed to see her Papa that night she could have persuaded him to take them all home. At the very least she would have made him aware of the harsh conditions and she knew that he would have done something to protect his children. Charlotte felt more and more that parents were being falsely informed and falsely led into believing that the school was thriving and the pupils along with it. Her sense of right and wrong and her moral indignation grew daily.

The winter storms and the wind and snow battered the school throughout December and January, the continuing hardships took their toll on all of the girls. The incidences of fever began to multiply and intensify until many of the girls became seriously ill and were unable to get out of bed or attend to any sort of personal care. Maria Brontë had been ill for some time with fever, sore throat and chest pain. She coughed day and night making a dry, rattling and hollow sound. She was kept in bed, where one of the treatments for her fever and weak lungs was to apply a blister or poultice to the worse affected side of her chest. Maria was too frightened of punishment to stay in bed for long and although she was still weak and ill, she attempted to get up and dressed with great effort and considerable pain.

On entering the dormitory one morning, the deputy superintendent spotted Maria struggling to get ready and regardless of her condition dragged her out into the middle of the room and shouted at her for her laziness. When Maria eventually made it downstairs to the schoolroom, the duty teacher punished her for being late. Charlotte, Elizabeth and Emily, along with many other girls, witnessed this persecution and they all knew that it was wrong and that Maria's illness was becoming worse each day. Her now constant cough could be heard throughout lessons and it irritated Miss Andrews who reprimanded Maria each time the rasping noise disturbed her. The Brontë girls could only watch in horror with a terrible and maddening helplessness.

Miss Andrew's time as superintendent came to an end. Although she still taught the girls, the role of headmistress was taken over by Miss Evans, a teacher with a kinder outlook and a more sympathetic nature. When Elizabeth had a nasty fall and hurt her head, Miss Evans took her to her own rooms and nursed her for a while. Of all the staff, Miss Evans appeared the most kind, but even she was subject to the harsh discipline and the overbearing command of the Reverend Wilson. One day she had produced bread and cheese because the lunch had been inedible. The girls were very happy but when Rev. Wilson discovered what had happened, Miss Evans was severely reprimanded.

'You must feed their souls not their bellies,' Rev. Wilson had shouted at her. 'These girls are here to learn that the harder their lives on Earth the greater their rewards will be in Heaven. They must not be allowed fancy clothes, fancy food and fancy behaviour. They are here to study the word of God at their peril.'

The man's large, red and angry face had frightened Miss Evans and she had promised him that she would never 'waste' food on the girls again.

Despite their repeated failure to recognise and alleviate their pupils suffering, the teachers eventually accepted there was a serious medical problem and a doctor was summoned to examine the girls and identify the on-going sickness. Too late for some, the fever, probably mixed with cases of tuberculosis, cholera or typhoid, had taken hold and the first deaths began to occur. In fear and horror, the staff began to send some of the worse cases home in a late attempt to prevent the further spread of the diseases and to avoid the cost of doctors, medicines and funerals.

In mid-February, it became apparent, even to the most strict and uncaring members of staff, that Maria Brontë was seriously ill. A letter was dispatched to the Parsonage, summoning her father to come and collect his daughter and take her home for a period of recovery.

Chapter Twenty-Three
Feb 1825

After Emily's departure to Cowan Bridge School and with only two children left at home, Mr Brontë had decided to economise on staffing. By Christmas, Nancy was engaged to a young man and was preparing to leave and get married; Sarah, with only two growing children left to nurse, was no longer needed. Mr Brontë tried to get Sarah a new post travelling as a lady's companion, but her mother objected and Sarah returned home to Bradford in February.

A middle-aged, widowed lady called Tabitha Aykroyd, who was living in the village, was approached by Mr Brontë to come to the Parsonage as cook and general maid. He had decided that once Anne had also left for school, probably in the following spring, there would be an opportunity for Aunt Branwell to return home to Penzance for a holiday, or even for good, depending how well things turned out for the girls' education. An experienced cook and housekeeper like Mrs Aykroyd would easily suffice for the needs of himself and Branwell.

However, things did not turn out the way Mr Brontë had anticipated. As Tabby Aykroyd took up her post at the Parsonage and before Mr Brontë could begin to make arrangements for Anne to go to school, he received the letter from Miss Evans with the terrible news that Maria was ill and he was expected to bring her home.

Although the letter played down her condition and talked only of her homecoming as a precaution, her father hurried immediately to the school and seeing the state of his child, took her straight back to Haworth.

On arrival home, and with the assurance from the school that his other girls were all well and happy, Mr Brontë, Aunt and Tabby all concentrated their love and care on trying to nurse Maria back to health. Tabby was kindly and old-fashioned. She liked children but her standards were not always to the exacting levels of Aunt Branwell and the two would sometimes disagree.

The joy felt by Branwell and Anne on the return of their eldest sister soon turned to fear as the severity of her illness, now diagnosed as tuberculosis, began to dawn on the younger children. Night after night, the sound of Maria's coughing and laboured breathing filled the dark rooms; Branwell and Anne, snuggled up together in the tiny bedroom next door to the stricken child, had their dreams interrupted as they listened to the awful sounds from the sickroom.

Maria, lying alone in the large double bed, once occupied by her Mama, felt sick and very frightened. Her head ached and her chest felt as if a great weight was laid across it. Every time she coughed her whole upper body shook and an awful pain shot through her ribcage. Looking around the room, she remembered her Mama's long illness, the shuttered windows, the dark atmosphere and the green coverlet that now lay over her own thin body.

When she first came home, Papa carried her downstairs for an hour each day, and laid her gently on the settle in the parlour. A vase of early spring flowers had stood in the middle of the polished dining room table. Daffodils, wild irises and fronds of catkins filled the air with their beautiful and intoxicating scents. A small posy of late snowdrops and early crocuses had been brought to the front door by one of the ladies from the church, who had heard that the little girl was poorly. These were carefully placed in Maria's hand by her little sister, on the one occasion that she was allowed into the room to see her.

'They are especially for you to make you better,' whispered Anne staring wide-eyed and breathless at her adored sister, before retreating to her little footstool by the fireplace. 'You must get better soon, Maria, because it is spring and it is sunny and Branwell and I want to take you on to the moors. We have got a new den and we know where there are some wild orchids. You must come very soon, before they are blown away in the wind.'

Maria smiled, feeling tearful as she remembered the times last summer before starting school, when they had all run across the moors, shouting and laughing, happy and free, with no worries and no problems. Surely those times would come again soon, wouldn't they?

When Papa came in to usher Anne away and carry Maria back upstairs, Maria asked her father when she would be well enough to go outside again in the sunshine. 'As soon as you are a bit better and when your cough has gone,' Papa had replied. 'You need to try and eat my dear and put some weight back on, then all will be well. Have some broth now and then go to sleep for a while.'

Maria did as her father bid, but the broth tasted strange and she could only manage a very small amount before it made her cough and she had to lie down and rest. Papa anxiously watched her reject her food and Maria knew from his look that he was more concerned than he was prepared to say. He stroked her hands, whispering to her that God was watching over her and that she was safe at home, and he and Aunt would make sure that she got better, but that it might be painful and uncomfortable for a while.

Maria drifted off to sleep happy that her father was so close and that she was at home. She tried not to think about school and how horrible, cold and scared she had felt there. She wondered how her sisters were coping and if the staff were being kind to them. She would be better before too long and perhaps Papa would consider her going somewhere else for her education. She did not want to go back to that place where she had felt so ill and frightened.

During the first few weeks back home Maria had just wanted to sleep and for the pain to go. She was not hungry and it was her cough that troubled her the most. As time passed she began to suffer from terrible thirst and extreme sickness. She often felt very hot and seemed to see and hear things that she was unsure of. She thought that she could hear people murmuring in low voices, she saw firelight and then, abruptly, darkness. Papa and Aunt would be in the room and then, suddenly, she would be alone in the big bed with no sight or sound of another being to comfort her. After days of wanting to sleep, Maria now felt scared to even close her eyes. She was frightened that she would fall into that terrible final sleep and, like Mama, she would go down to that awful, cold, black crypt deep beneath the church, where she would lie for all eternity.

Maria was also puzzled and perplexed. Miss Andrews had said that bad children died and went to Hell and good children lived and grew old, or died young and went to Heaven. If Maria were to die now, would she go to Heaven and be with Mama or would she descend into that terrible other place? Maria began to cry and longed for the comfort of her Papa who always knew what God wanted and what everything meant. Despite her tears and her pathetic, soft calls for help, no-one came to the room as she tossed and turned around the bed, with her head aching and the burning pain in her chest.

Looking down on the sleeping child some time later, Mr Brontë was worried by how troubled and anxious Maria seemed, even in her sleep. Her eyes darted around under her eyelids; she gave little whimpers and cries, whilst fidgeting and twitching under the covers. She was losing weight rapidly but could not touch her food. She was pale and thin. The awful, ever-present cough disturbed her days and shattered her nights.

Branwell and Anne tip-toed around the house; Branwell, desperate to see the sister he loved the most, tried various ways to get upstairs to see her. Unfortunately, not to alarm Branwell and Anne, none of the adults had mentioned that Maria's illness might be infectious and instead, just ordered the children to keep out of the sickroom. Branwell spent hours thinking up ways to get upstairs without being noticed, but the adults kept a close vigil and only once did he reach Maria's bedside.

As he gently pushed open the door, Maria started up in surprise and flung open her arms. 'Oh Branwell, there you are, I thought everyone had left me. Why haven't you and Anne been upstairs to visit me? Where have you been?' his sister called in anguish.

Branwell rushed into her embrace as Maria began to cough until she was choking. Spots of bright red blood began to splatter over Branwell's face and hair. The sight of the blood frightened Branwell; but he was so happy to see his sister that he allowed himself to be held in her skinny arms and be repeatedly kissed on his cheeks.

'Aunt and Papa say that we have not to disturb you,' moaned Branwell, 'but I jolly well fooled them and they don't know that I am here. I will stay as long as you like. Aunt's gone out and Tabby is asleep in the kitchen. Papa's in the study and Anne is playing with her doll on the kitchen floor. Why have you come home from school, Maria? Couldn't they look after you there? I am glad that you are home though, it's much better with you here, Anne is such a baby. Will you read me some stories when you are better and take me out for walks again?'

'Branwell!' Aunt's shout penetrated the house and Branwell looked around in horror, 'Oh, gosh, Aunt's back, I had better go. I will come back as soon as I can get past the grown-ups. Get better very soon, Maria, it will be lovely when you are well again.' Branwell ran out of the room and tip-toed rapidly back downstairs.

Maria did not get better. By the beginning of May, the terrible wracking sounds of her coughing could be heard night and day all over the house. Even people walking up the church lane could hear the noise of the little girl and they shook their heads at the dreadful sound. Maria began to slip into long episodes of deep sleep, waking to gasp for breath with blood and other foul-tasting liquids, erupting from her throat and trickling onto the pillow. Doctor Andrews shook his head, Papa and Aunt knelt beside the bed for long hours, praying to God to spare the life of this beloved child.

Finally, the terrible sickness stopped. The cough was silent. The long days and nights of fever came to an end; and Maria lay, like her mother before her, cold and dead in the large bed with the green coverlet drawn up over her small, white face.

Chapter Twenty-Four
May 1825

Numb with grief, Mr Brontë later went downstairs and hugged his two small children and tried to explain that Maria had gone to Heaven. A place where all her suffering was over, and she was happy and safe with their Mama in God's keeping. Aunt retired to her room, weeping quietly and refusing all food and drink for the next two days.

Branwell and Anne were horrified. How could Maria have died? She was their big sister. She was beautiful and they loved her. Where had she gone and would they ever see her again? The distressed children cried and cried. Tabby's hugs and kisses and Papa's warm and loving embraces, did nothing to take away their shock and sadness. Aunt finally emerged from her room, trying to comfort the children, but they ran from her and huddle together in the little study bedroom.

Maria's funeral was arranged for Ascension Day and that morning Branwell and Anne were playing quietly in the parlour as their sister's corpse, draped in a soft wool wrap, was gently carried downstairs by Papa. Tenderly and reverently he carefully placed her body in the small, narrow coffin arranged on a bier in the hallway of the Parsonage. Afterwards, Papa came to the parlour door and spoke softly to his two youngest children.

'It is time to come and say good-bye to your sister,' he whispered, 'you may kiss her and pray that she arrives safely into God's keeping. We will walk down to the church in ten minutes' time when the undertaker has made everything ready. Come now children. Come and say farewell and thank God that Maria is at peace.'

Lifting Anne into his arms, Mr Brontë carried the little girl into the hallway and raised her over the side of the coffin to kiss her sister's cold face. Anne stared at the body of the girl she had loved as her little mother. She began to tremble and cry, so her father returned her to the parlour as he rocked and soothed her.

Aunt Branwell moved forward with Branwell who was struggling to get away from her firm grip. Branwell had no wish to see his dead sister, no wish to further fuel his overwrought imagination and his morbid fear of death. Branwell was scared. As his Aunt lifted him up and over Maria's dead body, the boy screamed in fear and shock. This cold dead face: blue lips, and white, marble skin was nothing like his pretty sister. Those white hands and stiff fingers were not the ones that had tickled him and held his hand when out on the moors. This was not the girl who had read and sung to him or had snuggled up to him in bed when he was cold and scared of the dark. This was a lifeless effigy that bore no resemblance to his lovely playmate.

Branwell felt his fear rising and his breath disappearing. A blackness was beginning to overwhelm him and a dizzy withdrawal of his senses began to occur as once again he looked down to see the thin white hands, clutching a small posy of spring flowers.

The distraught boy fainted in his Aunt's arms, as the twitching and rigidity of an attack shook his body. Aunt hurried back into the parlour to lay him on the settle and give way to her own feelings of anguish.

Branwell awoke to the sound of a man's deep voice and was aware that the sexton was talking to him.

'Pull yourself together, lad, you need to get to the church in a couple of minutes. Now you come with me and I'll keep an eye on you. Be brave and let's not have any nonsense. Come on, stand up, young man, you mun walk behind t' coffin with your Papa. No crying now. You put on a good show for your Papa and your Auntie.'

Hauling him to his feet, Mr Brown looked down at him. 'Pity you're not a bit older, lad, I'd give you a good stiff drink, that would sort you out, never mind all that medicine. A drink would see you through t'mornin', but you're too young for that lark yet.'

'Would it stop my head hurting?' Branwell asked, standing shakily and feeling a throbbing pain behind his eyes.

'Aye, lad, it would, but it would hurt twice as bad in t' mornin'!' and with that Mr Brown gave a gentle laugh and pushed Branwell forward out of the parlour and down the front steps. The churchwarden, along with three other men, raised the coffin on to their broad shoulders for the short walk through the garden gate, down the path through the graveyard and on into the church.

Papa, with Branwell's hand held firmly in his strong grip, stood tall but walked with his head bowed behind his daughter as she was carried to her final resting place. Aunt and Tabby, sobbing quietly and each holding one of Anne's hands, followed behind. Branwell stepped down into the garden; the mournful tolling of the church bell rang out over the sad procession. Looking up he saw the long row of villagers lined up against the church wall watching in silence and waiting to follow them into the church for the funeral service.

Over the next few days Branwell and Anne stayed close to each other playing quietly together largely undisturbed by Aunt or Papa, Only Tabby seemed aware of the two lost children and tried to keep them cheerful by making special treats for them and giving them long smothering hugs whenever they entered the kitchen. The house seemed strangely quiet and no-one wanted to eat, talk or go outside in to the sunshine.

Chapter Twenty-Five
May 1825

Before Patrick had received the letter informing him of Maria's illness, Elizabeth, Charlotte and Emily knew only that Maria's condition had worsened and that Miss Evans was writing to their father to collect her and take her home. These two pieces of information struck fear and excitement in Charlotte. Firstly, Charlotte feared greatly for her sister's well-being and prayed that a spell at home would restore her to health; secondly, she was sure that this time Papa would be so concerned for their welfare that he would take them all home.

Throughout the following day, Charlotte tried whenever and wherever possible to look out for the arrival of her father. She thought of approaching Miss Evans, but she seemed to be spending much of her time in the sick bay and Charlotte's one enquiry of a member of staff as to her whereabouts had met with an admonishment to get on with her work. Charlotte guessed that Papa would arrive on the chaise about the same time as he had brought each of the girls, around early evening, and she tried to engage Elizabeth and Emily to looking out for their father.

Unfortunately, Elizabeth was also complaining of illness and pain. Charlotte felt it best not to expect her help, but was sure that another sick child would only increase the chances of them all going home. Instead, she commandeered Emily's assistance and told her to watch the main gate, when possible, or listen for horses' hooves or visitors, throughout the afternoon. By five o' clock, Charlotte was becoming desperate but an unexpected chance came when Elizabeth, who had been quiet and unwell all day, suddenly fainted. As she was carried from the classroom, Charlotte was told to go and find Miss Evans.

Amidst fear for Elizabeth but a soaring feeling that fate was working in her favour, Charlotte fled the school room and ran to the staff apartments, where a temporary sick bay had been fashioned from a couple of empty rooms. Calling and searching the rooms, Charlotte found only three sick children and no adult. She ran to the superintendent's office, but no-one was there. Becoming increasingly worried, Charlotte stopped and with a shock that made her gasp it suddenly dawned on her that none of the children in the sick bay had been Maria. With an awful fear the little girl ran towards the outer walls, As she reached sight of the main gate she observed Miss Andrews and Miss Evans sliding the large metal latch across and putting the bolt firmly into place.

'I am sure it will be fine, Miss Evans,' Miss Andrews was saying. 'The girls are all strong and I am sure they will recover soon. Mr Brontë seemed assured that we are just taking precautions and the others are all well and thriving.' Miss Evans was turning back towards the school, 'I hope you are right, this is so bad for our reputation and she did look very poorly. I hope we can contain this latest outbreak. You would expect this nice spell of weather to help.'

As she spoke she caught sight of Charlotte, breathless and trembling a few feet away, a look of horror on her pinched face. Charlotte was dumbstruck. Surely it could not have happened again? Papa must have wanted to see them; these women must realise how much they needed their father's love and reassurance, surely they could not have kept them apart, once more.

But, even as these thoughts spun around Charlotte's head, she knew. She knew the answers to her questions and in that moment she hated with a deep and abiding loathing the two women standing before her. They stood there, with the locked and bolted door firmly shut behind them, Charlotte was sure that another chance to gain her father's attention had been lost. The opportunity had in fact been brutally snatched away from her. Charlotte realised that she had absolutely no hope of seeing her father, let alone trying to convince him that they were all in grave danger.

'What are you doing here, Miss Brontë? Why aren't you in class? You bad girl! Go back at once, you have no right to be out here,' cried Miss Andrews moving towards her.

Miss Evans, however, put a restraining hand on the teacher's arm. 'It's all right, Miss Andrews, I will deal with this.' Taking Charlotte firmly by the hand, she led her back inside to her own office. Seating Charlotte on a chair and squatting down in front of her, Miss Evans took hold of both of Charlotte's hands. 'Now, Charlotte,' she said in a soft and rather kind tone that Charlotte had rarely heard before. 'Did you have a message for me or was there something else?'

Charlotte's dry tongue seemed plastered to the roof of her mouth. The shock of missing her father by minutes had rendered her practically speechless. She stared at this woman who, as far as Charlotte knew, had colluded with Miss Andrews to prevent her seeing Papa. Charlotte snatched her hands away from Miss Evans and as she made to get up, her tongue loosened, and a torrent of words came flooding out of her.

'I hate it here. I want to see my Papa. Why have you let him go without seeing us? How could you let him go? What is wrong with my sister? Why can't we all go home? Why is everyone so horrible to us? Why are we all being punished when we have done nothing wrong?'

The words tumbled unbidden from Charlotte's mouth, totally beyond her control. The little girl raved and shouted for some minutes before the tears and the sheer physical effort of expressing her deep fury, finally brought her to a halt. She sat in angry despair awaiting the terrible wrath of her head teacher. Charlotte was suddenly aware that Miss Evans was not shouting back at her, not marching her out of the room and not picking up the cane to thrash her. Instead, when Charlotte finally looked up her teacher was seated opposite her with tears in her eyes and a look of profound sadness on her face.

It was Miss Evans' turn to speak. With a kind and deliberate effort, to make Charlotte understand, she tried to clarify some of what was happening.

'I cannot explain to you, Charlotte, the trials and tribulations of running a school or the tremendous effort needed to keep all you girls well and educated. We have tried our best. Unfortunately things have not always worked out as planned, one or two girls have become ill and need extra care. You must now accept my word that we are all trying to put things right. We are sending your sister home only as a precaution and to prevent the further spread of illness. I have no wish to alarm your father and I suspected that you might make an effort to speak to him after your outburst following his last visit. Now, listen carefully Charlotte, for you to have cried and shouted and got upset, as you did then and have today, would have greatly distressed your Papa and that would have only made him more worried and anxious. He is a very busy man and he now has extra work nursing your sister back to health, although I understand that there is an aunt at home. The best thing you can do, if you truly love your father, is to be a good girl, work hard at your lessons and do nothing to upset him or your family back at home. Do you understand what I am saying?'

Charlotte stared hard at her headmistress. Was Miss Evans really doing her best for them all? Was it best for Papa to believe that they were all well and happy? There seemed to be some sense in what was being said. Was Maria's illness curable? Would she be back after a few weeks of Nancy's cooking and Aunt's care, fit and well? Was Charlotte being over-dramatic and worrying when there was actually nothing to worry about? Miss Evans sounded so calm, so genuine and so caring. Had Charlotte got it all wrong?

Charlotte became aware that Miss Evans was again speaking in that calm and kindly manner.

'All schools seem harsh when you are a pupil, Charlotte. They have to maintain discipline and hard work if children are to be educated and prepared for adulthood. Life can be difficult Charlotte, especially for women, and you must learn how to cope in the world. Now, I understand that your father was an examiner for a boys' school in West Yorkshire and I know that they are often much harder and rougher than we are with our young ladies. Ask your Papa about conditions in other schools Charlotte and you may be surprised to discover that we are not as bad as you may imagine.'

Charlotte was quiet and listened intently. She vaguely remembered Papa talking to Aunt a while ago about the boys at Woodhouse Grove School, only having one set of clothes and boys having to share their shirts and trousers when theirs were in the laundry. That did not happen here; in fact, the girls all had two or three sets of clothes. Miss Evans was now smiling kindly at her and Charlotte felt much of the fire and anger leaving her. She felt tired, exhausted and a little embarrassed. She must go away and think about what Miss Evans had said and perhaps things were not as bad as she had believed. Charlotte thought perhaps she should apologise for her outburst and thank Miss Evans for being so reasonable. She had been perfectly entitled to punish Charlotte for her bad behaviour.

Charlotte hung her head and was overcome with shame. 'I am sorry, Miss Evans, I did not understand and I apologise for being so rude. I will try much harder in future. I just miss my family and my home so much and I so wanted to see my Papa.'

'I am sure that all the girls would like to see their parents and go home for a while. By summer, you will all be returning home for your summer holidays and it is only fair that you are all treated the same. Remember, Charlotte, you are luckier than most of the girls as you have your other two sisters here to keep you company. Many of our girls are here alone and have no family around them.'

Miss Evans smiled and told her that she could return to her class and must pray for God to guide her and teach her to be more grateful and humble. Charlotte felt the blush of embarrassment cross her face as she quietly closed the study door behind her. What had she been thinking of? Ranting and raving at Miss Evans when all the poor woman was trying to do was to help her. Thank goodness she had not seen Papa and completely shown herself up for the spoilt and stupid child that she was with no discipline or self-control. Papa would have been so ashamed of her. Her face began to burn as she thought about how close she had come to total humiliation.

Charlotte set off towards the school room, aware that she had been gone for some time and that she would probably be punished for her absence. As she walked back Charlotte thought about all that Miss Evans had said. Perhaps things would be better now that she was the superintendent. Miss Evans had admitted that there had been problems that were now being sorted out. Perhaps school life would get better and lessons and meals would improve. Charlotte would so like to enjoy her time at school and when all this illness was over the school would possibly become a nicer place to live and work in.

As she turned a corner of the corridor her head full of Miss Evans' reassurances, an image suddenly struck Charlotte of Elizabeth unconscious on the schoolroom floor. With a terrible realisation, she remembered that this whole afternoon had started because Elizabeth had collapsed. Hadn't she been sent to find Miss Evans because Elizabeth was now unwell and possibly also in danger? Charlotte stopped in mid-step. Elizabeth was sick and in her panic to see Papa, she had failed to tell anyone. Miss Evans was unaware that another of her sisters was by now in the sick bay.

Whatever must she do? Dare she go back and tell Miss Evans that despite all her comforting words another child was poorly? Or, should she stop being dramatic and be reassured that illness was a natural part of childhood, and all children got coughs and colds and it was not necessarily a problem.

Charlotte stood trembling, unsure which way to turn, in complete turmoil. Who should she trust? Who was telling the truth? She was scared. It was all too much for her to deal with. There was no-one to consult, no-one to listen to her fears and no-one to advise her on what to do next. Should she try to find Mellaney and tell her what had happened? Should she let her heart rule her head or should she accept Miss Evans' reasonable explanation?

Charlotte's mind was made up for her when Miss Lord, who had been deliberately watching out for her, suddenly appeared in front of Charlotte and grabbed her by her arm.

'So, Miss Brontë, you think you can miss your lessons and go bothering the head teacher do you? You will miss tea and stay in the schoolroom for an extra hour this evening and write out one hundred times on the black board "I am a weak and stupid girl and must learn to know my place".' As she announced this sentence she cruelly dug her fingers into the flesh of Charlotte's arm and, bringing her face close to Charlotte's she whispered, 'You will never get the better of your elders and betters young lady. You are nothing but an ugly little wretch and you will never be any good to anyone or be of any interest. You are nothing. Now get out of my sight' and with that she flung Charlotte across the corridor and stalked away.

The outbreak of sickness and death at the school reached its height within the next few weeks. By that time, Maria had died and Elizabeth had been taken back to her home by one of the school servants. On seeing the condition of his second daughter and with no warning that she was coming home so ill, Mr Brontë travelled hastily to Lancashire to collect Charlotte and Emily, who with the other remaining girls who were still well, had been taken to the Rev. Wilson's holiday home near Morecambe.

Finally, and under the most harrowing circumstances, Charlotte and Emily came back to the love and shelter of their family and home.

Chapter Twenty-Six
May–June 1825

Arriving home with Papa should have been Charlotte's dream come true. but the joy of being back with her brother and sisters was cruelly spoilt by the grave nature of Elizabeth's illness.

The front bedroom was turned yet again into a sick chamber, where the thin and wasted little girl lay day and night, coughing and vomiting, crying out for her Mama and her dead sister in her delirium.

Mr Brontë left his church duties, abandoned his congregation and spent his days and nights with his dying daughter, totally bereft and praying to God for her soul.

Downstairs, the remaining four children played quietly; reading and whispering amongst themselves. The noise from upstairs frightened them all, but especially Anne and Branwell, for whom it was so familiar. It was as if Maria was back and the awful process was being played out over again.

'She will die, won't she, Charlotte?' sobbed Anne. 'This is just what it was like before. Whatever the doctor or Papa or Aunt can do, she will die, just like Maria. There will only be us four. Who knows who will be ill next time. Are we all going to die Charlotte? I am so frightened.'

Charlotte hugged her little sister and tried to comfort her. Looking over the top of Anne's head, she saw Emily weeping silently in the corner and Branwell scowling at the book he was holding but not reading a word of it.

'That's enough,' Charlotte cried. 'We cannot sit here waiting for the worst to happen. It is too awful. Look outside, it is almost summer, the sun is out and it is a warm, June day. The moors will have flowers in all our special places. Let us go and pick some and bring them back for Elizabeth. Go and get your cloaks and we will do something positive to help. Anything is better than sitting here doing nothing. Come, let us leave quickly, before any of the grown-ups realise that we have gone.'

Within minutes the little group were running across the back field and out on to the moorland. For the first time in days, they felt lifted and realised how much they needed the sun and the fresh air to ease their sorrow. Holding hands, they ran in a line towards the top of the brow along a track that would bring them to the side of the valley and eventually down to where the beck divided into two small tributaries.

Out of breath, but happy to be away from the horror and sickness of home, they sat on the large stones which stood in the water, delighting in the sound of the brook and the cries of the birds high above them. The grasses, bracken and mosses were green and luscious. Tiny harebells grew in the sheltered crevices and the blueberries were beginning to ripen amongst their lime green leaves. Buttercups and daisies nodded in the gentle breeze. Flies and bees flew overhead, water-boatmen skidded across the calmer eddies in the pools. Butterflies played amongst the grasses and a large cabbage white alighted on the back of Emily's hand.

'Look, Charlotte,' Emily whispered, 'Elizabeth has come to play.'

They all stared at the butterfly. As a couple more flew past, they all had the strange feeling that happy, friendly spirits were here, playing and flying amongst them. They felt a great comfort and Charlotte was glad that they had come to this beautiful spot.

'We were right to come here,' she announced. 'I think we were perhaps meant to be here. I do not know whether Elizabeth will still be alive when we get back but I feel that she is here, now, with us, rather than in that awful sick bed. We must not be frightened. Shall we say a little prayer for her soul?'

Jonas Sunderland was walking along the side of the ridge above Sladen Beck, on that June day on his way back to Top Withins Farm, when a strange sight caught his eye. Four of the Parson's children were knelt together in a small circle at the side of the beck, hand in hand, heads bowed, looking for all the world as if they were holding a prayer meeting. Jonas stopped for a few moments, removed his cap and rubbed his forehead. He believed in God and that religion had a place in everyone's life, but those little 'uns should be dashing about in the sunshine, not praying all day long. He would have a word with the verger next time he saw him. Perhaps the Reverend Brontë had a bit too much religious zeal where his children were concerned!

It was an hour after Elizabeth had finally softly sighed her last breath in her father's arms, that any of the adults became aware of the total silence in the house. Stumbling downstairs, blinded by tears, Mr Brontë went to the parlour expecting to see his four children, but the room was empty. Aunt was too distraught to know or care where the rest of the children were; Tabby, wise and sensitive, felt sure that they would be out together somewhere quiet and sunny, where they could think about their sister away from the awful scene upstairs.

'Don't fret Reverend, Sir,' she told Mr Brontë, 'they'll be out ont' moor and like as not be back for tea. You can tell 'um then. Though, I've a feelin' they already know.'

Patrick took his hat and walking stick and set off out of the back door. He was unable to face the horror that another of his precious children had gone. He felt a compulsion to be with the others, to assure himself that they were alive and well. He needed to see their faces, feel the warmth of their hands, and the sound of their voices. He had also to tell them the terrible news of their sister's death.

He strode out over the heath. The afternoon sun in his eyes and the smell and sounds of the moor all around, Patrick felt, despite his overwhelming grief, a grain of comfort. He had the feeling that here, amongst nature, God was still watching over him and that He had taken Elizabeth for a reason and that her death must be part of some celestial plan, of which Patrick had no understanding. The pain of the last two weeks had weakened Patrick's faith, had caused him to cry out in anguish as to why God needed to take first his wife and now his two daughters, from him. Here, amongst the wide open spaces the contrast with the sick room was overwhelming and strangely comforting.

Emily saw her father in the distance before the others noticed him. He was striding along the ridge, his shoulders drooped and his head down, and she knew in that instance what he was coming to tell them. Clutching Charlotte she pointed out the lone figure on the horizon and Charlotte grew still and stared across at her father's bent figure.

'What is the matter, Charlotte?' cried Branwell, jumping off a stone on to the beck side, 'What is wrong? Following Emily's direction, he too saw his father and with a little gasp sank to his knees. Anne burst into tears and unbidden set off up the track to meet her Papa.

That evening, the four children were ushered into the bedroom where Elizabeth lay under the green coverlet. Her soft brown hair was gathered in waves around her neck in contrast to the white, hollow face. Clutching a little posy of the delicate harebells, Charlotte laid them gently on her sister's chest, over her heart. Emily laid a bunch of buttercups and Anne a garland of daisies.

The children stood and wept with their Papa and Aunt, Branwell stepped forward and into Elizabeth's hand pressed his favourite tin soldier. Then, overcome with emotion, he was led sobbing from the sickroom.

Apart from the day of Elizabeth's funeral when, once again, the awful vault beneath the church was opened up to accept another child into its dark chamber, the remaining Brontë children took their sorrow out on to the moors. It was a beautiful summer and free of adult restraint, they spent most of their days playing amongst the wild flora and fauna, letting the sun and wind comfort their broken hearts.

Charlotte adapted to the role of eldest child and felt a strong responsibility for her siblings, ensuring that they ate, slept, played and talked about their sisters. Papa, Aunt and Tabby seemed too distraught to cope with anything but their grief. In the evenings, bold in her new role as the eldest, Charlotte would knock gently on the door of Papa's study and tell him what they had been doing throughout the day. Whilst her father could do little but nod and hug his daughter to him, he was immensely grateful for Charlotte's love and sensitivity and tried to rally some hope for the future.

'I am incapable at the moment of organising your lessons or seeing to your needs, my child. I must look to you, Charlotte, as my eldest living child, to care for the little ones until such time as your Aunt and I can think and cope with our tremendous losses. Try and look after them as best you can my dear, I am putting my faith in you as never before. You are now the eldest Charlotte. You will have to be the protector and comforter of the others, probably for the rest of your lives.'

Charlotte cried into her father's coat but relished the feel of his protective arms.

'I will do everything I can, Papa,' she whispered through her tears. 'I will try to make you proud of me and I will see that we all do our best to be good and follow the example of our sisters.' Charlotte felt sad but strong with her father. Her determination to carry out his wishes helped her to contain her grief in the following weeks and months.

Mr Brontë held his daughter close as he felt the agony and blame of sending his daughters to school. Should he have been more vigilant? Should he have insisted on seeing them and checking them over each time he visited the school? Had he let the fact that it was cheap and convenient override his resolve to home school them all?

Thoughts like this tormented him and added to his grief. He could not help wondering whether, if they had all stayed at Thornton, he would still have his wife and six children.

Chapter Twenty-Seven
September 1825

'97, 98, 99, 100!' called Charlotte as she lifted her head from the warm grey wall of the church tower. Looking around the surrounding grave yard, there was no sign of her siblings amongst the muddle of tombstones and long grasses, the laurel and the ivy, the stone surrounding walls and the pathways in between. It was a beautiful summer's day, Aunt was away in Keighley and Papa out on his parish rounds, and the children had come out to play their favourite game, hide and seek.

Charlotte was fully aware that neither Aunt nor Papa approved of them playing inside the graveyard. With such lovely weather, and Tabby too busy to escort them on to the moors today, the children had decided that they would spill over from their games in the garden and include the graveyard as their playground.

Suddenly, Anne darted out from behind a tall stone and ran towards her.

'Block you! One, two, three!' called Charlotte, tapping the tower wall three times and laughing at her sister's hopeless attempt to block her.

'Oh Charlotte, you saw me,' moaned Anne, 'I am always the first to be caught.'

'Never mind,' said Charlotte, 'it's a lovely afternoon to lay out. Look at all the buttercups and daisies. Why don't you make a nice long daisy chain whilst I go and look for the others?'

Halfway up one of the paths leading between the grave stones, Branwell had found the perfect hiding place. Some of the gravestones were laid flat, like low tables over the graves, instead of standing upright. He had found one just high enough to squeeze under. The grave stood at the side of the path leading away from the church towards the old vicarage at Sowdens. The grave was that of John Williamson of Stanbury who had been buried there in 1810, and his two daughters buried in 1817 and 1818. Over the last fifteen years the soft, damp earth had sunk down into the grave and the stone supports, with the weight of the flat tombstone, had been pushed down further into the ground, leaving a very narrow gap between earth and stone.

Forcing his way between the hard stone and the cold, moist ground beneath, Branwell wriggled, pushed and scrabbled until he was completely out of sight of anyone in the graveyard. He was deeply embedded in the bowl of earth underneath the stone. In the darkness and smelling of soil and damp, he continued to rummage around until his body was entirely nestled in his perfect hiding place. Reaching out his left hand he carefully pulled a few grasses and a nettle across the tiny gap he had wriggled through hoping that he could not be detected from the outside. Satisfied with his efforts, Branwell lay chuckling to himself that, for once, he had outwitted his clever sisters.

Emily had bolted up the path, gathering up her skirts and had actually climbed over the west wall. Gazing out over the fields and heath, she relaxed in the scented sunny air as she leant her head and shoulders against the warm edges of the dry stone wall. She could hear many different birds singing and calling across the great expanse of moorland and sky. The distant bleating of sheep and the occasional deep lowing of cattle could be heard from across the miles. Bees and flies buzzed around her and all the smells of summer; honeysuckle, heather, grass and hay, carried across the moors and filled the warm air with their evocative scents. Emily loved to be out here watching, listening and breathing in this wonderful and special "garden". Closing her eyes, feeling the hot sun on her face, she smiled inwardly and felt a great surge of happiness. She loved her home and the surrounding moors and hoped that she could live there forever.

Emily's reverie was rudely interrupted by Charlotte's voice as her head appeared hanging almost upside down over the wall. 'Oh Emily, you have gone out of the boundary,' Charlotte laughed, 'no wonder I could not see you, that's cheating.' She ran off all the way back across to the tower to slap the stone and call out, 'block you one, two, three, Emily.'

Emily heard her voice echoing in the distance but felt too warm and comfortable to attempt to follow or even to care that Charlotte had found her. She could quite happily sit here for the rest of the day, listening and thinking or gradually wandering off into a daze that allowed her imagination to drift. She stared up at the wide expanse of blue sky above her and the occasional small white cloud drifting slowly from the west, high up in the atmosphere. The church clock struck the quarter hour and somewhere behind her was the tapping of the stonemason's hammer. Someone shouted away over the hill towards the quarry, and the neighing of a horse in a nearby field mixed with the pleasant summer sounds.

This daydreaming was interrupted when a large round honey bee buzzed by her face and landed on a small ring of daisies beside her feet. Emily watched, fascinated, as it turned itself with its back to the sun and proceeded to drink the nectar from the tiny white and yellow flowers. Every few seconds, it rose a few inches into the air and then landed on a fresh flower. Its wings moved so fast they were just a blur. Its round, velvety striped body held Emily's gaze as she wondered at its ability to know where and how to find the nectar. Presently, it rose almost vertically into the air, hung in space for a few seconds and then swung away towards some wild roses, further along the wall. Emily was captivated by its performance and sat for some time wondering how on earth it managed to fly with its round cumbersome body and tiny delicate wings.

Suddenly, Charlotte reappeared and asked her if she had noticed where Branwell had gone off to hide.

'It's nearly three o'clock' Charlotte stated anxiously, 'and Aunt said she would be back on the 3.15pm cart. Can you come and help me find him. Anne and I have been searching for nearly half an hour. I don't know where else to look, unless he has gone out of the graveyard.'

'He has probably snook back into the house,' replied Emily, 'Tabby is baking cakes and buns for the Autumn Fayre I suppose that he is stuffing his face in the kitchen! He is such a sneak, don't bother looking for him, he will find his way back if he is still outside. You worry too much over him, Charlotte. He is not a baby, just a troublesome little boy.'

Charlotte scowled but did not fight back. She was protective of her brother. She was protective of all of them, as her father had requested. She was their extra guardian now, the eldest and the most responsible. She did not undertake that responsibility lightly. Helping Emily to climb back over the wall and calling for Anne, the three girls returned to the Parsonage. Branwell, who had fallen asleep in his cosy hiding place, was blissfully unaware that he had been abandoned.

Half an hour later, Branwell awoke to the sound of urgent calling from both his sisters and Aunt Branwell, who sounded very cross as her voice rang out from the front garden. 'Where on earth is he Charlotte? What have you all been up to? Am I unable to leave you children for a couple of hours without you losing one another? Go and look for him at once before your Papa gets home. I blame Tabby, why on earth doesn't she watch you properly?'

Realising that they were all in trouble Branwell sat up in alarm, forgetting where he was. His forehead smacked into the solid stone that was almost touching his head. The shock made him dizzy for a moment and then, in a panic to be out of his hiding place, he began to push and scrabble out of his den. His stiff arms and legs, rummaging in the earth, only served to force him further and deeper into the hollowed space. He became especially aware of the huge heavy stone above him which was so low that it was touching parts of his body. The more he struggled, the more he became jammed into the tiny space.

At first, the boy did not realise that he might be trapped. Using his hands and feet to try digging himself out he began to push the earth away from him and out from under the stone. However, this just helped to shore up the sides of the tomb and he sank further into the cold earth as the small piles of soil blocked out what little bit of light there was. After a couple of minutes Branwell was in almost total darkness and beginning to feel very scared.

With mounting panic, the frightened boy felt that the huge stone immediately above his chest, was getting closer to his body until he was sure that he could feel it pressing down on to his skin. He imagined that it was falling in on top of him, crushing him into the earth and down into the grave where he would encounter the dead people lying somewhere only a few feet beneath him. All Branwell's fears of death and bodies rose up inside him and he felt a horror take hold of his brain as his eyes stared out into the darkness.

Letting out a loud cry, the boy began to struggle and squirm even more. A cold sweat broke out on his face as his chest heaved. Feeling a sudden loss of air, Branwell's breathing started to come in rapid shallow gulps, he began to sob and wail with fright. What if no-one ever found him? He had found the perfect hiding place, but no-one knew where he was, he could die and never be found. With mounting terror, Branwell fought against the heavy stone. Trying to dig his fingers into the earth to create a space below him, he was convinced that the stone was descending closer to his face and body.

Crying and panicking, Branwell cried out for his Aunt, his Papa and his dead Mama, to come and save him. He started to scream as the world around began to diminish. Branwell felt a familiar sickness and darkness entering his head. A flashing light seemed to cross his vision and within seconds, the boy's limbs began to shake and shudder. Branwell felt as if he was falling, and he fell until a great darkness enveloped him and suddenly, mercifully, he succumbed to a black, soundless and welcome unconsciousness.

Unaware of the drama taking place only a few rows from him, the stonemason continued chiselling away at a huge headstone. He had to get the lettering finished that day as he had another six stones to cut tomorrow and they all had to be fetched by cart from the quarry and taken to his workshop in the barn across the lane. He slowly became aware of a lot of shouting and looked up to see Miss Branwell from the Parsonage, bearing down on him.

'Do you happen to have seen my nephew anywhere around, Mr Brown?' she asked, 'He really is too bad, we cannot find him anywhere and we think he may be hiding somewhere in the graveyard.'

'Well yes, ma'am,' came the reply, 'as a matter a fact I saw his red hair sticking out a while ago from under the Williamson grave stone, I think the young 'uns were 'avin a game of 'ide and seek. Don't know if e's still yonder, I ne'er saw 'im come out, but I've been too busy getting on wi' mi work.'

Hurrying across to where William Brown was pointing, Aunt Branwell sank down to the ground and began to call out Branwell's name. Following her through the graves, Mr Brown, who was also the church sexton and knew Branwell well, pointed to the grave where he had seen the little boy. He knelt down in the grass and after pushing aside nettles and earth, he then had to lie full length on the ground before he could just make out the boy's body wedged firmly and deeply under the heavy stone. Thrusting his long arm into the darkness, he could feel the boy's leg and clothing. It was drenched in sweat and smelt of urine. He brought his hand out, but there was no response from the child when his name was called.

''Fraid he's well jammed in ma'am and I dunno if 'es breathin'. I'll get mi tools.'

After running back for his bag, the stonemason began to scrape away some of the earth that was packing Branwell into the hole. 'I think 'e needs t'doctor first, ma'. I don't think I'm goin' to be able to dig fast 'nough with these tools and there's no knowin' if 'e is getting enough air. He's squashed and well and truly wedged in. I'll run and fetch Doctor Andrew and get some lads organised to dig 'im out,' he shouted as he sprinted off down the path.

Aunt Branwell knelt in horror as she peered under the stone and had the most awful feeling of dread. 'Don't let him be dead,' she whispered and, looking up to the sky she cried, 'Oh. Please, God don't let him be dead, I could not bear it.' Cries began to shake her body. She tried to shuffle further down to touch Branwell's chest or find his hand, but she couldn't reach far enough in to touch any part of him.

For the next few agonising minutes, Aunt Branwell rocked to and fro in silent vigil next to her beloved boy, praying to God that he would be all right. A white-faced Charlotte appeared on the path but was swiftly sent away to fetch Tabby and any other adult who she could find.

Mr Brown had alerted five men from the Black Bull public house as he ran past and they arrived in the graveyard armed with shovels and spades. Branwell let out a loud moan and began to shiver and sob. Aunt Branwell rose to her feet with great relief. 'I can hear him, I can hear him,' she called out to the men. 'Do please hurry. He is alive but he is stuck beneath this awful heavy stone. Please do anything necessary to get him out as soon as possible.'

It took the best part of half an hour to dig down without risking the great stone falling in and on to the boy. Branwell whimpered and sobbed, or shook and wailed, eventually drifting into unconsciousness. The men exchanged glances. They noted that the rumours of the Parson's lad having fits, was apparently confirmed.

Eventually, and as Dr Andrew and Mr Brontë came running up the path from opposite directions, Branwell was finally dragged out of his nightmare hiding place.

'Stand back lads,' the doctor called and with one glance at the boy who was now writhing and twitching in a great spasm of a seizure, he produced from his bag a large bottle of laudanum. 'This will calm him, we will soon have him settled, Mr Brontë. You can expect a fit in this situation, it'll pass, it's the lack of air and shock that's brought it on. Looks like he got himself wedged and couldn't escape. What an ordeal for the poor lad. Let's get him to the house and sort him out.'

A shocked and horrified Mr Brontë took his son in his arms and wrapping him in blankets, thoughtfully brought out by Tabby, he carried him swiftly but carefully back to the Parsonage where he laid him gently down on his own bed. He said a pray over the child as Aunt quickly stripped him of his damp clothes and wrapped him in a muslin sheet and a warm blanket. The doctor took his pulse and examined his little body before reaching into his bag for his magic tonic.

Branwell remembered very little of his escapade, except that he had had some special medicine that made him feel as if he was floating; all his panic and all his fear suddenly left him. Dr Andrew had given the remainder of the bottle to Papa with instructions to give him more if he began to feel unwell again. Branwell hoped that he would probably need to have some more as it made him feel so relaxed and happy.

That night, as Branwell lay warm and cosy in Papa's bed, each of his sisters came to see him. They had all been chastised by Aunt and Papa, and instructed to visit him and apologise for leaving him in the graveyard. Charlotte, as the eldest and therefore the ringleader, had received a good hiding from Aunt. She had obviously been crying when she showed up in the bedroom. She hugged Branwell and said how glad she was that he was saved and how sorry she was to have left him. Branwell gravely accepted her apology but warned her that in future he expected her to take better care of him. Anne burst into tears when she saw him and kissed him and hugged him until Branwell started to struggle for breath once more.

'It's alright Anne; it probably wasn't your fault. You are too young to know any better. I don't blame you, its Charlotte and Emily who left me. It's them that should be sorry and it's only because the doctor came and gave me some special linctus that I have survived. Let this be a warning to you, Anne, I am the only boy in this family and I need extra special care and attention.' Anne nodded her head and promised that in future she would help to make sure that he had everything that he needed and she would always make sure that he was alright.

Branwell smiled as she left the room, still crying, and was beginning to feel quite pleased with himself. He began to realise how much he could use this event to really get some attention and respect from his sisters. He had not, however, reckoned on the anger of Emily, who strode into the room with her face set and her fists clenched.

She looked him up and down and cried out. 'You horrible boy, what did you have to do that for? You must have heard us calling for you, you are so irresponsible. You had everyone worried to death. Now you have got us all into trouble and we are banned from the graveyard and we are not allowed on the moors for a week in all this lovely weather. Why haven't you told Papa what really happened? You got yourself into that hiding place you idiot. We have all got into trouble because of you. You are a nasty, selfish and thoughtless little boy.'

Unfortunately for Emily, Papa entered the room just as she was shouting the last sentence and a sharp slap sent her off to bed, crying and protesting all the way.

Emily sat on her bed angry and upset. Papa did not often hit any of them and she knew that she deserved a punishment for shouting at Branwell when he was sick. He had been stupid and they had all been punished by Aunt; Emily had to wash the hallway floor for a week, Charlotte had received a thrashing and told that she was to clean all the inside windows over the next few days. Anne had to peel the potatoes every day for a week, and they had all been banned from going out to play until Aunt decided they had been punished enough. Nevertheless, Emily remained defiant. Though her face stung, and she hated making Papa cross, she was secretly glad that she had told that stupid boy exactly what she thought of him.

Chapter Twenty-Eight
January 17th, 1826

In January 1826, Charlotte wrote Anne a little story and gave it to her for her sixth birthday. Anne was delighted when she received her present, written in tiny handwriting made to look like print and presented in the form of a miniature book.

'Oh this is beautiful,' exclaimed Anne. 'You are so clever, thank you very much. Look, Aunt, look what Charlotte has made me for my birthday.'

Aunt looked up from her sewing and examined the little leaflet. Only a few centimetres high and wide, it contained some cut-down paper sewn into a small booklet and had a cover made from newspaper scraps. The writing was so very tiny that she was unable to read the script.

'That is very nice, Charlotte, but my eyes cannot read the writing. Be careful, avoid writing in such small print, your eyesight is very precious and it is not good for any of you to strain your eyes. Well done, it was kind of you to make something for Anne.'

'I enjoyed doing it. I love writing. I could write lots of stories if we had more paper. Do you think that I could do more writing Aunt? Perhaps I could make up some poems or little stories or songs,' enquired Charlotte.

'Now, don't go filling your head with such nonsense, Charlotte,' replied Aunt sternly. 'You will be ten years old in April and you need to concentrate on your lessons and household skills. I know that your Papa wants you all to read and be knowledgeable, and that is good, but you may all have to earn a living when you are older and know how to run a household. Young ladies of our class only need to write letters to their acquaintances and shopping lists for their servants. As you get older, you will probably learn to speak and write a little in French, in preparation for teaching, apart from that you are not required to write anything else beyond your lessons. Charlotte, it is not befitting for you to waste your time writing. You need to concentrate far more on your needlework skills my girl.'

'I have finished my sampler, and you said that it was good,' Charlotte reminded her Aunt. She felt quite cross at Aunt's response to her little book and her lack of encouragement.

'Do not be cheeky, Charlotte,' remonstrated Aunt, 'Only practice will turn you into a good needlewoman. A sampler is just a demonstration of stiches. Now, there is a pile of mending to do and it is time that you started to help me more with it. Go up to my room and bring down the pile of shirts on top of my dresser. They all require some repair or alteration and I will show you what they need and how to do it. You can start immediately and you will find that you do not have the time to fill your silly head with writing and wasting paper. Off you go.'

Charlotte was cross, somehow a happy event had suddenly turned into a nightmare of endless mending. Charlotte did not enjoy sewing, although she was quite proficient at it. She hated to admit that she found it hard to see the tiny stiches and that sewing gave her headaches. She knew that if she complained her Aunt would think that she was being lazy and shirking her chores.

Charlotte started up the stairs and met Emily on her way down. She complained to her about the mending but Emily smiled.

'Don't worry, Charlotte, I don't mind sewing, I can help you. Actually, needlework helps me to think. I imagine all sorts of things when I am sewing. I find it quite soothing and it helps to concentrate my mind. I can almost go off into a daze when I am sewing.'

'Really?' cried Charlotte, 'I hadn't thought of it like that. I find it so tedious and it strains my eyes. I might try doing it your way and see if I can drift off into a fantasy whilst I am mending Branwell's shirts. I think that I am more likely to stab myself with the needle though.'

The girls laughed and ran up to Aunt's room to collect the shirts. Emily stopped by the dressing table and looked at some of the objects always on display. There was a lovely workbox, a delicate vase, a crystal glass dressing set and a lacquered Chinese box with her initials on it, E.B. Elizabeth Branwell.

'I love that box,' whispered Emily, 'It has my initials too. Isn't that strange, Charlotte, that out of all the letters in the alphabet, Aunt and I have different names but the same initials?'

'That has given me an idea for a story,' cried Charlotte. 'Why don't we gather all our alphabet bricks together and make up names of characters using whichever letters they fall on. We can throw them up in the air and see how they land. It will make us choose some really different names for our plays. Instead of pretending to be real kings and queens, we can be our own royalty with names beginning with X or Z or J, anything that the bricks decide. It will be like chance or fate as their names will be prompted by the bricks.'

'I like that idea,' said Emily, 'Tonight we will take the bricks to bed and roll three of them on the floor and each choose a character with the same initials, like William John Morpeth or Wilhelmina Julia Murgatroyd and then we can act them out. It will be fun trying to find names if they fall on X, Q and Z.' Emily laughed.

'Do you remember when Maria told us about the bed plays she and Elizabeth made up? I love our bed plays,' Charlotte replied. 'I wish Anne slept with us more often as it is better when there are three of us. I love acting out under the covers and pretending to be different people having exciting adventures.'

'It's best when it is just us girls,' Emily said. 'When Branwell sleeps in our room he always insists on playing soldiers and fighting wars. Do you remember that night he was acting like Napoleon and went charging across the landing straight into Aunt? We hid under the bedclothes and pretended to be asleep whilst she shouted at him and then he pretended that he was dreaming and sleep walking.'

'Oh yes,' laughed Charlotte, 'and then Papa came upstairs and told Aunt off for making so much noise and waking his children up! They hardly spoke for a couple of days. Do you remember?'

Aunt's voice suddenly called from the bottom of the stairs.

'Charlotte, what is taking you so long? Come downstairs at once with those clothes. What on earth are you doing up there?'

Charlotte and Emily grabbed the mending and fled downstairs. Aunt was happy to let Emily help but only for tacking the seams or sewing on missing buttons. She and Charlotte would do the fine stitching. It had to be done to a very high standard; the various stiches were practically invisible to the naked eye.

'Once we have finished this we have an errand to make down to the Greenwoods at the bottom of the town. I will take all three of you girls and I expect absolute courtesy and good manners. The Greenwoods are influential people hereabouts, as you know, and you must be on your best behaviour. Mrs Greenwood has some papers for your Papa and some journals. You will sit quietly and only speak when you are spoken to.'

Aunt Branwell was looking forward to this trip. She had met Mr and Mrs Greenwood at church and at the Parsonage and enjoyed their company. On various occasions she had called on them with messages or papers from Patrick and she enjoyed being in their lovely home, Bridge House, with its fine furnishings and sheltered location. These were people that she could identify with, people of the upper middle classes who had wealth and breeding. Aunt felt that these were the type of friends she would have had had she returned to Penzance. Patrick Brontë had a large parish and met dozens of people every day, but she was mainly confined to the Parsonage and the raising of the children. She longed for a social life amongst the local gentry and had taken Branwell to Bridge House a couple of times. Today she would take the girls with her, if only to show Mrs Greenwood what a good job she was doing, raising them as genteel and well-mannered young ladies.

After lunch, the girls washed and changed into their outdoor clothes. There was an icy wind blowing but the snows of December had not yet returned. The cobbled roads were damp but otherwise fairly safe to walk on; it would be a steep climb back up to the Parsonage after their visit.

Mr and Mrs Greenwood's beautiful Georgian dwelling adjoined their spinning mill. The mill overlooked the bridge over the Bridgehouse Beck, which ran through the lower part of the town. Mr Greenwood owned four mills around the town and was a church trustee and friend of their father. He was a generous, likeable man who, though a Baptist by religion, was never in conflict with their Papa. Mr Brontë liked this man and supported his work.

On arrival, Aunt and the girls were shown into the drawing room and offered refreshments. The girls looked to Aunt for her approval before accepting glasses of lime cordial. Mrs Greenwood appeared and chatted amiably to Aunt whilst the three girls sat silently with their drinks. None of them felt comfortable before this stern lady who was looking them up and down rather disapprovingly.

'Which one is which, Miss Branwell?' the lady enquired. Looking at Emily she said, 'I suppose this one is the eldest?'

Emily, at eight years old and two years younger than Charlotte, was a good six inches taller than her elder sister. Without thinking, Charlotte answered for her Aunt.

'I am the eldest, Mrs Greenwood, I am Charlotte and I am ten years old.'

Aunt turned to Charlotte with a horrified look on her face.

'And, who addressed you, young lady?' she demanded.

Emily and Anne held their breath as poor Charlotte looked bewildered.

'I am just saying that I am the eldest, not Emily. I think perhaps that Mrs Greenwood mistook Emily for me as she is a little taller than I.'

In the silence that followed Charlotte became aware that she had spoken completely out of turn. She had forgotten that she was to speak only if spoken to and she had now embarrassed her Aunt and made the venerable Mrs Greenwood think that the Mr Brontë's girls had no manners. With her face turning bright red, she mumbled an apology and stared down at the fancy carpet that covered most of the floor of the lovely room.

'Well,' exclaimed Mrs Greenwood 'I think this young lady needs to learn some better manners, Miss Branwell. Are you always this rude to your Aunt, child?'

Charlotte's face now looked and felt as if it was on fire. Emily and Anne dare not speak up for her as they knew that it would make matters worse and they remained silent with their eyes downcast. Aunt stood up and began to gather her belongings and the papers they had come to collect.

'We must return before it gets too dark,' muttered Aunt, 'Thank you for your hospitality, Mrs Greenwood. You are so kind. I will remember you to Mr Brontë and thank you once again.'

Aunt ushered the girls out of the front door and down the path. Her back was stiff and her face was set in a fierce frown. Not a word was said all the way up the steep hill back to the Parsonage. Charlotte kept wiping tears from her cold face. Emily and Anne walked with their heads down, arm in arm, as Aunt marched on ahead.

On entering the house, Charlotte could not decide whether to just walk straight on up the stairs to her bedroom or stay and be sent to bed. Aunt exploded as soon as the front door closed.

'How dare you show me up like that? You wretched girl!' she cried. 'How many times have you been told that you speak when you are spoken to? How dare you answer back to me and to Mrs Greenwood. I will never be able to show my face there again. You have no manners and no sense, you stupid child. Look what a disgrace you are to me and to your family.'

A loud slap hit Charlotte across her face and she cried out in pain and shock.

'Get to bed. Now, you dreadful child, I do not want to see or…'

The study door flew open and Papa stood in the doorway his face fierce and his fists clenched.

'What on earth is all this noise about?' he shouted. 'What is going on here, Elizabeth? Why are you shouting and why is Charlotte crying? I will not have all this disturbance when I am trying to work. What is the matter Charlotte? What has happened?'

Charlotte could not answer and set off running up the stairs with a loud wail. Her sisters also made to go after her but Papa's voice bellowed out.

'Emily, come into my study. Anne, go in to the kitchen. You, Elizabeth, may go into the parlour. I will speak to you when you have calmed down.'

Ten minutes later, after Emily had carefully and clearly explained to Papa the reason for Aunt's outburst and Charlotte's tears, her father sat gravely shaking his head.

'I will not have this behaviour in my house,' he stated. 'Thank you for explaining things to me, Emily. You did right to stay quiet at the Greenwoods' house. I will speak to Mr Greenwood myself. Charlotte was rude but it does not warrant a shouting match in the hallway. Go and ask your Aunt to come and see me and fetch Charlotte downstairs. She can apologise to your Aunt after I have spoken to her. It is Anne's birthday and I want you all in the parlour for tea at five o' clock sharp. I will not let this spoil Anne's day.'

Mr Brontë stared at his sister-in-law as she entered the study but offered her a chair and sat down opposite her.

'Well, Elizabeth, whilst I have every faith in your ability to teach my girls good manners and to take them into the town, on this occasion, I am disappointed in your behaviour towards them.' He raised his hand as Aunt attempted to speak.

'Children will always make mistakes and they will always need to be chastised. However, shouting and slapping, I do not approve of and certainly not in this case. Certainly not in the hallway of this house.'

'I am sorry, Patrick, I had no idea that you were in your study, I thought…'

'Ah,' pounced Patrick, 'No, Elizabeth, you did not think. You did not think about who was in the house or what important business they may have been engaged upon. I could have been entertaining the Bishop for all you knew. Furthermore, it worries me that you admit to behaving differently depending on whether I am in the house or out of it. That worries me, it worries me deeply.'

The two adults sat in silence both thinking over what Patrick had said. Aunt was truly sorry that she had herself, displayed such bad behaviour and was mortified that Patrick had overheard her outburst. She had been shocked when he appeared in the hallway and knew that her anger had overtaken her common sense. She felt humiliated at the Greenwoods, a family whose approval and acquaintance she was seeking. She punished Charlotte in a way not warranted by her misdemeanour. Aunt saw, now, that it was her own mistake in trying to curry favour with Mrs Greenwood that had made her behave in the way that she had. She could so easily have smoothed over Charlotte's indiscretion instead of making it into something so much worse than it actually was.

Aunt looked at her brother-in-law and then down at her hands.

'Patrick, you are right. You are absolutely right and I am deeply sorry. I had no right to behave like that in front of the children. I understand that it was false pride that prompted my actions. Please forgive me. Such an event will never happen again, whether you are in the house or out of it. You have my word.'

Patrick was looking at his sister-in-law and the words that had been ready to flow from his mouth dried up. He had been very angry with her and he had not expected such an absolute apology. He had been ready for a fight and was still ready to argue. However, he had received what he wanted without raising his voice. He sat looking at Elizabeth's small figure and at her obvious humility and remorse. He was overcome with forgiveness and the compassion that made him the man that he was.

He had said that his children made mistakes, he must now allow that their guardians also made wrong decisions and wrong choices, so did everyone. He recognised in Elizabeth a certain snobbery; an assumption that her southern ways were superior to those of the rough northern folk amongst whom she had found herself living. He knew that people, like the Greenwoods, were the ones that she identified with and wanted to be seen with and accepted by as a friend. He was painfully aware that Elizabeth had no female friend or companion with whom she could spend time or share female occupations. She had dedicated herself to his children and, now, he was angry because she had, for once, allowed her frustration and hurt to overflow over one silly incident.

Patrick looked again at this woman without whom he, his children and his household, would crumble and he felt a benevolence and understanding that he had not experienced before. He had not ever wondered what her life must be like. He realised now, more than ever, that her whole existence had been taken out of her control. This lady had been persuaded through duty and selflessness, to take care of him and his family. He felt ashamed for his neglect of her welfare.

Standing up, Patrick moved forward and held out his hands.

'Come, Elizabeth. You are forgiven and I know that in your heart you are a good and kind woman who would never knowingly hurt my children. This has been a lapse brought about by your need for company and friendship and I understand that. We must ensure that you have the time and opportunity to meet more people of your own station and sensibilities. I have not considered your feelings enough. I have focused too much on those of my children, and I apologise for that.'

Aunt was quite overcome by Patrick's remarks and had to wipe her eyes with a handkerchief before she could stand and place her hands in his.

'I am so sorry, Patrick, I have let us both down.'

'Enough,' cried Patrick, 'I will hear no more of it. It is over and done with and now, my dear Elizabeth, it is little Anne's birthday and we are to have a good tea and celebration. Let us put up a united front and go and cheer our little family. They are growing up, Elizabeth. The older they become, the more time you will have for pursuits of your own. Come now, let us see what delights Tabby has prepared for us all.'

Chapter Twenty-Nine
Feb 1826

It was a bitterly cold day, the children had spent most of the morning sitting around the table in the parlour doing some reading and writing. Papa was visiting Mr Paslaw, the parish clerk, who was gravely ill; Aunt Branwell was also out, having taken some boots to the cobblers. The four children were being "watched over" by Tabby who was actually in the kitchen preparing luncheon.

'I am so cold,' exclaimed Branwell, 'It is very cold in here. I think that you girls should change places and let me sit next to the fire. I am frozen and cannot learn all this work when my brain is slowly freezing over. Let me sit in front of the fire. You swap with me, Anne, and let me get closer.'

'We are all cold,' replied Charlotte 'and it is Anne's turn to sit there. Go and fetch some more clothes if you are not warm enough. Find your cloak and a scarf, Branwell. Stop complaining. You know that we can only have a small, damped-down fire until it starts to get dark. It is very expensive to keep this house warm. You know that. Papa is always telling us to be careful and economical.'

Branwell scowled at his sister. 'It's alright for you girls, you can share clothes. My shirts and trousers are too small and my cloak is getting short. I need a new jacket and some warmer boots but Papa says I have to wait until the spring. I need them now. What's the point in waiting?'

'Don't be so selfish, Branwell,' exclaimed Emily. 'We are all growing and as fast as we get clothes we grow out of them and it's not fun wearing hand-me-downs all the time. You always get new clothes, but we have to borrow, alter and mend.'

'You got new clothes to go to school and Papa said he couldn't afford to get me some as well.' Branwell retorted.

'It's a pity you're not at school now, Branwell. We could have some peace,' Emily hit back.

'Will you two stop it,' complained Charlotte. 'I have read this paragraph twice now. Stop bickering and don't even mention schools after what happened last year. It's because of that awful school that there are now only four of us,' Charlotte's lip trembled and she looked away out of the window.

'Go and help Tabby in the kitchen, it will be warm in there, Branwell,' ventured Anne, as an awful silence filled the room. Branwell just glared at her and muttered that kitchens were for women and servants, not educated young boys. He dragged his chair from round the back of the table and pushed it up against Anne's so that neither Emily nor Charlotte could see or feel the fire.

Emily got up, resting her hand for a moment on Charlotte's shoulder, she left the room and went to the kitchen. 'Do you need any help, Tabby?' she asked, 'I can't work in the parlour, Branwell is being horrible and it's too cold in there.'

'Now tha' 'mun do tha' studies, Miss Emily, tha knows, but tha' can 'elp wit bread, if tha likes,' replied Tabby. 'Prop your book up ag'in table and do a bit o' kneadin' like.'

Emily enjoyed being in the kitchen with Tabby and the heat in there was delicious after the cold parlour. It made Emily feel cosy and happy. She liked the cooking smells and the sound of Tabby's voice, with her dialect and odd ways of saying things. Tabby was often in the village visiting her family, or shopping and picking up all the local gossip. She had lived in the area all her life and remembered Haworth from the past. The children all enjoyed listening to her tales of what life in Haworth had been like before they began to build the textile mills. Tabby said that she remembered a time when there were "fairies" in the valley bottom and magic dells in the woods, where spirits and elves came out to play. Emily was only half sure whether these stories were just tales but she loved to hear them.

After half an hour, Charlotte and Anne appeared in the doorway. 'It really is too cold to sit in the parlour, Tabby. Do you mind if we go upstairs and play some dressing up games? Anne and I have finished our lessons and there is still an hour to lunch time.'

'Dun you childer be gettin' me in t'trouble with Miss Branwell. Tha's allus up to summat. Just be quiet and don't be matherin' me for stuff,' replied Tabby, as all three girls fled upstairs laughing.

'Right,' said Charlotte as they entered Aunt's bedroom. 'Today we shall dress up as Elizabeth the first and her courtiers. I shall be the Queen and you two can be my ladies-in-waiting!'

'What are ladies in waiting, waiting for?' asked Anne innocently.

'It doesn't mean that,' explained Charlotte. 'It's because they are waiting on the queen's pleasure, looking after her and doing things like dressing her and brushing her hair. Kings and queens are too important to do things for themselves and have to have people looking after them all the time.'

'I don't think that I would like that,' said Anne.

'I should hate it,' stated Emily, 'and I would hate having to meet everyone and be nice all the time and not be able to play in the kitchens or talk to the commoners, I would rather be me than anyone else.'

'Surely you would like to be rich and famous?' Charlotte answered, in surprise.

'Rich and famous people are usually men,' stated Emily, 'and men can be coarse and they are often very stupid.'

'You don't know any men,' said Anne, 'only Papa and he is very, very clever.'

'I don't mean Papa, silly,' Emily replied. 'I mean the ones I have read about and the curates and church people who come here. Some of the men and boys we see when we go shopping with Aunt are very rude and stupid.'

Charlotte smiled and thought how naïve her sister was! Charlotte would like, very much to be rich and famous one day and perhaps meet and marry a handsome young man. They would live in a big warm house somewhere near London or Manchester and she would visit her sisters in her carriage. They would all laugh about how they used to live in the Parsonage and remember how cold it was.

'Come on! Let's get the clothes out of the box. Quickly or we won't have time to play,' Emily cried as they looked out of the windows and made sure that Aunt was not in sight.

For some time now, the children had been going into Aunt's room to dress up, but only when they knew that she was out for a while. In a large trunk, underneath the window, were some blankets but also some of their mother's clothes, wrapped in tissue paper and interspersed with moth balls. Some of Mama's clothing had been cut up and altered to fit Maria and Elizabeth, but a couple of dresses were still intact. Two bonnets, a wool cloak and some boots were also in the trunk alongside two shawls and an assortment of gloves. These items had been used on occasion to act out plays and scenes from the books that they were reading. They all felt these things were precious because they belonged to Mama. No one had felt brave enough to actually ask Aunt or Papa if they minded the children playing with them. They thought that if they did not ask, then no-one could say no. They loved dressing up; it made their games and pretending come alive. They felt somehow that the grown-ups might not approve and so it was done in secret.

Emily was rooting deep in the trunk and began pulling out various items. There seemed to be more articles than usual and she was a little shocked to recognise the dress that Maria had worn to go to school and one of Elizabeth's shawls and her best bonnet.

'Look Charlotte, where have these come from? These are Maria's and Elizabeth's. Look, you can see where Elizabeth tore the corner of her shawl on the garden gate. There were only Mama's clothes in here last time we opened the trunk. '

Charlotte looked worried and felt instantly sad as she looked down at the items. Anne began to pull out the dress and also a couple of exercise books, one written in Maria's handwriting and the other in Elizabeth's.

'These weren't here before. Where have they been? why are they in this trunk?' Anne asked.

'I thought that all of their clothing had been altered for us to wear,' exclaimed Emily. 'Do you think that Papa knows that they are here?'

'Of course he does,' Charlotte replied softly. 'I have seen some of these things in Papa's room. He probably does not want to part with them so he has put them in here with Mama's things. I don't think we should touch them. Let's put everything back and leave it. We can play something else.' She turned abruptly and left the room calling back to Anne, 'Come on, Anne, I don't want to play dressing-up now.'

Emily and Anne looked at one another. Anne went to follow Charlotte downstairs. Emily stayed on her knees beside the trunk, she was running Elizabeth's shawl through her fingers, remembering the sister she had last seen lying in her coffin downstairs in the hallway. The memory was vivid. She felt the warm wool in her hand and instantly, the sound of Elizabeth's voice came to her along with the memory of the way she held her head, her smile and her laugh and the time that they had argued over some embroidery.

Tentatively, Emily reached for Maria's dress recalling the time that Maria had had the poultice applied to her side. Emily had been allowed a brief visit to her sick bed in Miss Evans' room. It had been the last time Emily had seen her. Emily picked up Maria's dress and smelt the cloth, hoping to get some scent; some lost smell of her dead sister but the overpowering aroma of mothballs had dispersed any lingering fragrance. Emily held the material against her body and cradled it in her arms. With her eyes shut tight, she tried to imagine her sisters standing in the room together, with her and watching her. The last person to wear the dress had been Maria, the last person to be wrapped up in the shawl was Elizabeth and the pretty bonnet had once perched on her lovely head of soft brown curls.

Without fully realising what she was doing, Emily stood and began to pull her own dress over her head and replace it with Maria's. Gently she wrapped the shawl around her thin body and hugged it to her. Then, just as carefully, she put her head inside the bonnet and deftly tied the ribbons under her chin. If only, she thought, I could be with them one more time. If only they were here now and they had not died.

Tears were spilling from Emily's eyes but she had a strange feeling of comfort, a feeling that she had somehow come closer to her sisters. By wearing the clothes that they had been the last to wear, perhaps she could somehow get inside them, inside their bodies and minds. Emily stood stock still, eyes tightly closed, holding her breath as she fought inside to become her sisters; to re-live Elizabeth and Maria, to feel and exist as they once had.

Emily felt a strange but exhilarating sensation pass over her as time seemed to stop and then reverse. The room, the Parsonage and the day itself, disappeared as Emily felt herself transported into a time and place outside of her ordinary existence. She concentrated in deep meditation on Elizabeth's voice, face, expressions: her whole essence. She sank into the happy memory of her sister. She imagined the warm feeling of Maria's arms, holding her in bed when she was little, kissing her face and enveloping her body. Emily could feel an excitement, a joy rising within her heart and mind; she could see and feel Maria within her, alive and breathing. An immense calm and happiness seemed to fill her soul. Were they here, now, surrounding her, within her? Had their spirits come back and were they here now in this room where they had both died? Could love and longing really bring back the dead?

Suddenly, somewhere in the real world, a door slammed and the noise of the birds and the church clock's chime, broke through her reverie. Opening her eyes, the beautiful feeling and serene calm begin to dissolve as waves of noise and reality began to rush in on her. Her moment of transcendence began to collapse. The room, the trunk and the sounds of the present, the here and now, blasted in like a storm and scattered all her thoughts and feelings. The magical moment was disappearing like the final remnants of a dream.

Breathless and agitated, Emily reached once more into the trunk and picked out Elizabeth's exercise book. Could she, for a few more moments try to become her sister? With her mind racing and her whole body rapidly losing the dream-like, tentative communion, Emily fought to restore her sisters if only for a few more seconds. Making an effort to mimic her sister's voice, Emily opened the booklet and began to read out loud as if it was her own thoughts and writing. 'Oh, goodness,' she said, 'my handwriting is such a mess. I must work harder at my lessons and not let the teacher give me a punishment. My handwriting is almost as bad as my little sister, Emily.'

A loud scream from the doorway dispelled the last of Emily's efforts As she fought to stay in her exquisite state, the reality of Branwell falling in a faint on the floor of the landing dispelled the last trace of fantasy. Emily became aware of clacking footsteps on the stone steps of the staircase. Aunt approached the bedroom and her look of sheer horror caused Emily to drop her sister's book to the floor. For a few seconds it seemed that everything went completely silent and still. Aunt stood as if in a painting. Her wide eyes, pale face and open mouth, her hands held up in horror as if to protect herself from some awful sight, broke into Emily's consciousness. Emily knew that she had done something dreadful, but was unsure what exactly had gone wrong. The sound of Tabby calling up the stairs, to ask what the matter was, broke the spell. The drumming of Branwell's heels against the steps and the banging of his head against the bannister restored Aunt to action.

'Tabby, come and fetch Branwell,' she shouted down to the servant as she advanced on Emily in two short strides. A resounding slap caught Emily full across her face, in a manner that brought her back into the present as surely and swiftly as anything could have done. The sudden pain and sharp shock made Emily cry out loud, it was promptly followed by another as Aunt fought to keep control of herself.

'How dare you!' she screamed, 'How dare you frighten me like that, you disgraceful, horrid child. How dare you come into my room and touch things that are none of your business. How dare you dress up and try to scare your brother half out of his wits. Get those clothes off, immediately. Go to your room, you wicked girl.'

Distraught, both by her Aunt's anger and the pain in her cheeks, Emily fumbled her way out of the clothes. Grabbing her own, she fled to her bedroom where she flung herself on to the bed and cried. Emily knew that she was crying not just because she had been hit and not just because she had done wrong and gone into Aunt's room and touched things that were shut away for a reason. She cried because, for an instant, she had seemed to be with Elizabeth and Maria. For one wonderful, brief moment the world had stopped and she had had a tiny glimpse of Heaven; a Heaven where her sisters were still alive and where she could be with them in spirit and almost in reality.

The realisation that she was back in her room, in Haworth, and that she was in trouble was hard for Emily to bear. Her sisters and her Mama were all dead and further away from her than ever, was what made Emily continue to cry long after her face had stopped stinging. Aunt's harsh words and actions had ceased to matter. Emily knew, in her heart, that whatever the punishment and however cross Aunt or Papa might be, it had been worth it, worth anything to have had that exquisite moment when her sisters had seemed almost alive again.

Emily woke some time later, cold and hungry. The church clock was chiming the half hour, but Emily had no idea what hour it was half of. No-one had come upstairs to see or comfort her and she realised that they probably would not. She would, no doubt, have to go without food for the rest of the day as punishment and the other children would have been warned to avoid her. They would be told that she was wicked and thoughtless and had deliberately tried to frighten everyone.

Tabby would be under strict instructions not to feed her. Aunt would be telling Papa, as soon as he came home, how naughty she had been. Emily vaguely wondered if Branwell was all right after his faint, but then felt, with some resentment, that he would be getting cosseted by Aunt and Tabby and that Charlotte and Anne were probably, at this moment, reading stories to him and generally pampering him.

Emily lay back on her bed and thought about her sisters. She had had a strange experience and it had thrilled and excited her. Had she experienced a ghost? Had they come back? Had she conjured them up by wearing their clothes and copying Elizabeth's voice and manner? She had felt so calm and happy. Was it wrong to try and reach out to them? Questions rolled around in Emily's mind as she fought to remember that enchanting feeling; that oneness and wholeness with her siblings. She wondered if it could ever happen again. Could she make them appear by thinking deeply about them and imagining them in the room? All these questions bothered Emily and took her mind off the trouble she was in and her rumbling tummy.

It was becoming gloomy as the light faded; the church clock rang out four chimes. It would soon be very dark in her room. Emily knew that with no food, no light and no comfort she might as well get into bed. If only Mama and her sisters were still alive. How different all their lives would be. Emily would have given anything at that moment for her Mama to reach across the abyss and hold her in her arms. She began to cry again softly, in long shuddering sobs that seemed to drain all her energy. Turning her face into the pillow, Emily felt as though her heart would break, with longing; she felt, in fact, as though it was already broken.

Chapter Thirty
Feb 1826

Some hours later as the church clock struck three quarters past the hour and the wind was blowing against the window, Emily became aware of someone in the room. Firstly a shadow, then a movement and then a soft hand was placed on her arm. For a fraction of a second, Emily's hopes soared and the excitement of her sisters' presence again filled her body. When a soft voice gently and quietly called her name, Emily knew that this was a living and breathing sister, come at last to offer comfort.

'Are you awake, Emily?' whispered Charlotte, 'Are you alright? Aunt wouldn't let any of us come to see you, but everyone is asleep now.' Emily sat up and pulled her sister to her in a long hug as tears again overwhelmed her.

'Thank you, Charlotte, I am so sorry if I upset anyone. I was only dressing up. Aunt was furious and she slapped me, really hard. I know I shouldn't have touched those things but I just wanted to be near Elizabeth and Maria. I was trying to bring them back.' Emily broke down into sobs and Charlotte climbed in beside her and began rocking her gently and smoothing her hair, Charlotte explained.

'I don't think it was the dressing up so much, it was the fact that you frightened Branwell and Aunt. They both thought they had seen a ghost. Branwell was hysterical for a while and had to have some of his special medicine. He thought that Elizabeth had come back when he saw you standing in Aunt's room. Apparently, you looked so like her in her clothes and Aunt told

Tabby that you were talking just like her when she went up the stairs. You scared her half to death. I think she was more upset than angry, that's why she hit out at you. I don't think she has told Papa the full story because when he asked for you at tea time Aunt said only that you had been sent to bed early for being naughty. Don't worry too much, I have confessed to Aunt that we have looked in the trunk before and played with Mama's clothes. She was a bit cross, but I said that we just wanted to touch Mama's things and we liked to feel close to her. Then she got a bit upset and said that we would discuss it in the morning.'

'Charlotte, I must tell you something,' confessed Emily, her voice rising so that it was high pitched and urgent. 'It wasn't like a normal dressing up game where we pretend to be famous people. This was nothing like that. Even though we wear each other's clothes at times, and wear cut downs and altered clothing from people who have died, this was different. After I put on Maria and Elizabeth's things, I closed my eyes and tried to pretend almost to be them. I began to feel strange and I almost felt that I was turning into Elizabeth. I could hear and see her, I could almost feel her. I wanted to take on her voice and movements and when I picked up her exercise book, I could feel myself talking and acting as she would have done. It was almost as if I was taken over by her and it was a wonderful feeling, one which I shall never forget. Do you think that was wrong? Have I done something awful Charlotte? Have I done something that Papa would not approve of? I am a bit scared that I may have tried to bring her back and that I shouldn't have done. What do you think?'

Charlotte was a little shocked at Emily's insistence and a little worried that Emily had gone too far. She chose her words carefully.

'I think perhaps that we should talk to Papa. He probably put those things in the trunk for safe keeping, perhaps knowing that they might upset us as they were all clothes that our sisters wore at school. If you recall, all our hand-me-downs are from before that time. I know that Papa has given some of their clothes to poor people in the parish. I don't think that he wants reminding about that awful place any more than we do. Also, Papa knows all about Heaven and what happens to people after they die and I don't think we should be scared of Mama or our sisters but I am not sure if we should actively look for them or try to magic them alive like we do the people in our stories. I am not sure if ghosts actually exist or whether we can make them appear just by being scared and imagining them. I am not sure if we are supposed to try and contact the dead. Tabby told Mrs Brown that Mrs Withenshaw holds séances in her house where she talks to the dead and that you can go there and talk to dead relatives, but Papa got cross and told her to be quiet and stop talking nonsense when he heard what she was saying. Papa is definitely the person to ask about this. We all miss Mama, Maria and Elizabeth, Emily, but they are safe with God and in a much better place. We should not try to bring them back to suffer here on Earth. I am sure that that is what Papa will say. We will talk to him in the morning. Now, you must go to sleep. It is very, very late.'

Emily, at last, felt comforted and snuggled down into the warmth of her sister's arms. 'Thank you for trying to make things better, Charlotte, I am so upset over my dead sisters that I am forgetting to be thankful for the sisters I have got. You are always kind to me and looking out for us all. I do love you but you must go back to your own room so that you don't get into trouble too.'

Charlotte slipped out of the bed quietly and tip-toed to the door.

'Night-night Emily, sleep tight, all will be well,' she whispered softly. The door closed silently behind her, she felt troubled and a little worried by Emily's behaviour and not a little afraid as she quietly returned to her room in the darkness. The yowling of a cat outside in the garden and the murmur of the wind in the chimneys and the rattle of its force against the window panes did nothing to alleviate her mounting fear. She finally drifted off to sleep, but it was a troubled, fitful slumber where her dreams were menacing with darkness and foreboding.

The following day dawned dull and overcast. A continuous heavy rain beat down on the Parsonage, the town and the whole of the north of the country. The wind shook the house and the cold seeped into the rooms. Tabby had lit small fires in the parlour and the study, but the gloom of the day spread over the house and all its inhabitants. Unsure of whether she was out of trouble or not, Emily washed and dressed, as usual, and ventured downstairs into her father's study at 7.00 am for morning prayers along with the rest of the household. This daily ritual was welcomed by everyone and so different from the harsh long prayer meetings of school. They always took place before breakfast, unless Papa was away on business. On this occasion, Emily stood at the back away from Branwell and Aunt, who both ignored her. Following prayers and a short sermon, Tabby left to prepare breakfast as the children waited to take their day's instructions from Papa and Aunt.. Today, however, Charlotte stepped forward and made a bold request.

'Papa, Emily and I are worried about something that happened yesterday and we need you and Aunt to explain things to us.' Aunt and Papa exchanged glances, but Mr Brontë was always mindful of the thoughts and feelings of his children and especially when they seemed troubled. Sending Branwell and Anne out to the parlour he invited the children to be seated. Unaware of Charlotte's plan, Emily was a little overawed and the stern look on Aunt's face did nothing to dispel her fear. Realising Charlotte had opened a door for her to express the worries and concerns they had discussed during the night, she too decided to boldly speak up. However, Aunt stepped in quickly at that moment to explain to her brother-in-law, her version of events.

'I am sure that the girls wish to discuss a little incident that happened yesterday, Patrick. I did not wish to disturb you too much after your long day. I could see you were tired. If you remember I told you that there had been a slight problem. I had to leave the children in Tabby's care for an hour yesterday.

Unfortunately, whilst I was out, Emily took it upon herself to enter my bed chamber and remove certain items of her sisters' clothing from the black trunk and proceed to dress up in them. When, on my return, I sent Branwell up to find her, the poor boy saw who he thought was Elizabeth standing in my room and fell down in a faint. Emily was, of course, chastised and sent to bed and I am pleased to say that Branwell, after much careful attention and some of his medicine, is now fully recovered.'

Papa turned in consternation to Aunt and demanded to know more.

'Whatever do you mean, Elizabeth? Branwell has been ill and I was not told. Emily has trespassed into your room and touched things that I have expressly instructed you to ensure that the children were kept away from. What has been happening in my absence? Charlotte, Emily, leave the room at once. Join the others in the parlour whilst I speak to your Aunt in private.'

The girls turned to leave the room. Charlotte made one last brave but disastrous attempt to mend what was becoming a seriously bad situation. She had no intention of causing any disharmony between Papa and Aunt, who had seemed to be getting on very well together lately. Nor did she want either of them to think that Emily was not sorry for what had happened.

'Papa, we only wanted to ask you and Aunt about what happened, Emily is very sorry that she upset anyone, she did not mean—'

'Silence,' shouted Papa, 'Leave the room at once, both of you. I will deal with you later.'

The two girls fled into the parlour where Anne and Branwell were sitting at the dining table vainly hoping for the porridge to be served.

'What's happening?' demanded Branwell, 'What is going on? We heard Papa shouting, is it to do with what happened yesterday?' The sound of Papa's raised and angry voice and Aunt's soft but urgent replies could be heard across the passageway. The children sat listening in horrified silence.

Emily squirmed in her seat, Anne looked worried and Charlotte bit her lip in anxiety. Only Branwell seemed unnerved.

'I bet Papa is angry because I was ill and no-one told him,' claimed the boy. 'I knew you would all get in to trouble for making me poorly. You especially, Emily, you tried to scare me to death.'

'Shut up,' hissed Emily, 'You always have to be the centre of attention, Branwell, just shut up. I did not deliberately try to frighten you. Anyway, Papa seems more cross with Aunt than us, at the moment.'

'This is awful,' cried Charlotte, 'Shall I try to stop them?'

'No,' replied Emily, a look of resolve on her face, 'I caused this, it is up to me to sort it out.' Emily stood and went to the door. She put her hand on the door knob, but it was flung open and Papa stood in the doorway, his face red and his fists clenched.

'Emily, come into my study, the rest of you, get on with your breakfast and then start your lessons.' Looking across at Branwell, his face softened slightly, 'Are you well, young man?' he asked.

'Still feeling a bit shaky, Papa, but I think I will be alright. It is just that it is so noisy this morning and its making my head hurt a bit,' Branwell replied, much to his sisters' disgust.

'Right. No lessons for you today, son. Go and have a lie down after breakfast and you can come out with me this afternoon if the weather improves.'

He led Emily back into his study. Emily marched in ready to confront both Aunt and Papa, if necessary, but the room was empty. Sitting down heavily in his chair and motioning for Emily to also be seated, Papa took a drink of water from the stand and began to fill his long pipe.

'I want to hear from you, Emily, exactly what happened yesterday in my absence and I want the whole truth.

For the next half an hour Emily repeated, as faithfully as she could, her extraordinary experience of the previous day. She held nothing back and took full responsibility for her actions. Emily apologised for frightening Aunt and Branwell.

She explained why she had worn the clothes and tried to convey to her father the strange feelings that they had evoked in her. Papa listened, silently smoking his pipe and occasionally nodding his head. Emily, emboldened to continue beyond her description, began to ask questions. Had she done anything wrong? Was she wicked, as Aunt had said? She did not understand and that was why Charlotte had asked for advice this morning. Emily told Papa how Charlotte had been a great comfort to her in the night and that they were both very troubled by the whole episode. She looked hopefully at Papa and awaited his verdict.

Papa said nothing. A tentative knock on the door by Tabby and a called reminder that Mr Brontë was due at an appointment in the church, went unanswered. Papa remained deep in thought and Emily sat with baited breath wondering what his reaction was going to be. Neither Emily, nor the other children were scared of their father, but they had a deep respect for him and were fully aware that his was the voice of authority in the house and what he said must be followed to the letter. He could be intimidating but was always fair. He might be loud and shouted on occasion but more often he was calm and composed. He did not play with them very often, but he listened to their games and solved their disputes. He encouraged their education and sparked their imagination; he could laugh at their antics or silence them with one look. Emily loved this thoughtful and slightly mysterious man, who spent so much time on his parish work yet still found time for his growing family. She knew that he loved them and she had the utmost faith in him. Consequently, Emily was not fearful of her father but she was always careful not to upset him.

Mr Brontë sat for a full five minutes. Hearing Emily's confession he was deeply troubled. The loss of his dear wife and two eldest children had hit him hard and deep. As a man who believed in and spent his whole life preaching the word of God, he had felt totally bereft. Had God forsaken him? Was he being punished? These and many other dark thoughts had filled his mind in the last few months and forced him to question his faith. What was God's plan for him and what would happen in the future to him and his remaining children? The Parsonage was part of his employment; if he died the children would be left orphans with no home and no money. The horror of these thoughts crowded in on him at times as he imagined his children as fodder for the workhouse. He must not let that happen. He must instil in his children the importance of good health, good education and moral fulfilment.

This episode with the children's clothing disturbed him and questioned his beliefs and made him think even more about their uncertain future. Elizabeth had failed him with regard to keeping the children away from the clothing that he himself had gently stored away in the trunk when too upset and too affected to be able to cope with seeing these treasured remains. He could not bear seeing the younger children wearing the special things that he had bought for his wife and eldest daughters at a time when he had had such high hopes for all of them.

Other issues regarding this incident also disturbed him. Elizabeth had struck Emily in anger and distress, something she had promised never to do again to any of his children. She had failed to inform him of Branwell's faint, despite his insistence that she tell him immediately if ever the children had an accident or showed any sign of illness. The loss of his two daughters had made Mr Brontë over-anxious and nervous regarding the health of his remaining family.

It was barely a month since the episode at the Greenwoods, when his sister-in-law had faithfully promised that she would never again let her anger override her behaviour towards the children. Yet, once again, he was well aware that without her it would be extremely difficult to manage his children, especially as he had neither the money nor the inclination to send them back to school.

Mr Brontë's eyes gazed across the room at Emily. He had a special affection for this proud and obstinate child. Tall for her age, fierce and scowling, but sitting straight and prepared in the chair, unflinching and resolute she was the one who most reminded him of himself. She may only be seven years old, but she was a child who had inherited some of his own characteristics. She was outspoken, angry at times and loyal to the death. She was a child who rarely lied and would always defend those she loved. This was a child he had always been able to talk to, one that he felt able to explain some of his feelings and behaviour to. He fleetingly wished she had been a boy.

'Well, Emily,' Mr Brontë finally broke the silence. 'This has been a sorry affair and it saddens me that I was kept in ignorance of the facts. However, no lasting harm has been done and I hope that you will not enter your Aunt's room again without her express permission and invitation. That said, I want you to realise one or two things, my dear.' Her father rose and walked across to the window.

'The loss of your dear Mama and our beautiful Maria and Elizabeth, almost broke my heart...' Mr Brontë coughed and cleared his throat, 'Each time I look at you, Charlotte or Anne, I can see your gentle mother. You have her eyes, Charlotte has her expression, and Anne moves her mouth in exactly the same way. Even Branwell can look so like his Mama at times and it is very hard for me to bear these sudden glimpses. As regards Maria and Elizabeth, your looks, movements, voices and personalities remind me every minute of every day, that we once had them and now they are lost, they were once alive and now they are dead.'

Papa stopped and his face shook for a moment before he managed to continue.

'It is a burden, Emily. A very heavy burden that I am struggling to carry. If at times I appear too busy, too distracted and too distant, it is not always the pressure of work and parish matters, sometimes it is too much to see and hear your harmless chatter and to watch you turn your head or move your hand in a perfect copy of your mother or your sisters.'

He moved away from the window and sat down again. 'I suppose that as you grow older, you will all change and as we will never know what your sisters would have been like as they matured these feelings in me may become less painful. You will all carry your mother's looks and ways throughout your lives and whilst at times it gladdens me, at others it can move me to despair.'

Emily stared at her father. Moved by what he had said, she began to understand the pain that her actions had caused. They were all suffering, all grieving and she had not realised it. Papa always seemed so strong and Aunt, always busy and organising everything. Emily had never realised that the adults were trying to deal with their pain as well; a pain that was perhaps even harder for them to bear because there was less opportunity to express and share their grief.

'I am not angry with you, Emily. I must ask you not to touch your mother and sisters' things again, not yet, not whilst our loss is so intense. Not whilst I still cannot bear to think of their deaths.'

Her father appeared to falter and he took a drink of water from the glass on his desk.

'As for the feelings that you describe, the way that you felt when you wore their belongings, I understand it fully. So many times I have wanted to see and feel your mother's presence. Often I have wanted to touch her hand, to hear her voice, that it has almost been the undoing of my senses. However, my dear child, death is part of life. It is all part of God's purpose here on Earth. We cannot and must not question His knowledge or our faith. We shall be with our loved ones again one day, in Heaven and it is to that great day that we must look and hold on to. Do not try to find your mother and sisters here on Earth, Emily, they are in a far better place and eventually you and I will know and understand that.'

Emily sat, enthralled by her father's words; she knew in her heart that he was right. Mama, Maria and Elizabeth were all dead to this life, but perhaps they really were alive and well somewhere in Paradise; together and waiting patiently for all the family to be re-united. It was a lovely thought and one that would sustain Emily, for a while at least. Emily felt her heart lift and she smiled at her father.

'Thank you, Papa, I will think about all that you have said and let it comfort me.'

'Good girl, Emily, you must go now and seek out your Aunt, who, I am afraid, I have been rather harsh towards. She has given up a great deal to come here as my helpmate and we must always remember that. She is a wonderful lady and a credit to your mother's memory. Go and find her and make your peace, my child.'

Emily left her father's study and set off in search of her Aunt. She entered the parlour and saw Tabby clearing away the remainder of the breakfast porridge and she realised that she had not eaten since breakfast the previous day. Hearing from Charlotte that Aunt was upstairs in her room and had not come back down for breakfast, Emily set off towards the stairs. With one foot on the bottom step she hesitated; much as she wanted to go and apologise, her rumbling tummy and light headedness got the better of her. Seeing the remains of breakfast standing on the kitchen table and fresh oatcakes on a plate by the oven, Emily dived into the kitchen before going upstairs to face her Aunt.

Chapter Thirty-One
June 1826

One day, Papa brought home some gifts he had bought in Leeds and laid them at the foot of the children's beds ready for their surprise in the morning.

Charlotte and Emily unwrapped their presents with great excitement and expectation. They were not used to receiving presents. Sometimes they would receive a gift on a birthday or a joint present at Christmas or on New Year's Eve, but these were usually things they needed rather than toys. From Charlotte's parcel fell a set of ninepins and a wooden ball and Emily had a small toy village with houses and people. They were both assembling their toys at the side of the bed when Anne arrived carrying a beautiful dancing doll. She was breathless with excitement and squealed with delight when she saw her sister's gifts.

'Oh, aren't we lucky?' she exclaimed, her little face lit up with pleasure. 'We will have such fun with all these beautiful things.'

Suddenly, the door flung open. Branwell arrived with his arms full of a dozen new, wooden soldiers. Jumping on to the bed he yelled, 'Look at these,' his voice breaking with delight, 'they are so much better than my old ones and they will make up a whole army to fight and conquer new lands.'

'They are wonderful,' sighed Charlotte. 'Can we share them, Branwell? Do you think we should share all the toys and then we could use them all as characters and places in our stories?'

'That's fine,' replied Branwell, too happy to disagree, 'but the soldiers must remain mine although you can each borrow one.'

'I should like this, smart fellow,' said Charlotte picking up a beautifully painted soldier. He shall be the Duke of Wellington; he shall be the Duke and the most famous of the twelve.'

Emily picked up the next, 'This shall be Lord North, the famous writer and member of Parliament. He is a good man, although he looks a little grave and serious.'

'Well I should like this one,' announced Anne, picking up a smooth but less brightly painted soldier. 'He will be Mr Parry, the famous artic explorer and he will discover new lands for our stories.'

Footsteps on the stairs brought them all to silence as Papa appeared in the doorway with a huge smile on his face.

'Now then children, what is all the noise about?'

The children all began to talk at once until Papa raised his hand for silence.

'Children, you have been very good lately and I know how hard this last year has been on us all. You are helping around the house and learning your lessons well. I am proud of each and every one of you and thought that you each deserved a gift. I hope that they will bring you much joy and happiness.'

All four children threw themselves at their father and their thanks rang out. Emily and Anne were both in tears by the time their Papa had extracted eight arms and legs from around his trousers. Setting Anne down gently on the bed as the others sat down on the floor, Mr Brontë looked at his remaining four children and felt near to weeping himself. They were such bonny, clever children and he loved them dearly.

'Now, now, my dears,' he whispered softly. 'I am happy that such small gifts have made you happy. However, there are lessons to be done and we must thank the Lord that we are all well and able to do His work. Dry your eyes and let us have you dressed and down for prayers before your Aunt realises that you are all still up here.' As he strode from the room, he clapped his hands and called back, 'Quickly now children, look sharp.'

It took the children a while to get ready. Charlotte was eager to start straight away deciding how they would use the toys for their stories. Anne's lovely doll could be a queen or a princess, ruling over rich lands and thousands of subjects. She would have handsome men at her bidding who would travel to foreign lands to bring back exotic gifts of jewels and cloths of gold and beautiful furs. Branwell's soldiers would be famous men from history who would fight battles for their beautiful queen and conquer lands all over the world. Her own ninepins would represent temples, pyramids and castles. The ball would be a huge ship that would sail around the globe full of brave men who would bring back all manner of animals, rich foods and beautiful ancient artefacts. Emily's village would be the start of a huge town; a metropolis, where they could create hundreds of people and stories and battles and buildings and-

'Children,' shouted Aunt from the hallway, 'you are late for prayers, come downstairs at once.'

The children tumbled into Papa's study clutching their new toys. Aunt looked disapprovingly at them all, and Tabby commented,

'You is all spoilt bairns, I'm sure. I dos'nt know what t'maister's thinkin' on spending all his hard-earned money on you bad childer',' but she was smiling at Mr Brontë as she ruffled Branwell's curly red hair. 'Yous all got cawld porridge, so you can calm rite down and think on.'

'Yes, that will do thank you Tabby,' remarked Aunt Branwell, 'I will see to my nephew and nieces, if you don't mind.'

Papa smiled at them all, and raising his hand brought everyone to silence ready for morning prayers.

Within a few days of their good fortune, the children were all planning new and exciting stories. During long afternoon walks on the moors and under the bedcovers at night, various ideas were discussed, mainly centred on the toy soldiers, or "The Twelves" as they had come to be known.

Chapter Thirty-Two
1827

Over the next few months, the children became more and more involved in their games of make-believe. Although there was plenty of falling out, especially with Branwell, who was always trying to dictate their play, the four children invented an imaginary kingdom in Africa. Their reading of history and geography and the knowledge they gained from newspapers and journals meant that they had been able to follow stories of adventure and daring taking place around the world. Early explorers in Africa had reported back to England and America, stories of great tribes of black natives who fought with spears and arrows, some of whom captured their enemies and proceeded to eat them.

Using their twelve soldiers, all in the personae of famous men, the children reworked the stories they had read and used their soldiers to invade part of West Africa, around the basin of the River Niger. This area was in reality ruled by the Ashanti tribe. In their play, the children fought and overcame these natives and eventually founded their own huge town. They called this metropolis of over fifteen thousand people, Glasstown. Here, they created in their imaginations, mountains and rivers, palaces and castles, wars and peaceful pastimes. There was a royal family and a parliament all based on the British social order. Having built this imaginary place, all their spare time was taken up with inventing lives and events for the huge population of this fantasy kingdom. At times the children's everyday lives; lessons, meals, exercise and sleep, mingled and became part of their extraordinary make-believe world.

This world was secret and known only to the four children. If the adults suspected anything at all, there was no written evidence. It is not unusual for children confined together so absolutely, to invent their own games and pastimes. Had their Papa and Aunt realised the intensity of their play and the length of time it lasted, they might have been concerned. For now, they had no idea of what fantastic events were going on in the children's fertile imaginations.

On one long sunny walk in late September, they were all playing happily in and around Sladen beck where it met the waterfall opposite the Virginia Water farm. The valley here was sheltered and the soft sounds of the water, the sheep and the birds was soothing and relaxing. This spot, about two miles from their home, was a favourite with the children and though Tabby complained about the walk, she loved to relax out here with her knitting or crocheting, whilst the four children played happily around her.

That afternoon, Branwell and Charlotte worked at the side of the beck shifting stones and boulders until they had a tall narrow construction. Branwell had been studying the tales of the Greeks and Romans with his father, learning of the ancient gods and deities and of their myths and legends. He shared these tales with his sisters and they all read Aesop's fables and The Arabian Nights. The children were fascinated by their book on nature and one on ancient myths and civilisations that described the ancient seven wonders of the world.

'We will make this into the Pharos Lighthouse and then we will build the great Pyramid of Giza, next to it,' stated Branwell. 'If we have time, we can construct all the seven wonders.'

'I love all these ancient stories and legends,' stated Charlotte. 'Do you think we can use some of them in our stories?' Charlotte's imagination was spreading every day. The more she learnt and read the more fantastic her tales became.

'Let's get the other two and we can build a city next to the water with all the wonders in one place.' Calling her sisters over from their flower picking and arranging, Charlotte explained the plan and suggested that they start on building a bridge of stones across the beck, on which to begin an ancient temple.

'We won't have time,' whined Anne, 'and those stones are too heavy for me.'

'I know,' said Emily suddenly. 'What if we were all Genii, like in *The Tales of The Arabian Nights*? We can imagine things or make them happen by magic, instead of actually doing them.'

Looking up at the waterfall on the side of the valley above them, Emily pointed out the trickle of water, the tumbling stones, the rocky sides and the lush green ferns and mosses, with celandines and purple orchids growing amongst them. Standing on the side of the stream and with both arms in the air she suddenly shouted out,

'I am Chief Genie Emmi and this waterfall is now The Hanging Gardens of Babylon, built for the King Nebuchadnezzar, to beautify his palace.'

The others stared at her in wonder, but took up the idea immediately.

'I am Chief Genie Branni,' shouted Branwell, 'I have constructed the Pharos Lighthouse this afternoon in this great river for all to see and wonder over, for ever more.'

Charlotte took up the call, 'I am the great Genie Tallii, and I am about to build the Great Pyramid of Giza, beside this mighty Nile River and inside this tremendous tomb will be buried the greatest Pharaoh of all Egypt.'

'Well,' piped Anne, 'I am the best genie of all and I am Chief Genie Annii and I am just going to build the Temple to the goddess, Diana, and it will be better than all the other wonders.'

For over an hour, the children worked hard moving stones and building their monuments, getting wet and muddy in the process.

A voice suddenly sounded out calling over to them all,

'Children! I am the Chief Watcher, Tabby Aykroyd, and you can all get out o' that water now and get ready for t' walk back 'afore it gets t' late.'

That night, as they sat in the kitchen after tea and before being sent off to bed, the children continued the discussion they had had all the way home from the waterfall. Branwell had insisted that he be the only Chief Genie as he was the boy, but this had brought a chorus of shouts and boos from his sisters.

Charlotte continued the argument, 'We must all be Chief Genii, Branwell, as we are all involved in the plays and must have the powers to perform the magic. We will all need to be able to alter our stories and create wishes and stop bad things happening. Most of all, I think we should all be able to make people reappear after we have killed them off or after they have died in battles, especially if they were good people. We are all the chiefs, the four chiefs and we have complete control over what happens, so we must be equal.'

'Well you and I are the oldest and we can read and write much better than Emily and Anne, so we could be the Chief Genii and they could just be Genii.'

Howls of protest arose from Emily and Anne. 'We have had this argument before Branwell and now you are forgetting your promise. You will never tell me what I can and cannot do,' shouted Emily at her brother. 'Not in our plays and not in real life!' and with that she pushed him off his chair and sent him sprawling across the hearth.

At this point, Aunt appeared in the kitchen doorway and sent the girls off to bed with threats of slaps and smacks if they did not learn to behave. Branwell got up, with Aunt's help, rubbing his shoulder and complaining that Emily was too fiery to be a girl and should be punished for her unladylike behaviour.

'You see, Aunt, they don't like it when I try to help them and show them the error of their ways. Because I am the only boy, I feel that I must protect them and help them to grow into good women. I do my best to be kind to them and I am sure that that is what you and Papa would want me to do, isn't it?'

Somewhere in the background Tabby gave a huge sniff and turned away. Aunt nodded her head and helped Branwell to the stairs, rubbing his shoulder and offering to check on him later to make sure that there was no damage done.

'It would be so much better if I had a room of my own, Aunt. It is hard for me to study and concentrate. The girls talk at night and keep me awake. I am growing up. I need to study more but in peace without their constant noise and nagging.'

'You may be right, my dear boy, now off you go upstairs and try to sleep. I will talk to your Papa.'

Branwell crossed the landing and walked past his sisters' bedroom, the door opened abruptly and a sudden sharp push in the back sent Branwell sprawling. He ran blindly back down the stairs shouting for his Aunt and howling with pain.

Despite knowing the consequences, a very happy Emily sat and waited for her Aunt to arrive!

Chapter Thirty-Three
April 1827

One morning, Aunt Branwell was having an argument with Tabby about the bedrooms. It had been a cold winter with a great deal of snow and now that spring had finally arrived, Aunt wanted all the mattresses turned and a general spring cleaning of rooms and bedding, as well as a re-allocation of rooms for everyone.

Bearing in mind her nephew's constant request for a room of his own, she was reluctant to move him during the freezing cold winter months when they had struggled to keep fires lit in the downstairs rooms; let alone upstairs. Aunt had spoken to Mr Brontë a few days ago and was now trying to persuade Tabby to enter into a new upheaval.

'It is awkward having three girls and a boy in the house and only four bedrooms,' Aunt was explaining, 'Now that the girls are getting older, I think we should have a complete change upstairs. I have spoken to Mr Brontë and he agrees with me, it is time to reorganise the sleeping arrangements. It is not healthy or wise to have the boy sleeping in the same room as the girls and they all need some privacy as they get older. Branwell must have either one of the back bedrooms to himself or the little room over the hallway that they currently use as a play room. We should be setting an example, we are after all a professional family and we have standards and morals above the villagers,' she added with a sideways glance at Tabby.

Tabby glared at Aunt, waiting to hear of what far corner of the house she was to be pushed. Perhaps her bed would be moved in to the back kitchen! She groaned inwardly as she thought about all the extra work; room cleaning, washing and drying of bedding and general chaos. Tabby thought of all the other houses in Haworth where children slept six in a bed until they left home as adults, and she could not help pulling a face.

'Well I mon need some 'elp if I've full top floor to see ti,' Tabby complained.

'Oh we will all help,' replied Aunt, with a wave of her hand. 'The girls are all old enough to change the bedding and help in the washroom. I am sure that we can get the sexton's lad in to do the heavy lifting, where necessary, and Branwell will be able to lift the smaller things. It will all be completed in no time at all.'

Tabby very much doubted this but had no choice but to go along with whatever arrangements Miss Branwell decided upon.

'We will start in my room today, Tabby,' continued Aunt. 'I will have Anne in there with me from now on as a permanent arrangement, in her own single bed. We managed that way until she was four, so I am sure that that will be alright. Mr Brontë will keep the bedroom over his study, Branwell can have the little room at the front for now and we will see how he manages. It will only take a small single bed and a chest of drawers. We had it like that when my poor sister was alive and Emily and Branwell slept in it. Charlotte and Emily can have the largest of the back bedrooms and you can keep the smallest back room for yourself, for now.'

After much complaint by Tabby and the children and a frown from Papa when he heard and saw all the carry on, everyone set about the rearrangements. Later the children were in the kitchen discussing the changes.

'We have nearly always had the little room as our special play room and study,' complained Charlotte.

'Why does Branwell get a room all to himself?' wailed Anne, 'I don't want to share with Aunt, she snores and makes funny noises and she will wake me up during the night. I shall have no-one to talk to when I go to bed. How will I know what is happening in Glasstown if you change things during the night? It's not fair.'

'It's only right that Papa and I should have rooms of our own,' replied a very smug Branwell. 'We have important matters to attend to and we need privacy and a good night's sleep. Besides, I need to keep control of the army and work out strategy or we will be overwhelmed by invaders. We may have to make more cities or make Glasstown even bigger. These are difficult times for our famous young men and I need to be able to think without you girls nagging about queens and princesses.'

Emily glared at him but turned to Charlotte rather than start an argument. 'I don't mind us sharing. I like us being together, Charlotte, but it seems very unfair on Anne. I should not like to share with Aunt, either.'

'Look,' insisted Charlotte deciding that, as the eldest, she should take the lead in this matter. 'Two things occur to me. Firstly, we should think ourselves privileged that we have this big house and we are not all sleeping in one room. Think how some of the people in the village live. At Tabby's cousin's house there are at least four children to a bed, and Mr Sugden has ten children and a two-bedroomed house. Where do they all sleep?'

The children became quiet and thought about what Charlotte had said. Were they being selfish and spoilt?

'Also,' Charlotte continued, 'How many times have we all changed rooms? After Mama died, after we lost Maria and Elizabeth, after Sally and Nancy left, when Aunt arrived. It changes all the time. Branwell will probably go off to school when he is a little older, or Papa may decide to send one of us girls away for a higher education and it will all change again.'

'Oh, I hope he does not,' cried Emily 'If he suggests it, ask if you can go Charlotte, I don't want to go away again.'

'I will be the next to leave,' announced Branwell. 'Papa is bound to send me off to some upper-class school to prepare me for Oxford or Cambridge or to study for a profession. You girls will not be sent to school again, you can be sure of it.'

'Do you think Aunt will leave and get married?' asked Anne plaintively, 'She has been here a long time now, do you think she will go back to Cornwall?'

'No, I do not think she will,' replied Charlotte, 'neither do I think that we should discuss that possibility. Aunt has dedicated her life to bringing us up, in place of Mama, and we should be eternally grateful.' Charlotte looked reprovingly at Anne, 'I am surprised that you would want her to leave, especially so that you could have her room, in fact I am quite shocked Anne.'

'Oh no, no, Charlotte, please do not think such a thing, I love Aunt, we all do. I only meant it as a possibility in the future. I want her to be happy. Won't we just look after ourselves as we get older? I didn't mean that I want her to go now. No, it's alright I will happily share her room I didn't mean that I wanted her to go.' Anne looked as if she was about to cry and Emily stepped in to the argument.

'We know you didn't mean that Anne and Charlotte totally misunderstood you, did you not Charlotte? Don't get upset Anne, no-one wants Aunt to leave. I know that we have all slept together in the past, but we are growing up and there is room for us all to spread out a bit. We can't sleep with Tabby as she is not family and no matter how much we like her she is still a servant and that would not be proper. Aunt and Papa have probably come up with the best arrangement for the time being. Let's wait and see. Everything will change again before long. You see, everyone, the baby Branwell will probably die of cold in the only bedroom without a fireplace or he will be so frightened on his own in the dark that he will come creeping back in in the middle of the night to share with us, won't you Branwell?' Emily pushed him gently in the ribs, but he was not amused.

Branwell had, at last, got what he wanted. He had his own room and he couldn't care less where everyone else slept. His various conversations with Aunt about how he needed somewhere of his own for peace and quiet away from his sisters, had finally worked. Aunt had discussed it with Papa again recently and he had eventually got his own way. Now he could read and write in his little room and make up stories and study pictures and do whatever he wanted and not have to rely on, or share with his sisters. He had not told his sisters yet, but he had started to write a little book. It was a story about his toy soldiers and he had called it "My Battel Book". He didn't have much paper so he had kept the writing very small and printed part of it so that it looked like a proper book. He would keep it a secret for now.

Branwell was happy to still play with his sisters, especially Charlotte, and to help them when they got stuck, but now he could be more independent. He would make sure that he was in charge of their stories and he would organise more battles and get the people into more wars with neighbouring lands. The girls were too soft and were always trying to create royal marriages and soppy girl things.

Branwell did not realise that his conversations with Aunt had served as a prompt for her to discuss the growing girls and their need for privacy and the moral and social rules that dictated that children of the professional classes should not sleep together after childhood. Communal undressing, sharing of beds and chamber pots, was not acceptable in a family of girls and boys rapidly approaching their teens. Aunt and Papa had discussed the issue many times and for the whole of the previous evening.

'My children are still young,' Mr Brontë had complained. 'Charlotte is not quite eleven and Anne only seven. They have led a very sheltered life here in Haworth. I have deliberately not exposed them to the moral corruption of some of the townsfolk and they have had a good Christian upbringing. Dear Elizabeth, I am sure that you are being hasty.'

Aunt Branwell, was, in some ways, more wise and better informed than her brother-in-law, who chose to see the good in all and could not contemplate any problems in his own home or amongst his own beloved children.

'I just think that if they are separated now, whilst they are young, it will save problems later, brother-in-law. The girls are silly at times and can be quite naughty. They have make-up play which displays such flights of fancy. They have such wild imaginations and read all sorts of magazines and books, I sometimes wonder whether it is such a good thing. We do need to be careful. There is a fine line between educating and corrupting.'

Mr Brontë looked quite appalled at this speech but chose, on this occasion to give in quietly.

'Whatever you say, Elizabeth, you know far better than I what young ladies require. I am sure that, as a woman, you know what is best for my daughters. However, where Branwell is concerned, I must have the final say in all things. He must have the best education and the help and support of the whole family. It will be his destiny to look after you all when I am gone to meet my maker. Branwell is my hope and my family's future, and we must make absolute provision for all his needs.'

'Of course, of course,' agreed Aunt, nodding her head vigorously, 'the boy is a credit to you and his education must continue and flourish. That is one reason why I feel it is time for him to be separated from his sisters. He must not be distracted by the needs of the others and they must learn that he comes first. I am sure that they all realise that. They are good children and their petty quarrels are only the normal childish ways of their age. They will all grow out of them. I will continue to teach the girls according to their station in life. They are all clever and willing to learn. I am sure that they will succeed as teachers or governesses. I can teach them all I know, but to be the best they may still need a little further refinement when they are older; a young ladies' academy for a year or two perhaps, finances permitting of course? I do have an annuity and some shares of my own, Patrick, as you know, and I would be willing to help out if necessary.'

Mr Brontë stood and began to walk around his study, where they had both been sitting having their discussion. He was touched by his sister-in-law's generosity and felt humbled by her kindness. He laid a hand on her shoulder and his voice shook as he spoke.

'I know that we have had this conversation before Elizabeth and on that occasion we were both left angry and misunderstood. I want you to know that I have no idea what I would have done without you when my darling wife died. You have been my constant helpmate and companion. I am grateful for all you do for my little ones as well as for me. The smooth running of this house is down to your expert housekeeping and ability to organise Tabby and the children. If you think that it is time for Branwell and the girls to be separated, then I bow to your womanly wisdom. With regard to their education, you have made a wonderful gesture. I sincerely hope, however, that I will never have to call upon you to use your nest egg to finance my children's future. It is I who should be paying you for all you have done for us. Thank you, Elizabeth. Thank you from the bottom of my heart.'

Mr Brontë left the room and taking up his walking stick and cloak from the hallway, ventured out into the cool evening air.

Aunt Branwell felt quite overcome with emotion. Her brother-in-law was, she knew, a kind and honest man, but he had had to be tough for all of his life and he could appear distant and even hard, at times. He had never spoken to her in such a manner as this, even when they had both been overcome with the deaths of her sister and nieces. Grief had kept them apart rather than uniting them. They had both gone about the tasks allotted to them in harmony with each other, but not in any particular close contact.

Aunt Branwell realised that Mr Brontë was a lonely man, lost without a wife and who, ideally, needed a new one to help him overcome the past and look forward to the future. Unfortunately, he was fifty years old and weighed down with his ministry. With four growing children and a household to administer, it was unlikely that another wife would come along.

Heaving a sigh, Aunt Branwell got up to leave the room in the knowledge that both their lives had been irrevocably altered by Maria's untimely death. The law barring a man from marrying his dead wife's sister had led to them never attempting to show too much emotion or affection towards one another. They would probably go on sharing the same house until one of them died; two lives led in close proximity but never together. She knew that they could not afford to cultivate a fondness that could never be fulfilled. The loneliness of the years stretching out in front of both her and Patrick caught her with a sudden and overwhelming sorrow as she made her way slowly up the stairs to bed.

As she reached the landing the low murmuring coming from the back bedroom where Charlotte, Anne and Branwell were currently sharing and still awake, caught her ears. Emily had been disturbing the others with toothache and a cold and had been sleeping in Aunt's bed for a week. As she climbed into bed beside the hot but sleeping child Aunt felt that she was right to separate the children, in fact she was sure of it. They were growing up and were developing into different characters with different needs and requirements. If they had all been girls it might have been different, but she felt that she must protect her nieces from the eyes, ears and male curiosity of their brother, and any other male who came within the vicinity. As daughters of a clergyman, their behaviour and their morals must be spotless. Their actions must be above and beyond those of less Christian families. If she were to do this job properly, and for the sake of her dear sister and brother-in-law she must, the children needed to be guided and guarded by her good sense of right and wrong. She must protect them all from anything that might bring trouble or sadness to them, either individually or to the family as a whole. That was her role and part of her promise to her dying sister, and she would make sure that it was done, as in all things, to the very best of her ability.

Chapter Thirty-Four
May 1827

'Branwell, where are you?' Mr Brontë's voice rang out from the back door of the Parsonage.

Branwell was sitting in the privy watching a spider weaving a web in the corner, marvelling at the long thin strands of gossamer silk escaping from it and being woven into its beautiful concentric patterns. On hearing his father's voice he hurriedly snatched up his clothes and ran to the house.

'Ah, there you are, my boy,' his father exclaimed. 'I have to walk down to Keighley this afternoon and collect the newspapers and to call on the Reverend Drury at the vicarage. I wondered if you would like to accompany me? We could have a talk along the way about your studies and I wish to see what the next series of lectures are at the Mechanics' Institute and whether they might let you attend.'

Branwell was thrilled. He loved to go anywhere with his father and was particularly pleased when it was just the two of them, with no girls involved.

They set off after lunch and chatted amiably during the four-mile downhill walk to Keighley; a much bigger town than Haworth and a few miles from the large, industrial city of Bradford. Despite being early May, spring was late and they had a cold, strong wind behind them. Branwell knew that it would be a hard uphill walk back with the wind in their faces. It had been a bitterly cold winter with much snow and even now there were small, high areas of the north-facing moorland where frosted snow still remained. Nine-year-old Branwell and his father were well wrapped up in cloaks and hats and wore long boots against the wet and slush on the roads. There were little or no pathways, it was not an easy walk.

Keighley stood in the bottom of the Worth Valley, a manufacturing town of mills and industry. It had seen a lot of unemployment in the last few years due to the mill owners' stand against the Trade Unions and the loss of a local bank. There was much poverty and life was difficult for many of the population. Disease was rife, and coupled with the harsh winter; both young and old had succumbed.

As they walked, Mr Brontë chatted about the state of the country and Keighley in particular. Branwell could listen to his father for hours talking about wars, politics, the economy and social reform. Today they talked also about the literature Branwell had been studying and how he was finding the poetry his father had recommended.

'When I was a young man,' his father informed him, 'I read John Milton's long verse "Paradise Lost", until I knew great chunks of it by heart and you would do well to do the same my boy.'

'I have started,' replied Branwell eagerly, 'I can quote the first sixteen lines,' which he promptly did, to his father's great satisfaction.

'Well done, my boy,' his father praised. 'And what of John Bunyan's *Pilgrim's Progress*?' There is another work of prose that will stand any young man in good stead. Literature of this nature tells you about life and about God and you will do well to learn as much of both works as you possibly can.'

Branwell was loving this walk and talk with his father, but unwittingly spoilt it by innocently asking if Papa had plans to send him to school.

Papa's face clouded over and he was silent for a while.

'My dear boy, the loss of your sisters was an enormous blow to me and their deaths were made all the more likely, from what I gather from Charlotte, by the conditions at their school. I am loathe to send you anywhere where you may be subject to an organisation and a discipline that is beyond your constitution. I do not wish to discuss the subject any further.'

This exchange halted their conversation and both were silent for a while. Suddenly his father put his arm on Branwell's shoulder and in an attempt to cheer the boy said, 'Besides, we do well, my boy, you and I. There is plenty yet that I can teach you. Enough time to worry about going away to learn when you are much older.'

Branwell smiled up at his father but was, however, perplexed by his school prospects. He would be ten in two months' time and would have enjoyed leaving the Parsonage full of women and learning amongst boys of his own age. His move to a room of his own had, as Emily predicted, isolated him from the others and he was, as she had rightly stated, quite scared of being on his own in the dark. Many nights he dreamt of Maria and Elizabeth or saw them again in their coffins and he got out of bed to wander on to the landing or open the shutters to try and find some light to dispel his fears.

Branwell lacked male friends and companions. There were only the sexton's sons, whom he saw regularly to talk to. John, the eldest, was much older than Branwell but told him tales about the villagers and hinted at things that went on in the public houses and the pleasures of drink and women. Branwell always laughed with John, but he was confused and innocent regarding much of what he heard.

Branwell had secretly hoped that Papa would take him to have a look at Woodhouse Grove School at Rawdon, a Wesleyan Methodist establishment set up for the boys of clergymen, on the outskirts of Leeds and Bradford. He wished that Papa would take him there one day and let him decide whether he would like to go there for a while as a boarder. However, Branwell also knew that his father would not be persuaded to do anything that he did not wish to do. Charlotte's tales of the school at Cowan Bridge had surely been exaggerated, but Papa had been affected by them and if Papa now said no to school that would be the end of the matter.

A man approaching from across the road suddenly waved and shouted. By coincidence it was Joshua Fawcett, a Leeds man whom Mr Brontë knew from Woodhouse Grove School.

'Good afternoon, Sir,' Patrick called, raising his hat in greeting.

The two men talked for a while about various matters before Mr Fawcett turned to Branwell with the words. 'Well young man, will we be seeing you at Woodhouse Grove before long? How old are you boy, about seven or eight?' He tapped Branwell's cheek with his walking cane and Branwell stared back at him.

'I am almost ten years old sir and I am educated at home,' he answered politely but crossly. Branwell was not a tall boy and had been mistaken before for being younger than his age.

Mr Fawcett turned enquiringly to Mr Brontë, 'Nearly ten, sir, and still at home! I am sure this young man would benefit from a good Methodist education, what! Think on it Brontë, we have a good school full of bright young boys. I am surprised you have not considered it before now.' He walked away up the hill.

Branwell did not look up but was aware in the silence that covered the last two miles that his father was very annoyed. He was glad when they reached the edge of the town. The people, noise, dirt and general activity soon relaxed both father and son as they made their way, firstly to the printers and then on to the vicarage.

The Keighley vicarage was a stately home compared to Haworth Parsonage and the Reverend Theodore Drury was a large, jovial man who seemed delighted to see them.

'Such news, Patrick,' he shouted as they were ushered into a large parlour and offered drinks and cakes. 'Mr Wilberforce, the man himself, is coming here in July for a visit, you must come and meet him and bring the boy.' He smiled at Branwell and offered him a large slice of cake which Branwell gladly accepted.

'Really, that is wonderful,' replied Mr Brontë and turning to Branwell explained how William Wilberforce, Member of

Parliament for Hull and the man trying to abolish the trade in slavery, had sponsored Patrick many years ago when he had started as a student at Cambridge University.

'It would be a wonderful opportunity to meet him,' stated Mr Brontë, 'You are most kind, Theodore, and I would love to take up your invitation.'

For the next hour, the two men talked church matters whilst Branwell sat and read a book from a range in a bookcase which ran along one whole wall of the room. A lovely copy of *The Pilgrim's Progress* in a green leather binding attracted Branwell's attention and this did not go un-noticed by his father.

The excitement at meeting Wilberforce in a few weeks' time lifted Mr Brontë's spirits and sustained the pair on the long climb back up to Haworth. As Branwell had foreseen, the wind was strong and blowing directly off the moors to the west. It was getting dark by the time they reached home and Branwell was tired but pleased that he and Papa had spent the afternoon and evening together in male companionship. When his sisters enquired what they had been doing and where they had been, Branwell was able to smile enigmatically and tap his nose with his finger.

'You girls have no idea what business Papa and I have in Keighley. We men have meetings and discussions that you would not even understand.'

'Don't be so pompous,' replied Emily, 'tell us what you did or I shall tell Tabby that it was you who left all the mud on the staircase yesterday.'

'Mud, mud!' sang Branwell, 'What do I care about mud, when I, Patrick Branwell Brontë, have been summoned to Keighley in two months' time to meet none other than the great Mr William Wilberforce. So there!' he marched out of the parlour grinning from ear to ear.

The girls stared after him in wonder.

'He is lying,' stated Emily.

'He can be so annoying' observed Charlotte.

'He is just saying it to try and make us jealous and cross,' added Anne.

Two minutes later Papa flung open the parlour door and announced,

'Such news girls, I have been invited to meet my mentor, the great and good Mr William Wilberforce; the man who is doing his utmost, both in our country and abroad, to abolish slavery. A great statesman, a philanthropist and a benefactor of scholars. Such an honour and young Branwell has been invited to come along too!'

Chapter Thirty-Five
July 1827

For almost a year now, the children had been using their toys, books and their father's newspapers, to create their Young Men's plays based on the twelve wooden soldiers. Branwell's insistence that he lead their stories and that the young men were always fighting battles, was annoying the girls more and more.

'It is time we had a new game,' announced Emily one day in July. 'Let us go for a walk this afternoon and plan some new people and places.'

Setting off over the moors after luncheon, the four children argued over a new imaginary world.

'We can still use the "twelves" as a beginning,' insisted Branwell, 'but let's alter them and let them each have their own kingdom.'

'They are such clever fellows,' answered Charlotte, 'shall we make them all six miles high like the characters in the story in Aesop's fables.'

'Oh, yes,' laughed Emily, 'although the chief fellows can be ten miles high so that they stand out from the others'

'So how big will their houses be?' asked Anne, 'and what about the animals and birds, will they be enormous as well?'

'We need to choose our chief men,' announced Branwell, ignoring his sister's question. 'I will call mine Boaster.'

'Mine will be Hay Man,' decided Charlotte.

'I will call mine Clown, seeing as they are to be such silly fellows,' laughed Emily, 'and mine shall be only four miles high, ten is too lofty for a clown.'

'I will call mine Hunter,' declared Anne. 'He will hunt all the animals on his island and then come and invade your islands looking for more.'

'He will have a fight on his hands when he gets to my island,' warned Branwell. 'I shall gather an army of twenty thousand men and five thousand horses and they will all have swords, muskets and a mighty cannon and they will kill your Hunter and invade your island, Anne.'

'Branwell, you sound as if you are becoming Napoleon again,' remarked Emily. 'Is it impossible for you to live on your island in peace and harmony?'

'Well, Anne had better not try and invade, then,' answered Branwell. 'I have to defend my men and my country.'

'I think that I would like my island to be more like Paradise,' Charlotte suddenly announced. 'I would like thousands of trees and flowers, cold clear streams and waterfalls and beautiful palaces. I have had enough fighting, Branwell, it is all you are interested in. Let us have places where people live in peace for a change.'

The arguments continued as the children strolled along and Tabby listened in to their chatter.

Tabby often wondered about these children. She was very fond of them all and liked being at the Parsonage. She had been quite flattered when the handsome parson had offered her employment as the cook-cum-housekeeper but she resented Miss Branwell's frequent interference.

These four children were not like the youngsters in the village or the children of her cousins, nieces and nephews. They were strange little creatures, always together, often arguing or just as likely to close ranks and collect in a band that no-one could separate. They were either slapping each other or fiercely loyal and protective. Branwell was the one that caused most of the disharmony amongst them; being the only boy, she supposed it natural that his sisters would irritate him. Charlotte obviously adored him, Emily fought and stood up to him and Anne was often caught in the middle.

Tabby was happy to observe their odd ways and recognised that they were obviously intelligent and certainly quick to learn. They all read and studied, beyond anything Tabby had ever seen. Her own schooling had been minimal and she could barely read. She marvelled at how clever and knowledgeable they all were.

She was brought back to the present by a loud cry. Branwell, who had been balancing on a large rock had slipped and cut his knee on the stone. The girls all gathered round him and, as usual, he made great play of his injury, which was little more than a long scratch.

'Go and dip my 'anky in that stream Charlotte and I'll give it a bit of a rub,' Tabby instructed as she sat down beside the crying boy.

'Tha's too old to be yellin' like a bairn, Branwell, Give over now, tha'll send me def,' she complained as Charlotte arrived back with the dripping handkerchief.

'He is such a baby,' remarked Emily, scowling down at him. 'Get up Branwell, what sort a soldier sits and cries on the battlefield? Napoleon would have had you shot,' she laughed as she ran off.

Branwell scowled after her and was even more put out when the other two girls followed her.

'Well, you can't blame 'em,' said Tabby, shaking her head. 'Tha's ten now lad. Ther's yung 'uns in't town, years less than you is workin' int' mills all day and 'alf the nite. Tha dunt know tha's born playin' around all day long. There now, hold that cloth in place an it'll stop bleedin' soon enough.'

Branwell sat on his own nursing his knee as Tabby moved off and took out her knitting.

Branwell knew that Tabby was right. There were young men, children even, who worked in the mills and the quarries and on the farms, or in the sweat rooms of their own homes, who spent hours and hours in hard labour, six and seven days a week. He had seen their skinny bodies, their bloodshot eyes and their dirty clothes, when he had walked down into Haworth or over to Keighley. They were poor, ragged children who looked worn out. He had also watched from the Parsonage windows and heard the funeral bell as one after another, children had been buried in the graveyard after dying from hard work, disease and poverty. They were wretched unhappy children and Branwell, for once, felt ashamed.

Pulling himself up onto his feet he walked over to Tabby.

'Thank you for your handkerchief, Tabby, it is better now,' he assured her. 'I think I will go and find the girls.'

'You do that lad and think on,' Tabby replied, not even looking up from her stitches.

After he had left, Tabby laid her knitting across her lap and thought about this odd boy. It made her cross that he got so much attention and yet seemed oblivious to all the hardship around him. She had been brought up in Haworth, dragged up would be more accurate, and she had found the young Brontës' childhood a stark contrast to her own. They were well clothed, well fed, had lots of schooling, had lots of books to read and healthy exercise. They had their father and Aunt always looking out for them and they had that lovely house to live in. They were in church every Sunday, very God-fearing and Christian. What more could children want? On top of that, here they were most days, running wild on the heath without a care in the world.

Tabby shook her head and picked up her needles. They must be the luckiest children in Haworth she thought. Privileged, that was the word she was looking for. They were privileged and had no idea how the rest of the town managed. She had been going to make them some cakes for tea but now she had talked herself out of it. They were spoilt, all four of them, and she was sure that she was not going to put herself out for them, none of them.

Half an hour later and just as Tabby was drifting off to sleep a hand gently shook her arm.

'Look Tabby, look what we have been doing,' whispered Anne.

Tabby looked down and saw a great pile of dark blue, fat bilberries piled in Charlotte's shawl. There must have been a few hundred of them.

'We know you like them and can make jams and pies and preserves, Tabby,' continued Anne, 'We picked this for you too, to thank you for coming out with us even when you don't always want to.'

Anne held out a little bunch of heather, just beginning to turn to a lovely dark purple and Tabby could see where the tough stalks had cut her hand.

'Well, now,' beamed Tabby, 'My but you are all such good and thoughtful children. I was just sat 'ere thinkin' as 'ow when we gets back a mun bake some nice cakes for y'all for tha's teas. Come on all of you, pull mi up and let's be getting' back. I could eat an 'oss.'

The children pulled her up and gathered up the bilberries. They had spent the last half an hour chatting about their new play as they picked the wild fruit. "Our Fellows" was the title that they had chosen and after tea they were going to plan their first adventure.

Chapter Thirty-Six
Sept 1827

It was a warm breezy day and Emily had just finished dressing and was washing her hands and face when Papa knocked on the bedroom door. 'Emily, my dear girl, I am hiring Blackitt, John Hartley's horse today. I have a few calls to make, would you like to come with me?'

Emily's heart quickened and she ran to the door. 'That would be wonderful, Papa, I would love to come, are we going now?'

'We will leave straight after breakfast as soon as I have fetched the horse from the barn' replied her father.

After morning prayers and much to the envy of the others, especially Branwell who was most upset that he had not been chosen, Emily arrived at the breakfast table flushed and excited.

'It's not fair,' moaned Branwell, 'Papa should take me.'

'You went last month over to Oxenhope on Mr Hartley's horse, Branwell. Let someone else have a turn and don't be so selfish,' Anne reminded him.

Emily shot her sister a grateful look as she crammed a bowl of porridge oats and warm water into her mouth and was told off by Tabby for her unladylike manners. Today, however, nothing could stop Emily's sheer joy at the thought of a day on horseback, riding with her Papa on this warm autumn day.

Father and daughter set off as the church clock struck 7.30 am. Emily sat side saddle between her father's arms with her legs dangling over the horse's side. Papa straddled the large black horse with his feet firmly stuck in the stirrups and his hands clasping the reins. The rough, thick material of Papa's huge black cloak wrapped around the little girl and his fob watch brushed against her cheek as she settled on a folded piece of cloth arranged over the hard, leather saddle. Papa had placed various things into the saddle bags on either side of the animal. In these large leather pockets he had carefully stored a Bible, some special water in a bottle and other objects that Emily recognised from the church.

The plan, her father explained, was to offer comfort to Mr Samuel Feather, who was very poorly; give a short service at Ponden Hall for the safe delivery of the toddler William, who had had whooping cough; and to talk to the squire about the proposal for a new Sunday school to be built in Haworth, near the Parsonage. They also had things to deliver and collect at various other homesteads. There were documents to interpret and a funeral to arrange at Middle Withins Farm. Emily felt giddy with excitement.

Papa turned the horse towards the moors and they set off across the back field to the little village of Stanbury, north-west of Haworth and about two miles away. They maintained a steady trot as Papa steered the horse over grassland, cobbled streets and up dirt tracks, waving to people as they passed. Mr Brontë reminded some that he had not seen them in church for a while and others that there was a band practice at the church on the following Saturday to start raising funds for a new Sunday school.

This was a project that Mr Brontë had been putting a lot of work into lately. Other churches in the town already had Sunday schools attached and some of the mill owners had contributed to the funding as they felt that it was important that their workers had a place for education and religious instruction. Emily was aware that if enough money was eventually raised it would help the poorer children in the village and would provide a place where they could be helped, looked after and taught the lessons of the Bible.

The Brontë children went to church every Sunday to hear their father, or visiting parsons and curates, preach from the high, three-decker pulpit and although Emily was already aware of many of the Bible stories and loved to hear the church music and sing the hymns, she found some of it more frightening than comforting. God seemed always ready to punish and to scare children into being good. The Devil was always waiting to pounce and death seemed to be everywhere. Emily found it hard to understand why bad things existed in the world and why God didn't just make everything nice and sunny and beautiful. He could stop people dying and bring her mother and sisters back to life if He was so powerful and all-knowing and all-seeing and then everyone would be happy for ever, wouldn't they?

Papa pulled the horse up outside Samuel Feather's cottage in Stanbury and tied the reins to an iron ring set into the stone wall. Lifting Emily down gently onto the rough path, he gathered his Bible and a crucifix from one of the panniers. Inside, Mrs Feather and a toddler sat at a wooden table where the lady was mashing up gruel to give to the small child.

'Sam's upstairs at t'loom, parson, but 'e's no fit for work,' she exclaimed. 'Leave young 'un 'ere and I'll watch 'er. You gan up.'

Papa disappeared up a narrow staircase and Emily looked around the hot, dark room. There was a table and three wooden chairs, a small dresser and a crib with a sleeping baby inside. A fire with various pans and kettles hanging down over it was smouldering under a heavy layer of peat; the smoke from which was partly filling the room. The fireplace took up half of one wall and in the ceiling above, a long creel had washing hanging from it but also yarns of dark wool. As Emily's eyes became accustomed to the dark and the smoke she could make out another child sitting quietly in a corner pulling and teasing out wool from a large untidy pile on the floor.

'Say 'ello t' parson's lass,' demanded the mother, but the child just stared at Emily. Emily had no idea if it was a boy or a girl and felt too shy to ask any questions. She turned her attention instead to the toddler who was now reaching out to touch Emily's cloak and had bits of gruel round its mouth. 'This is Liberty, she's nearly two,' Mrs Feather informed her, 'and baby Martha's six month' but she's a bit sickly, like.'

Emily felt obliged to answer this information with some of her own. 'I am Emily Brontë and I am nine years old,' she replied.

Silence followed and Emily felt that she must fill the gap. Perhaps the lady wanted to know all her details and that was why she had imparted her own. Thus, when Mr Brontë and Samuel Feather arrived downstairs five minutes later, Emily was still reciting the names, ages and in some cases addresses, of as many family and friends as she could remember. Thankful that Papa had arrived and becoming overwhelmed with the heat and worried by the silence from the Feather family, Emily stopped her chatter and headed for the door. Back safely on horseback she questioned her father about the strange family she had just witnessed.

'You have to be aware Emily,' Papa explained, 'that we are very lucky to live where we do in a large house with good food, shelter and godliness. Many people surrounding us have very little in their lives and are very poor, despite their willingness to work. Sam Feather, for example, the chap has stagnant lungs and will likely not live out another winter. They all have to live and work amongst that stifling heat and the wool has to be combed morning and night in order to sell the cloth at the market and make enough money to feed the family and pay the rent. There are eight children altogether, the two eldest are already working down at Ponden Mill in the valley. There were three girls upstairs helping run the loom and the three young ones downstairs. They are all living in a couple of rooms where they have to keep the fire burning day and night to keep the loom and the wool running. I don't know how they will survive after their father's gone.'

Emily thought about this for a minute. 'Why do they have all those children, Papa, if they have no money to feed them?' she asked. Her father did not answer immediately but looked at the far hills and steered the horse out of the village towards the higher ground of the moors out to the west. It was a few moments before he replied.

'Because, that is what the Lord has decided and we must not question his wisdom. Children are a gift from God and every child should be loved and wanted, just as you and your brother and sisters are.' This was said with such force and finality that Emily felt it wise not to question her father any further on the matter, but instead, as she looked out over the hills and watched the clouds scudding across the moorland she felt a renewal of happiness and pleasure in her surroundings.

'We are going to two of the Withins farms later but our next call is to Ponden Hall. We must pay the toll and then you must sit tight and we will go a bit faster along the paved lane.' Papa paid the one penny toll for the horse and they cantered away down the narrow lane. 'It's about a mile further on down the valley,' explained Papa 'You have met Squire Heaton at church. He is an important man, part of the local gentry and a church trustee. He owns Ponden Mill below Stanbury as well as other mills and property in the area. We will ride past it shortly. The quarry on Penistone hill is also theirs.'

'I know, Papa, and we sheltered at Ponden the day that the bog burst. Mrs Heaton was very kind to us.'

'Of course, and I forget that you meet so many of the parishioners at church. They are a good family, my dear, and the squire kindly lets me borrow books from his library at times and I have a couple to return. He has two little boys, Robert and William, and a new baby due any time soon. They are important people in the district and you will note how different they are from rough mill workers and farmers. The Heatons are a family that have helped to build up wealth for the area and invest in new ideas and new manufacturing, stone quarries and industry. I am hoping to discuss the new Sunday school project with Squire Heaton. Be on your best behaviour and do not speak unless spoken to.'

Fifteen minutes later they entered the flagged yard of Ponden Hall and dismounted in front of the beautiful home of the Heaton family. Emily had walked past it once or twice since the day they had sheltered there, but they had not felt socially able to call on the residents. It was a lovely seventeenth-century house facing south with its long rows of mullioned windows and old stone walls. The original house, on the right hand side, had a kitchen garden at the front, with vegetables and herbs and a large field at the back with horses and fields beyond with sheep and a few cattle. Above and to the left were the newer buildings, attached to the original house but altered and added around twenty-five years previously. Emily looked up at the wall above the yard and saw an inscription with the date, 1801, inscribed on a stone plaque. Outbuildings housed chickens, geese and dogs, all of which suddenly appeared to greet them.

The noise brought out a servant and four of the Heaton family, two cousins, John aged about fourteen, and twelve-year-old Michael. Behind them was the young master, Robert aged five and, toddling behind him, his two-year-old brother William. The older boys were polite and friendly to her father, but Emily felt uncomfortable at the way they looked at her with slight contempt and pushed in front of her as they ushered them into the house.

From a flagged-stone entrance corridor, they turned to the right and entered the charming sitting room which faced south across the valley. Sun shone through the windows and lit up the polished wood of a long dining table and a huge sideboard dresser. It was a lovely room and Emily marvelled at the flagged floors, the sturdy oak furniture and the expensive chairs with their tasselled coverings. A woven carpet covered the centre of the floor and a long wooden settle ran down one side. Everywhere was polished and shone in the sunlight. Books lined a long shelf and a small piano stood in the far corner.

Squire Heaton had been sitting at a small side table reading a leather-bound book, he rose and greeted Mr Brontë with a handshake and an offer of a "noggin" for the traveller. Emily had no idea what he was talking about and remembered to stay silent, even when Mr Heaton called her a wee bonny lass and tweaked her cheek, rather painfully, with his big paw-like hand.

He called to his nephews to take Emily round the house and yard whilst he and Mr Brontë conducted their business, Emily was unceremoniously dismissed from the lovely room and left at the mercy of the Heaton boys.

The next hour stayed with Emily for the rest of her life for, despite their uncle's lovely home, education and privileged position in the neighbourhood, the young Heaton cousins were rude, cruel and disgusting. They tormented Emily for every minute that she was in their company. They dragged her into various rooms, punching and nipping her, calling her poor, simple and stupid. The boys tried to look under her skirts and slapped her hands and face when she pushed them away. They threw mud at her out in the yard and spun her round and round in one of the barns until she felt sick and faint. They pulled her hair mercilessly until tears poured down her face, then called her a cry-baby and pushed her into a tiny privy in the farm-yard and locked the door.

In the dark and amongst the awful smell of human waste, Emily cried but dare not shout out in case Papa was interrupted and it caused a scene. Emily knew how important the Sunday school project was to her father and could hear his warning to be good and polite at the Heaton's and only speak when spoken to. Outside, a huge dog was barking and growling and jumping up at the door to Emily's prison. Realising that the boys would have to let her out before her father was ready to go and that their uncle was probably unaware of their bad behaviour, Emily remained silent.

Suddenly, the privy door was flung open by Joshua, the third and eldest of the Heaton cousins. At sixteen years old, he was a tall, blond youth, with rather delicate, but ugly features.

'What have we here?' he demanded 'What is going on? Come out of there, you don't belong here, what are you doing here on my uncle's property? This is private land and you are trespassing.' He pulled Emily's arm, cruelly twisting it at the same time. 'Get off our land, you witch,' he shouted in her face. 'Girls who come up here get what they deserve,' he yelled as he began to push Emily towards the farm gate. 'Come here again and I'll set the dogs on you.'

Emily had had enough of this awful family and spinning round on her heels she kicked him hard on the shin. 'Let go of me you horrible lout!' she shouted, 'I am here with my father and you and your disgusting brothers will be in trouble when he hears how you have treated me!' Emily was unaware of the dairy maid, two farm hands, three goats and a goose, who were all watching the proceedings. The little girl was furious and had never been treated like this before in her life.

A manservant strode into the farmyard from the house shouting, 'Now, now what is all this young sir and what is all the noise about? The master is in business with Reverend Brontë, we cannot have them disturbed. What is going on?'

Joshua Heaton stared at Emily as he rubbed the front of his right leg. 'I am just throwing this little vixen off our land Phillips, she was hiding in the privy and obviously has no right to be here.' He stormed.

'She spat at us and called us names,' piped up Michael and John.

'We were only trying to show her around,' said Michael, 'but she has dirty hair with things crawling in it and she can't talk properly and then suddenly she attacked me and we had to lock her in the privy in case she killed one of us.'

'Throw her off uncle's land, Phillips, and set the dogs on her,' Joshua demanded.

'On the contrary, young sir, this is Miss Emily Brontë, one of the Parson's daughters and she is our guest. I suggest you boys all calm down and show this young lady some courtesy. Go back into the house all of you, at once.'

John Phillips, Mr Heaton's man-servant stood with his arms folded and his stern face showed that he meant business. 'Your uncle will hear of your appalling behaviour boys, this is no way to show Heaton hospitality and it is far time you learnt some manners. You are also guests here, remember!'

Phillips held out his hand to Emily and guided her back to the house and handed her over to, Eliza, the kitchen maid, with instructions to show her where to wash her face and generally tidy herself up before returning her to her father.

'I do apologise for the boys Miss Brontë,' Phillips continued, 'I am afraid that they get a bit boisterous at times but they don't mean any harm. They don't see many girls up here and they forget their manners. They have no mother you see. Mrs Heaton does her best to add a female influence, but they are an unruly bunch. I do hope you will overlook their high jinks and not feel the need to inform your father. I am sure that there is no harm done. Perhaps Eliza here can find you some small cakes or a few sugared sweets to take back for you and your Mama.'

Phillips, looking Emily in the eye throughout this speech, felt sure that the little girl would be placated with the offer of some small gifts. He was surprised when the child replied, 'I don't have a mother either, but my sisters and my brother and I know how to behave and we all have good manners even if we do not live in a big house or have lots of money.'

Emily allowed herself to be led into the kitchen and washed her hands and face. 'Ooh,' said Eliza, 'you is brave talking t'butler like that, we'd lose a week's wages for saying owt round 'ere. Them lads is out o' control, everyone knows it. Sorry if they 'urt you miss. T' tell truth, they have hit me a few times and other things. It's 'orrible livin' 'ere but mi mam was in service 'ere and it's all there is for the likes o' me in these parts. I 'ate livin 'ere, I wish I cud get work down in 'Aworth but there's nowt at t'moment. 'Ere take these few scones and a bit o' barm cake for t'family and if you tak' my advice…'

'Eliza,' Mr Phillips voice rang out, 'Mr Brontë is leaving, is the young lady ready?'

By the time Emily was back on the horse and the cakes carefully wrapped inside the pannier, she felt able to look up from the safety of her father's arms at the three boys pulling faces at her from an upstairs window. 'Come again, any time,' shouted Mr Heaton as they set of at a trot up the lane further on to the moor, 'the boys love to have children to play with.'

'I trust you had a good time with the Heaton cousins, Emily, and showed your good manners. They are such a charming and distinguished family. Did you thank them for their hospitality? How nice of them to share their baking with us. What splendid young fellows those Heaton cousins are. They spend a lot of time with their aunt and uncle, since they lost their own poor mother, God rest her soul. It would do Branwell some good to come up here and seek their acquaintance. They have a superb library in one of the rooms upstairs that would benefit the boy. Mr Heaton seems quite taken with the Sunday school idea, too. What a very satisfactory visit indeed!'

They continued on their way and the higher they got the more spectacular the views became. They could see far across the moors in all directions. Looking west were the high Pennine hills and the pack-horse route to Heptonstall, the small town over the brow of the farthest hill top. Looking east down the valley was Haworth about three miles away with only the very top of the church tower visible. Facing south Emily could see undulating moorland and hill tops and to the north, more green hills stretching away in to the distance. Far below them was Sladen beck running in a deep fold between the hills. At various places along the route, becks, streams and little rivulets crossed their path and the horse had to be held firmly by Mr Brontë as it slithered in the mud.

'This whole moor is running with water that collects at each rainfall and snowfall and finds its way down into the becks and eventually the River Worth,' Papa informed Emily. 'It is what is known as a watershed; a huge holding area of water. It is very necessary for the mills and the population in the valleys but it can be unstable at times of very heavy rain and the streams can burst and gallons of water run down the valley causing floods. That is what happened two years ago when the bog burst. It is a difficult place to live and the farmers up here have a hard time of it. A few cattle or sheep, a couple of pigs, chickens and a bit of hay are about all they can manage, especially up on the higher ground. It's a wild area to live,

Emily, and the people can be rough and ready. It is part of my work to bring them nearer to God and help them to live in a Christian manner.'

Emily was becoming more aware of the role that her father played in this far-flung community. He was always busy; visiting his parishioners, helping the sick, writing letters, studying the Bible and preaching his sermons and generally trying to get things done in the area to help the townsfolk. Emily was proud of her Papa and felt privileged to be spending the day with him. She loved being on these lovely moors, high up on horseback with the wind blowing in her face and the sun shining in her eyes. Emily was aware of all the smells and sounds of the moor; the birds and the flowers, the water and the sky, the heather and the peat banks, the colours and the wide open spaces. Emily felt happy deep within the natural landscape, away from people who could be cruel and unkind and away from the sadness and pain of ordinary life. Up here, there was nothing but the natural elements: the sun, the wind, the heath, the waterfalls and the ancient rocks.

Chapter Thirty-Seven
Sept 1827 (Same Day)

Emily and her father continued along the top of a slope and then dipped down before following an uphill track that led them directly up to Top Withins Farm. They slowed as they made their long uphill approach. The farm was perched high on the top of the moor, facing south and west, built with huge slabs of millstone grit. As they reached the high ground, Papa drew Emily's attention across to the east.

'It is said that this is one of the highest spots in the county and between here and the Ural Mountains in Russia, there is no higher ground. On occasion when the wind blows from the east, it can come from those mountains, three thousand miles away.'

Emily gazed in wonder following this information and imagined the wild wind blowing snow and sleet across the North Sea from Russia, over the eastern side of England and into the heart of the Yorkshire dales and moors. It was a wild and wonderful feeling of land and weather working with and against each other.

Top Withins farm stood at the very end of this eastern blast, the highest farm on the highest point of the moor. The farm was in two main parts with a few outbuildings and a stunted tree bending over it in the wind. It was built into the side of the moor, almost growing out of it, Emily thought, with its stone walls and heavy, flag-stoned roof. There was one long row of windows on the upper floor and a few other single ones set deep into the 3-feet-thick walls. It had been built to resist even the most extreme winter weather with a main door set into a deep porch to keep out the constant wind, which blew, whatever the weather, at this height.

They dismounted and Papa shouted hello as he knocked on the door. The door flew open, helped by the wind, and the round, red cheery face of Mrs Sunderland greeted them, 'Come away in, your Reverend Sir, and you too Missy, its rite grand to si' thi'. Cum away in now.'

Emily gazed around her at the comfortable room, its walls covered in a light blue wash against which the shadows danced from the flickering fire. A large dresser stood against the back wall and a wooden table and a few chairs took up most of the rest of the floor space. The floor was flagged and two dogs were stretched out on it in front of the large fire place.

'Jonas's ovet int fields wit' beasts, Reverend, but a ken send lad to fitch 'im. We is just 'int dairy, butter's about ready and Joseph's churnin'.' Mrs Sunderland laughed and showed a mouth with few teeth but she seemed a pleasant and cheery person and Emily liked her at once. 'Well fancy, t'parson comin' up all this way today and wit young un. What's tha called missy?'

Emily gave her name and age and would have recited her address but Papa held up his hand. 'Perhaps Emily can give a hand in the dairy Ann, whilst Jo goes to find Jonas. It is important I have a word about some common land that might be useful to him.'

Calling out to her son, Mrs Sunderland took Emily's hand and led her through to the dairy, which was situated in a low room at the back of the farm against the east wall. A young boy of about ten or eleven years old with a mop of black unruly hair and sun-tanned arms was busy turning the handle of the butter churn. He smiled at Emily and said hello. 'Give churn t' lassie, Jo and go and find thi father. Reverend's 'ere an' this is 'is little lass, Emily, be quick now.'

Jo surprised Emily by grabbing her hand and placing it on the handle, under his own. 'You mun keep it going 'til I gets back Emily else butter'll spoil,' he stated, giving her an encouraging smile. 'When it's done I'll tak you owt and show you me hens and stuff, if tha's interested.'

The boy shot off in search of his father and Mr Brontë and his mother went back into the "house" as these hill people called the parlour. Emily took both hands to the handle and felt quite proud to have been given such an important job, although it wasn't long before her arms began to ache and she wondered how long she would be left in charge of the butter. Looking around she could see various milk churns on the flagged floor and some big bowls spread out on a table with muslin cloths laid over them. Emily had watched Aunt and Tabby separating milk for curds and whey, but they did not make their own butter at the Parsonage. Butter and milk were bought from various shops and used mainly for baking. They had their own hens and shares in a pig, but no cow. Various wooden butter pats of different sizes were leant against the table top and the whole room had a lovely clean, fresh smell to it. Emily heard voices and Jo arrived back to take over the churning.

'It's probably 'bout done now. Go an ask mother to come an' check it and we can go out for a bit if tha likes?' he offered.

Within minutes, and after being given a cup of lovely fresh creamy milk from one of the churns, Emily and Jo set off for a tour of the farm. Chickens roamed all around and there were two pigs, Daisy and Mathilda, in an outbuilding. Jo informed Emily that Mathilda was 'wit 'litter. Emily was pretty sure that that meant that the pig was having babies but didn't really like to ask. The young boy took her all over the farm and then they walked further away towards an intake field; a field that had been gradually altered from moor to grazing land, where seven cows were feeding on the coarse thick clumps of grass. Jo explained how the cattle were their livelihood and each day he took the churns on a hand cart to Stanbury to sell the milk, cheese, whey and butter to the grocer. Jo showed Emily where he had tried to dig a small garden at the south side of one of their fields but apart from a few potatoes and turnips he had been mainly unsuccessful.

'We can grew 'erbs int t'ouse, but they's no much'll grow in these parts, 'sept grass an hevver. Mind it's grand at t'moment wit' t'hevver all out and last month we 'ad a good crop o'bilberries. We 'ad a right good feast then.'

Jo walked Emily across the brow of a hill and pointed out the spire of Heptonstall church to her. 'It's rite grand livin up 'ere an' it's wild as 'ell int winter.' He immediately blushed and apologised, 'Sorry, lass, we use lots of wods up 'ere that Reverend would ni approve of, don't mean to offend like.' Emily smiled and assured him that it was fine. Living in Haworth and hearing many different people in church every week meant that Emily heard a lot of language of which her Papa might not approve.

'Do you live here with just your parents?' Emily asked him.

'Heck, no, there were nine of us, but young 'uns died. I've two sisters an' a brother married and livin in 'Eptonstall. Our William and me 'elp dad on't farm an' our Nancy's in service at Stanbury, wit' Taylors. Then tha's young Jonas, who is t'eldest, after first three like an' he was named after mi dad, then there's all grandchilder' what comes up overt top and stay for a bit.'

'Stop, stop,' laughed Emily, 'I have lost track. Does that mean that you are the youngest then?'

As Emily spoke she stepped backwards and her foot caught on the edge of a stone and slipped in to a little hollow where it was immediately drenched with water. She cried out as her ankle twisted. Sitting suddenly and unceremoniously on the heather she rubbed her foot. Although the pain was sharp, she tried desperately not to cry in front of this nice boy, who immediately dropped down beside her, his face full of concern.

'Shall I go fetch mi ma? She can 'ave a look an' see if it's ok and put some balm on't.'

'No, no' cried Emily, 'please don't cause a fuss, it will be alright, I just slipped on that stone. I didn't see it,' replied Emily rubbing her foot vigorously with her hands. 'If I can just sit a minute, I am sure that it will be better.'

Despite the pain in her ankle, Emily felt happy sitting up on the heather with this pleasant boy.

'What 'bowt your place?' Jo asked suddenly, 'I've ony bin t'Aworth a few times. Seems pretty busy like. How'd you cope with all them people and noise? It'd drive me daft.'

Emily described the Parsonage and what they all did on a typical day. She told Jo about the loss of her mother and sisters and he shook his head in sympathy. He seemed to know the awful pain that it caused.

'It's 'ard life up here, and mi ma has lost a couple o' young uns like. Still a'd rather be up 'ere than down there,' he said, pointing down the valley.

Jo explained that he was never lonely or stuck for something to do. He only got down to the school in Stanbury now and then, and with so much to do on the farm and the whole moor as a playground, he was very happy with his life. He spent many hours setting traps for rabbits and grouse which lived all over the moor and were part of their diet. When times and the weather were hard, they had little more than porridge to eat and rough oat bread. Despite the cattle they drank mainly water as the milk was too precious to waste. Milk was their main source of income. Sometimes, they had wool to weave and he also had a brother working at the quarry at Penistone, but money was scarce and depended very much on the animals and the wool and milk they produced.

Emily felt the sun on her face as Jo talked about his life and gradually the pain in her foot subsided. Jo helped her to stand, taking her hand and walking her slowly back to the farm. They stopped for a minute at a little spring running through the heather on a slope beside the farm and the water tasted wonderful to Emily, far sweeter than what came out of the well in the Parsonage garden.

Emily's foot was almost dry and only hurt a little bit when they returned to the farm porch where Papa was just packing away the Bible into the saddle bag. Jo's parents were standing beside the horse and both smiled at the children, hand in hand, windswept and breathless from their walk.

'Now then lass, has our Jo been looking after thee rite?' asked Mr Sunderland.

Emily thanked everyone for their kindness and said she hoped that the butter would not be spoiled and that she could come and see them all again in the future. Mrs Sunderland bent and gave her a kiss on both cheeks and said what a bonny lass she was and how she would be welcome any time. Mr Sunderland and Jo both shook her hand and she felt quite thrilled at all the attention from these kind people.

Emily and her father climbed onto the horse and began the descent towards the lower, Middle Withins Farm, on their way back to Haworth, waving and calling goodbye. Jo walked with them the few hundred yards to where the path divided and they took the one going north-east towards a larger farm about a quarter of a mile away. He waved and made an elaborate bow as the horse picked its way along the path and Mr Brontë called back to remind him that he was to visit the church more often. Emily waved and watched as he disappeared out of sight feeling strangely sad to see him go.

'We must hurry, Emily, we still have two calls to make and its already nearly three o clock,' said Papa as he delved into his pocket and brought out some oatcake that was still warm from Mrs Sunderland's oven. The pair ate as the horse descended down the track to the next farm.

This farm was much bigger that Top Withins and had long low roofs over the main house and two low, wide outbuildings. Papa explained that they did wool combing and hand loom weaving here as well as running the farm and looking after the various animals. They had more land and their fields were more arable on these lower slopes. A few sheep as well as a small herd of around twenty cattle roamed the enclosed fields and the usual chickens, geese and a few ducks came out to greet them as they entered the farm yard. Two horses in the back field cantered up to the gate and whinnied in recognition of Blackitt. As they dismounted a cacophony of barking welcomed them as three sheepdogs pelted down from a nearby field. Amongst all the noise and clamour Mrs Jackson appeared in the doorway and welcomed them in.

Within minutes and after a lot of whispered discussion they were ushered into a small back room where on a long wooden settle a body lay under a cream linen cloth. Papa had explained to Emily that their purpose here was to arrange the funeral of old Benjamin Jackson the father of Robert Jackson, the current farmer. Emily was not alarmed at being in the same room as the dead man. She was fairly used to being around death and funerals. She knew that in these farming areas, as in the towns, living was hard for everyone and illness and accidents meant that only a few lived to a ripe old age.

Old Mr Jackson had been one of the lucky ones. He was in fact eighty-two when he had finally passed away two days before and his family where keen to arrange his burial as soon as possible. A body kept in a warm house at this time of year soon deteriorated and even as they sat listening as Mr Brontë read a passage from the Bible and said some prayers, the undertaker arrived to measure Mr Jackson for his coffin. They arranged Friday for the funeral and discussed the carriage of the body on a pack horse to Stanbury. At this point the body would be transferred to the funeral cart for the rest of the journey to the church. Mr Brontë proceeded to the back of the house where he had documents and deeds to explain to Mr Jackson's son. Also in the room, rocking backwards and forwards in a creaking rocking chair was old Mrs Jackson, Benjamin's elderly wife; a rather tiny old lady, in her late seventies. She was making a strange crooning noise, as she rocked, which quite alarmed Emily.

Emily was sent out into the farmyard with a cup of water and another oatcake and spent the next half hour sitting on a low wall watching the sheep and listening to a couple of curlews. Her ankle was still painful when she put her weight on it, but it did not bother her too much and she saw no reason to burden her father with any worry about it.

After a while, the old lady approached Emily from the farm building. She was muttering to herself and seemed quite odd in her black clothes and long straggly hair, with her limping walk and her trembling hands. Emily tried not to think of the witches in her story book as the old lady came and sat next to her, whilst patting her eyes with a piece of linen cloth. She seemed to be talking about her dead husband but she had no teeth and her mouth seemed to droop to one side. Emily just nodded in sympathy when she felt she should respond.

In the background, Emily could just hear Sladen Beck running below the farm, with the water rushing along as it came down the valley. Skylarks were flying high above the moorland and singing in the afternoon sunshine and the sheep added their baaing and bleating to the overall noise. Emily kept looking at the old woman, who was clearly distressed, but felt unable to help. She decided to do what she had at the other farms and told the old lady her name, age, date of birth and where she lived. Emily smiled at the woman and asked her if she would like to hear about her brother and sisters as well, but to Emily's horror the lady began to cry and rock herself backwards and forwards making the same awful high-pitched noise as before. Emily stood up in alarm to go and fetch Mrs Jackson but the old granny grabbed her wrist and clung on to her arm as she continued with the strange sound. Emily felt trapped and in despair shouted for help.

A young woman came to her rescue, clambering over a nearby wall and gently releasing Emily from the old lady's grasp. 'I could see you from mi window up there, where we've a loom runnin'. I thought she was mebbe bin a nuisance. It's all rite granny. It's me, Annie,' she soothed, 'it's all rite you come away yon with me now, let's get thee back int 'owse.' She smiled at Emily and apologised, 'She's mi great gran and with towld man havin jus' died, she dun't know what's apnin'. She's not been rite since she 'ad a funny turn and now she keep's lookin' for great granda and canna find 'im. Poor owd lass ud be better off we 'im if you ask me, but that's t'Lords job.'

The girl led the old lady away into the farm house and Emily continued to sit on the wall. It was unusual to see people this old and Emily wondered if she was over a hundred. She mused over what the old lady must have looked like when she first came to live here, where she was from and what they had worn in those days. That girl had said she was her great grandmother, so at least four generations of the family lived here, constantly being born, living and eventually dying in the same house and amongst the same moorland. What would they all be like in another hundred years? She wondered, when the young woman she had just seen was long dead and her great grandchildren would be living here. That would be the year 1925. Would any of her own family still live at Haworth? Emily wondered. What would they be like? It all goes around Emily was thinking. The years, the seasons, the days and nights and life and death, it was a great wheel that drove forward from time way in the past to now and then on thousands of years into the future.

'Come on Emily, be quick now, we still have another call to make,' shouted Papa.

Emily blinked and pulled herself out of her daydream. She got up from the wall, the stones of which had been around since ancient times. These stones, these hills and this land had stayed unchanged for thousands of years and Emily felt quite strange as her father lifted her up off the ground as if she was just passing over the Earth for a few brief seconds in time.

Chapter Thirty-Eight
Nov 1827

There was no possibility of taking a walk that day, as heavy rain beat against the windows. Charlotte and Branwell were sitting in the parlour after lunch playing with the twelve soldiers, unaware that Papa was standing behind the door listening intently to their game.

'I think that Napoleon is the best and bravest soldier that ever lived,' Branwell was saying and Charlotte was arguing that The Duke of Wellington, known as the Iron Duke, had fought Napoleon for many years and finally defeated him at the Battle of Waterloo and he was therefore the best.

As the children's voices rose and their discussion turned to argument, their Papa put his head around the door.

'Children, children,' he exclaimed, 'there is no need to shout at each other. What are you arguing about?'

Both children began to speak at once but Papa held up his hand and sitting down he began to talk to them.

'Now then, if you wish to know about Napoleon's defeat at Waterloo, you only need to ask me. I can describe the entire battle as if I was there. I remember reading about it in the papers. In fact, all the Peninsular wars and all the major conflicts of the early part of the century were bread and butter to me. The newspapers were full of famous men and the battles they fought.'

'Waterloo took place in the year before you were born Charlotte, in June 1815. Maria was toddling and Elizabeth a young baby. Your Mama and I had recently moved to Thornton, where you four were all born. After the Duke of Wellington's victory there was great rejoicing in Britain and throughout Europe. There was a street party in Thornton for all the children and your Mama took the little ones along to it. I seem to recall that Maria was given a little flag to wave,' Papa halted and cleared his throat before continuing.

'People were so glad that Napoleon's stranglehold on Europe had finally come to an end. I remember well the reports in all the journals of the day. The battle took place in Belgium about twelve miles south of Brussels… Just a moment, we need soldiers, lots of them! Go and fetch Emily and Anne and come back with as many toys and things that we can use. We will have a battle, here on the dining room table. Quickly children, use your initiative and bring me my warriors whilst I prepare the battlefield!'

Charlotte and Branwell were thrilled. Papa was not only going to tell them about the battle but was going to enact it in their parlour. They shouted for Emily and Anne and ran upstairs to grab as many soldiers, dolls, ninepins and other toys as they could find.

The four excited children gathered around the table and saw how Papa had laid his walking cane under the heavy velvet cover to produce a ridge and had placed books to represent buildings.

'We need more battalions and more cavalry,' Papa cried, thoroughly enjoying the game. 'Go and fetch more recruits, children!'

Emily and Anne ran off to the kitchen and seeing a pile of carrot tops and potato peelings on the table Emily gathered them up in her apron. Tabby looked on in complete surprise as the girl ran off with bits of carrot falling on to the floor behind her.

Anne went into the back kitchen and came out with an apron full of wooden pegs and dashed back to the game.

'Wonderful,' exclaimed Papa. 'The strong pegs will represent Wellington's men and the soft carrots will be

Napoleons battalions. Now then, we will use your toy wooden lion to represent the Duke and one of Branwell's wooden soldiers as Napoleon.'

Gradually, Papa set up the entire table with the opposing forces, explaining to the children as he worked.

'There were actually three main battles fought over three days involving the French, the British, Dutch and the Prussians. The Prussians were led by a brave old general called Field Marshall Gebhard von Blucher and he led 120,000 Prussians against the French at the town of Ligny. Despite their efforts they were overcome, but Blucher swore allegiance to Wellington and set off with his remaining soldiers to meet up with the Duke at Waterloo on the 18th June. Meanwhile, on the 16th June, Wellington's men fought the French, led by Marshall Ney at the town of Quatre-Bras a few miles south of Waterloo and both sides suffered heavy losses. The outcome of the battle was a draw and both sides withdrew to meet again at Waterloo two days later where Napoleon would lead his men.'

Papa pointed at the table, 'This is the layout for Waterloo. Wellington gathered his men behind this northern ridge and Napoleon marched up from the south-west joining forces with the remainder of Marshall Ney's troops. Now children, Napoleon was good, very good, and he had conquered most of Europe in the previous ten years and the French adored him as their Emperor. He was a very clever man and Wellington had fought his troops in Spain and Portugal for seven years, in what is now known as the Peninsula Wars. However, on this occasion, Napoleon made a huge mistake. Thinking that Wellington might try to move his men around to the east, here, to attack from the side, and also to stop Blucher coming to Wellington's aid, from here, Napoleon sent a force of 33,000 men under Marshal Grouchy to intervene. This proved to be a fatal mistake and when orders were sent for Grouchy to return to Waterloo the messages were misinterpreted and this enormous back-up of men failed to come to Napoleon's aid. Blucher got through to Wellington just as the English and Dutch troops were being overcome and saved the day.'

Papa was moving pegs and carrot tops, nine pins and soldiers all over the table as he spoke, 'This poetry book represents the Chateau d'Hougoumont, and this one the farm of La Haye-Sainte and that the farm of Papeloote. Each one was in a strategic position where Wellington's men could take refuge and try to stop the Imperial Guard getting through to the ridge.'

The children stood around the table spellbound as they watched and listened to their father. This was so exciting and he knew so much about what had taken place. Charlotte and Anne, neither of whom was very tall, strained to see what was happening as they tried to take in the full view.

'Can you all see?' Papa suddenly asked. 'Pull out the chairs and stand on them, I want you to see the full battlefield to appreciate how it all happened.'

For the first time, the children were allowed to climb on to the dining room chairs and it made them feel like birds flying over the battle field and seeing all the action. Papa was in full flow, describing attack and counter attack, moving battalions and squashing whole regiments. Carrot tops and bits of potato peelings ended up being flung onto the fire in defeat and Anne had to cry out to stop two pegs following them.

'All day the armies fought. All day rain poured down as the Heavens opened and drenched the land and the soldiers, making the fighting even harder to control,' Papa cried. 'Firstly, the joined forces of the Dutch, Belgians and English, under Wellington, battled against the French cavalry, infantry, gunners and the imperial guard, the cream of Napoleon's men. Blucher, heading the Russians and Germans arrived around mid-day. The British troops were each headed by famous fighting men, Ponsonby, Uxbridge, Gordon, Mercer, and many others whose names will live on throughout history. Wellington on his huge battle horse, Copenhagen, rode backwards and forwards all day long urging his troops on and leading them into battle. The noise of musket fire, bugles, cries and cannons, the clashing of swords and the screams of agony rang out all day. The smoke from the guns and cannons and the mud and rain greatly handicapped the soldiers but did not prevent them fighting to the death.'

Papa looked around the room at his four children wide eyed, flushed and utterly absorbed in the tale. 'Men whose horses had been slaughtered under them, ran forward with their swords drawn, cutting down the enemy in their hundreds. Battalion after battalion of British troops advanced in waves in special formation that helped to prevent the enemy getting in amongst their ranks. Everywhere wounded and dying men had to be trampled underfoot as the armies clashed and gradually gained or lost ground. Neither Wellington nor Napoleon shirked their duty and both could be seen in their splendour charging up and down the ranks of men, calling them forward to defend the cause and defeat the enemy.'

The front door opened and closed with a bang and seconds later Aunt Branwell popped her head round the parlour door. The sight that met her eyes was one of the strangest she had ever seen. All of her nieces and her nephew were standing on the parlour chairs shouting encouragement to their father who was flinging bits of vegetables into the fire whilst calling on his children to beat back the French!

Aunt stood with her hand on the door knob and her mouth open, too shocked to utter a sound. For a minute no-one even realised that she was there until Papa snatched up the farm of La Haye-Sainte and moving towards the door was about to fling it on to a pile on the floor. The sight of his sister-in-law brought him to an abrupt halt.

A complete silence followed as each child became aware of their Aunt and stared in fascination at their Papa as he stood in front of her with a sheepish grin on his face.

'Why, good afternoon, Elizabeth, we were wondering where you were.' Mr Brontë coughed and turning to his astonished children issued his orders.

'Children! That is enough of your history lesson for today. Now let us have this table cleared and the cloth replaced whilst your Aunt goes into the kitchen and has a cup of tea.'

With that he brushed past their Aunt and walked across the hallway to his study, leaving the children feeling rather confused and silly standing on their chairs. The look on Aunt's face galvanised them into action and they all scrambled down and rushed around to clear the table of all the detritus of battle.

Aunt said nothing but turned abruptly away and wandered off to the kitchen shaking her head. Tabby only half listened as Aunt muttered that there was no discipline in this house; the children were all deranged and even Mr Brontë had become completely unbalanced!

Chapter Thirty-Nine
Dec 1827 – Jan 1828

At the end of the year 1827, the four remaining Brontë children were aged between seven and eleven years old, and could all read and write to a greater or lesser extent. They worked hard at the lessons set by Aunt and Papa and enjoyed their studies, even when the room was dark and cold in the winter months. Papa encouraged them to read widely but wisely, all books and journals that were interesting and educational and would feed their enquiring minds. These included Blackwood's Magazine, with its dark tales of adventure, and the Keighley Argus newspaper. These papers reported local events but also commented on political matters in Parliament and the lives of the royal household and famous events in science, war, the arts and social change. Story books, poetry and nature and travel books were all encouraged along with classical Greek and foreign languages. Also, of course, they each continued to study The Bible and Common Prayer books, of which they had their personal copies.

By now the four young Brontë children, kept together day and night with almost only themselves for company and amusement had naturally become inter-dependant on each other. They ate, slept, played and studied together and all their games and expressions of imagination were shared and combined. For as long as they could remember they had enjoyed this 'making out'.

"Making out" was still their favourite pastime. Very few stories were written down but some generated occasional drawings and sketches, short verses and battles or plays, to be acted out. Sometimes their games became so boisterous and noisy that, on one occasion, Tabby fled from the house, claiming that: 'Yon childer's all gooin mad, and aw darn't stop in t'hause ony longer wi' 'em.'

The new bedroom arrangement had thrown Charlotte and Emily together; they had invented more special bed plays. When they had been sent to bed early or could not sleep, they created more and more stories or acted out the parts of famous men and women, queens and princesses, noblemen and peasants, even mythical people or animals from the stories and fables that they read or heard about. Emily liked to pretend to be a dog or a cat whereas Charlotte might be a rabbit or a fox. Sometimes Charlotte was Queen Elizabeth the First and Emily was Mary, Queen of Scots. It didn't matter whether they knew the real lives of the people they enacted they just used their imaginations and pretended or "made out" whatever came into their heads, until one or both fell asleep dreaming of fantastic people and lands.

However, the organisation and content of their stories was still in its early stages. Glasstown was growing in their imaginations but each child had different ideas about the characters and there was not always harmony. Neither were there any constructive, chronological events. Sometimes they left it alone and at other times only one child would be working on it and so there was much confusion the next time they all tried to act it out. Suddenly, one dark and cold December night as they were sitting around the kitchen fire trying to keep warm, everything changed and a new, more organised series of plays began.

Charlotte and Emily were trying to get Tabby to light a candle, but she told them it would be wasteful and if they were bored and tired they should all go off to bed.

'I would rather do anything than that,' replied Branwell, and the girls agreed.

'Well,' remarked Tabby, 'think up some nice place to be.'

'What if we each had an island?' cried Charlotte, as Tabby's remark sparked her thoughts.

'If we had an island each, I would choose the Isle of Man,' said Branwell.

'I would choose the Isle of Wight,' replied Charlotte getting excited at the prospect.

'The Isle of Arran would be for me,' said Emily.

'Mine would be the Isle of Guernsey,' said Anne.

'Right,' cried Charlotte, 'now that we each have our Island, who shall be the rulers? I will have The Duke of Wellington as my Chief of Men.'

'Lord Herries will be mine,' said Branwell, warming to this new idea of each of them having their own kingdom rather than a shared one.

'Walter Scott, shall be mine,' chose Emily.

'I shall have Lord Bentnick,' said Anne. 'Shall we start new plays, Charlotte, and new books each writing about our chosen islands?'

'Yes,' replied Charlotte in great excitement, 'let us start the Tales of the Islanders. They will be full of exciting stories and people who have all sorts of adventures. We can begin with…'

The sound of the Grandfather clock striking the seventh hour sounded its way into the kitchen and Aunt appeared, as if from nowhere, to summon them all off to bed. For once, however, they were all too excited to complain and sped off upstairs full of ideas to discuss about their new islands. That night after whispering under the covers and calling between bedrooms they dreamt of their new kingdoms. The four great Genii were back in command.

Chapter Forty
1828

From now on and for the rest of their lives, the children would imagine, act out and write stories from their imaginations. Many of their ideas came from the articles and events they read about but as many came from their own thoughts and emotional experiences.

Music, art and literature increased as part of their lives, as they grew older and their social circle expanded. They walked to Keighley and occasionally visited Bradford and Halifax, taking note of all the sights and sounds of the towns and cities. At home, they listened to all the news that came into the Parsonage from the many visitors who called to see Papa. Village gossip was also at hand, usually repeated by Tabby following visits to various members of her family nearby.

One day when the children were all keen to get out onto the moors, they had to wait for Tabby who was standing near the Parsonage wall on the path leading out across the fields. The children, all wrapped up warm against the biting wind, were wanting to run up to Penistone Hill but Tabby had been stopped and drawn into conversation by Mrs Brown, who lived in Haworth and was on her way back from a visit to her father in Stanbury. The children stood around in the cold, politely but impatiently, waiting to start their walk. They listened to the gossipy conversation between the two women.

The dialects in West Yorkshire, the language adapted and spoken by each area, valley and upland, varied considerably.

As in all parts of every country, the language is affected by who is speaking and where they have heard the language spoken. People had widely different accents and dialects and ways of phrasing their words. Added to this, the children read all sorts of books and listened to church liturgy and poetry, songs and local people of various social classes, from farm labourers to the Bishop of Bradford. The whole made for a blend and mixture that produced the way in which they each communicated. Tabby and her neighbours certainly spoke in a different dialect from the children and it was probably difficult for the children to follow and understand. When the dialect was produced rapidly, by two middle-aged women speaking of things that the children had very little interest in, their dialogue must have sounded almost like a foreign language.

However, the children loved to copy and to mimic people and their speech. It wasn't long before they began to listen in to the conversation and then try to reproduce what they had heard. Branwell started it, and as they ran off up the hill he began to imitate Tabby and Mrs Brown. He had had a nasty cold and with his bunged up nose and attempt at dialect, it came out as gobbledegook and the girls all laughed at the strange noises coming from their brother.

Charlotte took up the joke and squeezing her nose to imitate her brother, she too began to talk in strange nasal tones. Soon all four of them were holding their noses and talking utter nonsense.

It was Emily who suddenly saw the potential of using this strange speech for their imaginary people.

'Charlotte, Branwell, Anne! Stop and listen,' she cried. 'Why haven't we thought of this before? We act out our plays in secret. Why don't we also have a special language so that we can talk about them in front of the grown-ups?'

Anne bumped into Branwell who had stopped abruptly when the sense of what Emily was saying struck him. Charlotte, too, stopped running and came back to where Emily was standing.

'My goodness, Emily. Why didn't we think of that before?' Charlotte cried, 'you are a genius, of course we must have a secret language as well.'

'It will have to be English,' stated Branwell, 'but we can use bits of Latin and Greek and French and Yorkshire and Irish and lots of other languages and, well, anything we please really.'

'As long as we hold our noses and speak from the back of our throats,' said Anne, practicing as she spoke, 'we can say anything we like.'

Branwell had no idea what Anne had just said, so carried on speaking and taking charge of the new language. 'I know a lot of Latin and Greek now, so I will organise you girls and let you know what the words mean and you can find out some French and perhaps a few words of German. I will write it all out and then we can each learn to talk to each other and then we can let our characters speak in the same way. It's a brilliant idea, well done Emily for suggesting it, I have been thinking about it for some time, myself.'

Emily pushed her brother and he fell to the ground where he pretended to be hurt.

'You are despicable!' Emily shouted, but she was laughing as she ran off with Anne up to the top of the hill and along the edge of the quarry.

'Actually,' said Charlotte, hauling her brother up from the ground and pretending to be concerned that he was hurt, '…Actually, I think that we have already got a sort of language, even if it is accidental. If you think about it Branwell, I know that we write an awful lot in our lessons, but our writing lacks grammar and our spelling is dreadful. You are always saying how Emily and Anne's writing is especially bad. Emily only had half a year at school and Anne has had none. Our punctuation and sentence structure is very poor compared to that in books and newspapers.'

'I see what you mean,' answered Branwell, rubbing his legs and wincing in pretended pain. 'All that makes it even harder for other people to read and understand. It's a pity that we don't have paper to write our stories down. We barely have enough for our lessons.'

'I can hear it all in my head,' responded Charlotte, 'I know how all my characters speak, whether they are rich or poor, peasants or noblemen, but I cannot always write it down, even if I wanted to and we had masses of paper.'

'Does it matter though?' replied Branwell, tentatively testing his ability to walk. 'As long as we four all know our stories well enough. Do we need worry about writing them down or proper grammar? You and I can write well enough, it's only Emily and Anne who struggle. They are not very good are they, Charlotte, you must admit it, their ideas are very childish. I have actually offered to write things down for Emily when she gets stuck.'

'Oh, how generous...' retorted Charlotte in a sarcastic voice, 'and how will she improve if you do it for her, Branwell? Emily and Anne have some excellent ideas actually and Emily is very talented at all sorts of things, especially music. You are not the only clever one in this family Branwell, be careful that we girls don't do pretty well ourselves in the future.'

'I am just trying to help and be nice,' whined Branwell, but Charlotte was already striding away from him in search of her sisters. Branwell ended up hobbling off to find Tabby whom he hoped would fuss over him and help him to struggle back to the Parsonage where he would receive an edible reward for his suffering.

That afternoon, the children were upstairs in the little room which Branwell was using as his bedroom. They were each talking about their islands and the characters that they were developing.

'I am not sure that four separate islands works,' Charlotte suggested.

'I am getting confused,' Anne complained, 'I can't keep all your islands in my head along with my own.'

'Would we be better with one island?' suggested Emily. 'One island where instead of everything being wonderful and fantastic, there were children trapped there who lived in a massive underground room, locked away where they were punished for being naughty.'

'Is that because Aunt makes us stand in the cellar for being cheeky?' Branwell asked.

'Well,' Emily replied, 'we have battles and wars and fights, but we never have anything bad happening that involves children or their punishment. I think that we should have an island that is fabulous above ground but that has dungeons where children are held captive and—'

'You can have what and who you like on your island, Emily,' cried Branwell, 'but on my island children will be banned. I am going to have an island with men only. Women and children will not be allowed anywhere near it.'

Their arguments continued until Tabby called up that tea was ready.

Seated quietly round the table, Aunt asked Emily to pass the bread. Emily could not recall afterwards what on earth had possessed her to suddenly grab her nose and, speaking from the back of her throat, reply to her Aunt in a voice and a language that was unrecognisable.

Two hours later when she was allowed out of the dark cellar and sent off to bed, she had all the ideas for her new island, firmly organised in her head.

Chapter Forty-One
August 1828

The children had several plays and stories on the go at once. Real events both in the Parsonage and those reported in the newspapers were all mixed in to their fictional world. The lack of paper or spare writing materials meant that little was written down in the first couple of years but the children were constantly producing ideas and talking about their characters and making up stories and adventures for them to experience. The "Young Men's" plays and those of "Our Fellows" and "The Islanders" were all well established by 1828 and often the events of one became confused and mixed with those of the others. Still using their toys, especially the wooden soldiers, as symbolic figures, the children continually renamed and re organised their chief of men.

Time had little effect on their characters and some could live for hundreds of years whilst others lasted for half a day. The Duke of Wellington would metamorphose into his two sons, The Marquis of Douro and Lord Charles Wellesley, whilst Napoleon dissolved and became Young Soult or Northangerland or Boaster or Captain Tree. The changes were ongoing and it is little wonder that Emily and Anne often felt confused as their older siblings changed names and locations and storylines, whenever they chose.

Many of the children's stories copied the events that were actually happening in Britain and the colonies. The newspapers continued to focus on political, social and legal events and made much of the lives and beliefs of the famous, including the Royal family. The events in the courts and palaces were also reported and eagerly followed by a reading public who almost never saw their monarchs but only read about them. Many wars were in progress throughout the known world as colonisation spread and many changes were taking place in Britain as the Industrial Revolution progressed.

Papa was an intelligent and active man who wrote regularly to the papers about events that he felt strongly about. Slavery, public health, emancipation, education and religious matters all found their way into the letters page of the local newspapers. Papa explained and argued his ideas and beliefs with his children almost as if they were adults and so they became very well informed about local and national issues.

One morning Papa entered the parlour clutching the Leeds Mercury newspaper and interrupted the children's lessons.

'Children,' he barked, 'what do you think about this? The Catholic and Irish activist, Daniel O'Connell, has been elected as political member for County Clare in Ireland. He wants to enter the House of Commons in London as a member of Parliament, but as you know, as yet, the Catholics do not have the vote. If they were emancipated they could put their own Catholic member's into Parliament. What do you think about that? Is it a good thing or a bad thing? Should the Protestants and the Catholics put aside their past fights and join together or should we stay separate in our religions and our beliefs? Charlotte, you first, what do you think should happen?'

Charlotte sat for a moment trying to gather her thoughts. She had noted several letters in the papers about this and she had read about the catholic fight for the right to vote following the Act of Union between Great Britain and Ireland. She wanted to give her father an intelligent and informed answer.

'Well, Papa,' she began, 'They have fought for a long time and were promised the vote by Mr Pitt when he was Prime Minister, but nothing came of it. That was twenty-five years ago and now they are becoming angry and frustrated. King George argues that because we are a Protestant nation, it is against the constitution to allow Catholic emancipation and consequently Catholic politicians. However, this may lead to the Catholics becoming violent and then they may start to fight and cause a lot of upset both in Ireland and in England.'

'Yes, a very good answer, my dear,' replied her father, who was impressed by Charlotte's obvious knowledge and understanding of the issues. 'And what do you think, Branwell? The British have fought over the centuries to deny Catholicism and many have died in the cause. Should everyone now be given the vote, despite their religious beliefs? Should everyone in Britain decide who should rule the country alongside the king?'

'I think not, Papa,' replied Branwell. 'That would mean that even women would be able to vote and that would be just silly. I know that there are some clever ladies but men are far more capable of ruling countries and making laws. Women should be running their houses, should they not, Papa?

Papa turned to Emily and looked at her quizzically.

'Branwell can be so silly, Papa. He thinks that females are somewhat inferior to men and that they have no intelligence. I do not see anything wrong with educated women voting, but as for the Roman Catholics, I am unsure. Would it be safe for them to make decisions about our Parliament? They are not Christians in the same way as us are they? I thought that our country was Protestant. Doesn't that mean that our politicians have to be Protestants too?'

'A very important point, Emily,' replied Papa, 'and one that the King argues for very strongly. Should we remain a Protestant country with a Protestant king and a Protestant Parliament? Now Anne, what do you think, should the Irish Catholics be able to vote and elect their politicians to the House of Commons?'

Anne had been listening and thinking hard whilst the others were speaking and she had thought about what each had said. She did not want to appear less knowledgeable than the others. After a while she smiled and answered, 'I think that as you are Irish Papa and as you are a good Christian man, then you should decide and we should all follow your leadership.' Anne looked triumphant as she made her statement.

Aunt smiled at her and the others clapped their hands. Papa looked around at them all and having announced that he had never encountered such clever children he left the room as suddenly as he had entered.

Mr Brontë was correct; his children had extraordinary knowledge that many other children of their age and similar social station had neither the need nor the inclination to develop. This information they twisted and infused with the stories they read and the pictures they observed and the music and dialogue that they heard. Their father felt that there were very few subjects on which they did not have an opinion, and that pleased him very much.

In the Parsonage study, above the fireplace and around the walls were engravings by the artist, John Martin. These showed biblical scenes including "Belshazzar's Feast" and "The Last Judgement". There were also colour paintings of Kirkstall and Bolton Abbey. These pictures were seen every day by the children and along with their Bible studies and Papa's sermons they built up fabulous ideas of Heaven and Hell, abundance and poverty and good and evil. Everywhere that the children went they listened, read or observed and much of what they learnt went into their stories and plays. It seemed that there was as much political debate and argument in Glasstown as there was in the Houses of Parliament.

By the middle of the year 1828, the children now aged between eight and twelve were living an almost dual existence. Reality and fantasy were becoming more and more transposed and eventually the children themselves became confused. There was an urgent need to write and record. Branwell and Charlotte had tried to secrete scraps of wastepaper in order to document some of the events. Yet they did not have enough left over from their lessons; there was always the danger that Aunt or Papa would find it and discover their secret worlds.

Chapter Forty-Two
August 1828

This situation of recording their stories was finally resolved by the children, almost by accident, a short time later. Anne and Aunt were in the parlour. Aunt was reading a very tattered copy of Blackwood's, that everyone in the house but she had already devoured cover to cover. Anne was sitting by the window threading a needle with cotton in the late afternoon light.

'What is the matter, Anne?' Aunt enquired as she heard her niece sighing.

'Oh Aunt, it is this sampler. I am trying so hard to do all the stitching but it is getting dirty and the needle seems blunt and the stitches I did yesterday are not straight and will all have to come out again.'

Anne held up the square of linen on which she was working. Charlotte and Emily had both achieved the level necessary to be given mending and making of clothing and now it was Anne's turn to finish her final work. It was this close needlework, often done at night, using only fire or candlelight, which ruined the eyesight of so many young girls and women.

As Anne struggled, Aunt came over to help.

'You should be doing better than this Anne, you are eight years old,' Aunt gently admonished. 'When I was your age, I could make shirts and turn collars. Your stiches are too big and you are using the wrong sized needle.'

'Aunt, you are so good at needlework and so neat,' Anne replied, 'I will never be as good as you if I sit here until I am fifty years old.'

'You girls spend such a lot of time reading and chattering. You would do far better to concentrate on more household matters. I am sure that I do not know what on earth you find to talk about, closeted up in your rooms or down in the cellar. What are you all up to?' Aunt looked across at Anne hoping that she would enlighten her.

The children had made a pact that their make believe and plays would be kept secret from the rest of the household. More and more ideas and characters were being produced at such a rate that it was taking up all of their leisure time and distracting them as they performed their household tasks. They had now discovered a way of writing their stories down that would fool the grown-ups and this was making their play even more secret.

Anne was torn as to what to say. Would it do any harm to tell Aunt what they were doing? It wasn't anything wrong but Charlotte and Branwell had insisted that she and Emily promise not to say anything to the grown-ups about it, ever.

'We just discuss our lessons or play games or read,' replied Anne, but her pale, thin face was already turning pink.

'Is that so?' stated Aunt, looking her niece in the eye. 'You are certainly all very keen to dash off to play. What a pity that you cannot put as much effort into your sewing.'

It had started one Saturday a few weeks before. Aunt had been tidying her room and had gathered some old letters and journals and scraps of rubbish that she was going to throw away. Amongst them was the little book that Charlotte had given Anne on her sixth birthday. Anne, sharing Aunt's room, had slipped it into one of Aunt's drawers for safekeeping.

That morning Anne had observed Aunt sorting out her bedroom drawers and later had watched in horror as, whilst feeding various papers and bits of wood on to the fire in the parlour, her little booklet had been amongst them.

'Oh Aunt, please don't throw that away, it is one of my treasures,' she pleaded.

'There is too much stuff cluttering my linen drawers, Anne, and you are older now and it is written in such tiny writing that no-one can read it anyway. None of you have good eyesight and you must not strain your eyes writing so small nor reading such miniscule print.' She made to throw it into the fire but Anne started to cry and Charlotte begged Aunt not to dispose of it.

'Please, Aunt, let her keep it. It took me ages to make. Promise Aunt that you will not read it, Anne. Just have it as a keepsake.' Charlotte instructed Anne. With Anne's assurance Aunt reluctantly handed it over.

The two girls had left the parlour, taking the little book with them, and entered the kitchen where Emily was sitting at the table watching Tabby mixing bread dough.

'Why are you crying, Anne?' Emily had inquired and when Charlotte explained, both Tabby and Emily were indignant. Tabby gathered Anne in her arms for a hug and Emily asked,

'Why would Aunt want to throw it away? It hardly takes up any room. Do you think that it is because she cannot read it Charlotte, and she does not want to encourage us to write things that she may not approve of?'

'But it is a lovely little story,' protested Anne from the safety of Tabby's embrace, 'and Charlotte made it especially for me, didn't you, Charlotte?'

'Yes, I did,' replied Charlotte as she thought about what Emily had just said. A plan was slowly beginning to form in her head. For two years now, it had worried Charlotte that keeping track of all their tales and characters was getting out of hand. She was aware that many of their stories were confused and disjointed. Each child contributed different things at different times and each had different ideas in their heads that did not match or link in with the others.

They had managed to keep it mostly secret, although Tabby knew that they talked a lot about their stories and acted out some of the scenes when they were out for walks with her. Tabby saw it as natural that the children should invent a game. That was what children did. It was what she had done as a child, pretending to be an important person or being rich and famous. What Tabby and no-one else realised was that these games or "making out" were becoming an obsession, and one that would last for many years.

Charlotte realised that if they wrote down their ideas and inventions, in tiny script in tiny books, none of the grown-ups would be able to read them but it would also help them in their creations and organise and record their fantasies. Charlotte had become more and more excited at the thought. Their attempts at a secret language had failed in front of grown-ups, although they still practiced it when alone and it always ended up in fits of laughter. If they could record their stories in writing that was small enough so that only they could read it, they could write anything they pleased. No-one else would know what they were doing or be able to enter into their special world of make-believe.

'Do you realise what you just said, Emily?' Charlotte had asked excitedly.

Emily and Anne just stared as Charlotte fled the room shouting, 'I must find Branwell, where is he?'

Branwell was upstairs in his room on the floor with his soldiers. 'Oh, hello, Charlotte, you are just in time to help me with one of the Peninsula wars. Can you get Wellington ready, I am occupied with Napoleon. He is having trouble with some of his generals.'

'Branwell, quickly, put them away and come down to the cellar; I have an idea and must tell you all, come quickly.' She had flown downstairs to drag Emily and Anne out of the kitchen.

Chapter Forty-Three
1828

Hidden in the gloomy surroundings of the cellar Charlotte had explained her plan. They had all read their Papa's stories and poetry and each one of them had marvelled at his skill and knowledge with words. Papa had had stories, papers and poems published and the children knew how much he valued seeing his work in print and how important it made him feel. All the children could now read well and it was one of their favourite pastimes as well as part of their lessons. Charlotte would often read newspaper articles out loud to the younger children so that they could all discuss what was happening in Leeds or London, Bradford or Birmingham.

They knew about foreign wars, about industrial changes, about social reforms and about the leading men and women of the nation and, in their isolated but enjoyable childhood, they eagerly sought out what was happening in the rest of the world. From Africa to America, Belgium to Brazil, India to Ireland, they eagerly read about the world and its people and each event and culture was reworked and re-enacted amongst their imaginary characters.

Sometimes, Aunt would try to limit their reading and complain that they needed more practical training. She would make the girls sew rather than read and would complain to Papa that reading would ruin their eyesight; almost suggesting that sewing would make it better!

Whilst Papa seemed happy to give them free range to read whatever books or materials were at hand, even he would complain if their play got too noisy or if he felt that they were discussing matters that were not Christian or not fit for young children.

'Now,' explained Charlotte, whispering in the semi-darkness, 'we all love making up our stories and acting them out. What if we began a book or a magazine, in a similar way that Blackwood's magazine or the Leeds papers are produced and we wrote it in keeping with our characters? We could give our young men or the islanders their own newspapers, in a size and type that would fit their size?' She looked around her silent siblings all staring at her in the gloom.

'Think what we could achieve. Our paper would be modelled on proper grown-up ones and we would fill them with stories and events set in the cities of our fantasy countries. It means that we could all write them and we would all know what was happening. We would record events and it would help us to put things in order. We would not lose sight of what was happening. We could even have more than one paper eventually. We could also include letters and poems, just as there are in the real newspapers.'

Charlotte stopped again for effect. 'But, and this is the best part, we would write them in a tiny script that only we and our characters could see. That would mean that no grown-ups would ever be able to read them and we could write whatever we wished. We are trying to organise our stories but with nothing written down it is hard for us all to coordinate our thoughts and actions. This way we can keep a history of our characters and testimony of what is happening and we four will all know where we are with everything and what we are doing.' Charlotte's eyes shone as she beamed at her brother and sisters.

The other three stared at her as they thought about what she had said.

'You are right, Charlotte,' Branwell cried with mounting excitement. 'What a good idea. Nothing we wrote could be read by the grown-ups. We could write about ANYTHING, good or bad! You are so clever Charlotte. We could write about battles and wars and, and, and, oh, anything we wanted.' Branwell's eyes were also now shining with excitement.

'Oh, Charlotte, you are so clever,' said Anne. 'I get so confused, especially now that we have an island each. I cannot keep up with what is happening in all your other islands and I have forgotten where we are with Glasstown. Could we have separate journals for each kingdom? It would make it all so much easier to follow.'

Having realised the potential of Charlotte's idea, Branwell now tried to take control.

'Perhaps Charlotte and I should do most of the writing,' he stated looking at his little sisters. 'You two are a bit too young and your writing and spelling is still awful. But Charlotte, what about your eyesight? It's not very good, is it? Perhaps I should be in charge of all the writing? I will write down your ideas and put them into a proper and organised miniature newspaper.'

'No!' cried all three girls in horror.

'You cannot comment on my eyesight, Branwell you do not see too well either, and you will write about nothing but soldiers and wars!' shouted Charlotte.

'I can write very nicely, sometimes,' complained Anne.

'You will never even imagine some of the stories I can write,' added Emily.

'No,' stated Charlotte firmly, 'We girls need to write our stories as well, Branwell. You cannot just take charge. We will all write and record and all join our ideas together.'

After further discussion and argument Emily suddenly pointed out that they had very little writing materials, except that which they were given for their studies. Paper was very scarce and only Papa had clean new paper for his important letters. He did not even write down his sermons most of the time; he would just stand in the pulpit and talk to the congregation in his lovely voice with its beautiful Irish accent.

'We have no money and no means of getting our hands on fresh paper,' Emily reminded them, 'Aunt has made me write across my exercise book and up and down it and sideways, to save paper, so what will we use and where will we keep it if it is to be hidden?' she questioned.

'Well,' replied Charlotte, 'We cannot start straight away, obviously, but we can start to prepare. If we keep our writing and our books miniature we can hide them easily, probably down here somewhere, and we will need only a minimum amount of paper. We need to start collecting scraps and asking the grown-ups to save bits for us. Emily, you and Anne ask Tabby to save as much as she can from shopping and deliveries in the kitchen, sugar and flour bags, that sort of thing.'

'You tackle Papa and Aunt, Charlotte,' suggested Branwell, eager to start on their new project but seeing himself as chief writer not the collector of paper.

'I think we will get more if you ask,' observed Charlotte wisely, knowing full well that the grown-ups would be more likely to oblige him and would assume that it was for his lessons.

The sound of Aunt calling for them for tea had broken up their meeting and they had all dashed back upstairs.

After their meal, the four children had sneaked off into the back garden for another meeting whilst Aunt was busy arguing with Tabby. Charlotte suggested that Emily would gather all the paper together and she and Anne would cut it to size and sew it into little booklets. Then they would all design a newspaper and write about the events in Glasstown or on their islands.

'That still sounds like a lot of paper,' remarked Emily. 'Surely it would be better to confine our writing to one kingdom, to have one newspaper that records all the events.'

'Look,' explained Charlotte who had brought a copy of her father's newspaper outside for them all to look at. 'We have all looked at this, and the format that it uses. We have always used our story and lesson books and the newspapers to create our stories, now we can just follow the same form for our characters' newspaper. If we can't get enough paper together, Emily, we will perhaps do alternate ones, one week for Glasstown and another week for the Islanders.'

'Charlotte is right,' exclaimed Branwell, 'and I have lots more knowledge than you girls as I study Greek and Latin and I am learning all about ancient history as well, so I can bring in lots of information about foreign politics and philosophy, that you three know nothing about.'

'You don't know anything about philosophy, Branwell,' Emily sneered, 'You can hardly say the word.'

'Stop arguing you two,' Charlotte snapped. 'If we keep it all written in tiny script in our little books, we can write anything we want to,' Charlotte reminded them.

'Anything at all?' questioned Branwell, looking slyly at his sister, 'what even rude things or bad language or foreign words or things grown-ups would tell us off about? I know some things that would shock you girls, things that no-one knows I know about, things that Robert Brown has told me.'

'I am sure that we don't need to know tittle tattle from the sexton's son, Branwell,' cautioned Charlotte, glancing at her younger sisters. 'We don't need to write vulgar things Branwell, just secret things.'

'I will probably write some of my own stories then,' replied Branwell, 'in fact I have already written some things of my own, so this is not your idea Charlotte, it was mine, ages ago. I will write things and not show them to you girls, you are all too delicate!' he added, sneeringly.

'Actually, Branwell, I started this when I made the little booklet for Anne's birthday when she was six, and you know I did,' countered Charlotte, 'However, that is not what matters, the thing is that it is now time to take that idea and really use it for all our stories.'

'Well, I have got special stories of my own and I still think that I have more knowledge and writing skills than you girls and I should do the writing. Women and girls do not write. They spend their time on more frivolous things,' Branwell insisted.

Before anyone could argue, Charlotte stepped in again.

'I am afraid Branwell is right. All our books are written by men; The Bible, poetry, stories, our history books, the newspapers, hymn books, everything we read. It would be nice if women could get books published. I think that when I am grown up I will write a book and everyone will be shocked to find that it is written by a woman.'

'Good for you, Charlotte,' Emily added, 'It is time that women were given a chance. I am sure that there are plenty of women with important things to say. I am sure that there are plenty of clever women who know far more than Patrick Branwell Brontë!'

'You are talking nonsense, Charlotte, no woman will ever write a book unless it is about sewing or babies. You will all be sorry,' shouted Branwell before he stormed off back into the house, 'when I am a famous writer and you are all working in service. I shall ride past you in my fine carriage and remind you all of what nonsense you used to speak, especially you Emily.' He disappeared, leaving the girls to continue discussing their ideas.

As they re-entered the house some time later, Aunt was coming down the stairs and eyed them suspiciously. 'What is happening, girls, what have you three been doing outside? There is sewing and cleaning to be done. Anne, is your sampler finished yet? And you, Charlotte, have you tidied your needlework box as I asked? Come now, all of you. Let us have some work done. Emily, go and find Branwell. I asked him to go to the apothecary half an hour ago, where has he got to? Your Papa is asking for him. Just check to see if he is in the lane, my dear. If there is no sign of him come straight back, don't go into the main street on your own.'

Emily quickly grabbed her shawl and set off down the lane. She was thinking about the idea of writing all their stories down when, as she reached the church she heard shouting coming from across the graveyard. It was the raised voices of young boys squabbling or fighting.

'Leave me alone,' a familiar voice rang out 'Leave me alone or I will tell my father!'

Without hesitation, Emily ran into the churchyard and headed up the path towards a group of six young lads all standing in a circle pushing and shoving a very scared Branwell to the ground. Each time he tried to get up they pushed him back.

'Give us your money and we'll let you go!' shouted one.

'Yes, and you can git us some more tomorro', we know you've got plenty livin' in that posh 'ouse.'

'I spent it all in the village to get my Aunt's shopping,' wailed Branwell, 'which you have stolen. Leave me alone and let me go home.'

The group were too busy to see Emily reach for a large stone and hurl it at the lad nearest to her. They all jumped as he let out a loud scream and fell to the ground.

'My father and some men from the village are on their way and you will all get a beating,' screamed the furious Emily, 'Get away from my brother, leave him alone.'

Within seconds, the boys scattered in all directions, one of them holding his hand to the back of his head. Emily ran to Branwell who was now shaking and wailing out loud. His clothes were covered in grass and twigs and his face was scratched and swollen. Emily began to drag him up from the ground as his whole body began to shake violently and his eyes seemed glazed.

'Sit down here for a minute, Branwell,' Emily calmly encouraged as she took his hand and sat down beside him. Branwell lay back and rested his head on a tombstone. He was still shaking but gradually his breathing slowed and he opened his eyes.

'Thank you, Emily,' he gasped, 'I was really scared.'

'It is alright,' his sister assured him. 'We will walk slowly back to the house. Just lean on me and I will explain to Aunt what happened. It wasn't your fault, Branwell. Do not be scared now.'

Later that evening, as Branwell lay on the couch in the parlour, and just before the others went to bed, Emily crept in to see her brother. He had been dosed with laudanum and his face had been bathed in witch hazel. He was awake when she knelt beside him and took his hand.

'Are you better?' she whispered, 'I hope those boys did not hurt you too much.'

Branwell looked up at his sister and began to cry. 'You were so brave Emily, I thought that they were going to kill me. You charged up like Boadicea in her chariot. You saved my life. I will never be able to repay you, and I am so mean to you at times. I am so sorry for being such an awful brother.'

Emily hugged him to her. 'You are not such a bad brother, Branwell,' she murmured 'those boys were just bullies. They are always the same when they are in groups. I think I frightened them off as they believed that there were men coming to beat them.'

'You were very brave,' repeated Branwell, 'You would make a good soldier Emily. I was very scared. If there is anything I can do for you in return just let me know. If you want me to do any of your work for you or any lessons or writing then that's fine, you only have to ask. I didn't mean it when I said I would write our stories on my own it's just that I write better and faster than you and Anne, that's all'.

'Thank you,' replied Emily, 'I have got lots of ideas. Everyone knows that I can't write very well and my spelling is awful. It is odd but all the letters seem to get jumbled up and jump about on the page. They don't come out right and I make lots of blots and spill ink on the pages.'

'Well, just tell me your stories and I will write them down for you,' offered Branwell.

'What! Even when I am grown up and writing famous books, like Charlotte?' Emily teased.

They both began to laugh and were still laughing when Aunt arrived to shoo Emily off to bed.

Chapter Forty-Four
Christmas Day, 1828

It was snowing and the air was bitterly cold in Haworth on the 25th December 1828. At breakfast Aunt had announced that there would be no lessons today but that they had a busy morning ahead. The shops would all be closing at noon and they needed extra supplies collecting before they all went to church. The girls were also expected to help Tabby with the Christmas dinner. Christmas Day was one of the children's favourite days. They loved the rich smell of the food, the excitement of the church celebrations and goodwill that seemed to fill everyone with hope and happiness.

Tabby, red-faced and flustered, kept shooing the children out of the kitchen and then shouting them back in to help. By ten o'clock, and after a quick walk, into the village for sugar, tea and pudding rice, they had all gone into the church to listen to Papa preach his Christmas sermon. The church was full and everyone had sung the carols and enjoyed meeting and greeting their neighbours.

'I love this time of the year,' announced Charlotte to no-one in particular, I love the way that it seems to bring everyone together and people seem kinder and more agreeable. The church seems warmer as well and I love the Christmas carols and the music.'

The church musicians had played extra loudly and the noise of the instruments could be heard all over the top of the town.

Even the non-church-goers had stopped in the street to listen and to sing along with the carols.

Emily linked arms with Charlotte after the service, as they wandered around the church they now knew so well. The soft candle light was soothing and there was a general feeling of calm and welcome. A number of the parishioners remained seated in the pews, enjoying the atmosphere and others wandered around chatting to neighbours or admiring the decorations. A doll laid in a wooden crib, to represent Jesus in the manager, was set up below the altar. Mary, Joseph and the shepherds, made out of rough papier-mâché and painted with blues and reds, gathered around. As the girls looked at the scene, their eyes drew inevitably towards the crypt, beneath the small Lady chapel to the right.

'Maria would have been nearly fifteen now,' commented Charlotte, 'and Elizabeth fourteen come February. I still cannot believe sometimes that they are not here with us. And Mama, it's over seven years since she died. Do you think our lives would have been very different Emily, if they had lived? I think about them so often, and miss them dreadfully. Can you still remember them? Do you remember Mama? You were only three when she died.'

'I can remember kneeling next to her bed and her fingernail got caught in my hair,' whispered Emily. 'I have tried so hard, but that is the only memory of her that I can recall. I cannot remember what her voice was like or even what she looked like really. I just remember her hand on my head and a green cover on the bed.'

'Oh, yes,' replied Charlotte, 'that awful green coverlet. It was in Aunt's trunk. She hid it because she said that it upset Branwell, but I am not sure why. It's gone now, she gave it away to the butcher's wife when their shop was destroyed in that fire.'

Emily strolled away from her sister and sat in the front pew. Christmas was not a particularly happy time for Emily although she enjoyed Christmas Day. It was nice that people celebrated the birth of Jesus and people were more kind and generous than usual, but Christmas and the New Year meant another year had gone by; another year when Mama, Maria and Elizabeth seemed to be moving further and further away. Emily's memories of their lives seemed to be drifting somewhere far beyond reach as even their family began to forget how they looked, what they wore, how they sounded and the feel of their skin and the sound of their laughter. It made Emily sad.

'Come on,' called Charlotte realising and recognising Emily's sudden withdrawal into melancholy. 'Let's go out into the snow and have a quick walk across the back field, before we go in for Christmas dinner. Come, we shall have to be quick.'

Grabbing Emily by the hand, Charlotte pulled her sister up and out of the church, up the lane and out on to the field beyond the Parsonage where they could look out towards the west and across the moors. It was snowing hard now and the strong wind was in their faces. This was what Emily enjoyed, wild weather and nature all around.

'Try not to be sad, Emily, today is a day of celebration. There are carols and music and nice things to eat and Papa will give us all the new pens and quills he has promised and Aunt will be full of joy and a little beer and we can all be happy, even you,' Charlotte shouted against the snow as she hugged her sister and then lifted her face to hers, 'I have got some new ideas for stories, all about Christmas and the presents that the Three Kings brought from foreign lands. I will share them with you tonight. We will start a new bed play and you can choose who you want to be.'

Emily cheered up immediately. 'I think that tonight I shall be the snow queen but I will be a good queen and bring ice cold diamonds from the North Pole and leave them around the town at all the houses where they cannot afford nice food for Christmas. I wonder how the Sunderlands up at Top Withins farm are managing in this weather. It will be desperately cold up there today. I wish I could spend some time with them when the weather is like this. I know it's a hard life out on the moors, but it is thrilling and wild and I love the way that everything is ruled by nature and the seasons. I love all the smells and the wide open spaces and yet, oddly enough, I don't ever want to go away from home. I should hate to live in a big city or in another part of the country. I just want our house and the moors, nothing else.'

'You are a strange girl,' laughed Charlotte, 'and if we don't go back indoors soon you will have your wish as we shall both perish in this cold. Be quick, I will race you back.'

The girls arrived at the kitchen door, breathless and red-faced from the wind and the snow and with wet boots and skirts. Tabby was cross that they had taken so long to return from the church, there were plenty of jobs that needed doing.

'Where have you two bin?' she demanded, 'and look at t' state of you. I'm sure you all go stark ravin' mad at Christmastide. Hast tha finished beatin' the puddin' batter Emily? Have you peeled all the parsnips Charlotte? Anne's done most o't pottaties hersen. She was back from t'church twenty minutes since. Now get those wet things off 'afore you catch yo'r death or Miss Branwell catches you. Whichever comes first, t'end 'll bi t'same.' Tabby laughed at her clever remark and the girls ran off upstairs to get changed.

As the girls were carrying their wet clothes down to dry on the clothes rack which hung from the kitchen ceiling over the fire, Branwell emerged from his little bedroom. He called the girls into his room to examine the tiny manuscript that he had just started.

'Come and read my latest story of Glasstown. It is very good, I am sure that you will agree. I thought that we could add extra characters using the set of Indians I got in Haworth. If they join the Ashantees, there will be an enormous battle. I have written a story where they attack one of our Islands and they are currently besieging the castle where the Islanders have all fled and are surrounded. I think you need to set to work on getting The Duke of Wellington's forces to invade and Parry and The Duke of York need to get involved. Where is Anne, we need her to rally some more forces too.'

Branwell was red in the face with excitement as he related his tale of the coming battle and the girls too picked up on his enthusiasm.

'We have to take these things down and help Tabby with the Christmas meal Branwell but we will come back with Anne, as soon as we are finished,' cried Charlotte. 'Remember all that you have in your head and as soon as we have finished in the kitchen we will get together and arrange the siege. This is wonderful. I can see it all now. Go and find the soldiers and the Turkish musicians and the Indians that are in the parlour, there are some scattered near the window, Branwell. We will be back as soon as possible. Oh, and find Blackwood's latest magazine and see what is happening in Parliament so that we can keep it up to date. I haven't had chance to read it yet. Come on, Emily, quickly, the sooner we get done, the sooner we can get started on our story.'

Branwell ran around the house collecting books, toys and newspapers and managed to evade Papa's call for him to come and meet a visiting preacher who was coming to Christmas dinner. The girls finished their kitchen chores whilst Anne and Aunt laid the parlour table for the special meal and arranged garlands of holly and ivy. They all met again in Branwell's bedroom and arranged the toys in a circle on the floor and the main soldiers, one held in the hand of each child, organised the siege of the Islanders.

'You girls arrange the characters and I will write down what is happening,' cried Branwell. 'Papa has given me some paper and a new pen today. It is perfect for our new newspaper. There is enough paper to make lots of little journals.'

Engrossed in their play, the children did not even hear Papa call up that Christmas dinner would be served in ten minutes. Aunt finally came upstairs to find them and was astonished that they were so loathe to leave their toys and come downstairs for the lovely food. A full goose had been prepared and two curates and the churchwarden had all arrived to share in the festivities. Aunt was a little cross to find that the children were not prepared and ready to greet the guests but, because it was

Christmas, she held her sharp tongue and sent them all downstairs. The smells from the kitchen and their healthy appetites soon got them all settled around the table in the parlour.

After a long grace, where Papa thanked God for his goodness and for providing such a wonderful feast, everyone was served with the lovely Christmas food. The children were unusually quiet. Their minds were back upstairs, working out how the Islanders would survive such overwhelming odds. Charlotte felt that they needed more leaders to counteract this huge invasion and she would check the list of current members of parliament and the Duke of Wellington's men to see who she could recruit. Branwell was secretly on the side of the Islanders and decided that when they returned upstairs he would produce a new hero who would match whoever Charlotte put up against them. Anne was thinking about introducing a queen or a princess who was visiting the island but of whom hardly anyone knew the true identity. She would be incognito but a few of the Chief Islanders would know her identity and would have to protect her to the death. Perhaps a tall, dark stranger would emerge who would suddenly reveal himself as a king from another country and, after all the fighting he would be the one to save her.

Emily was pleased that a new idea had emerged. A siege in a castle would be good, as they could shelter for months no matter how many tribes attacked. Emily thought about the Islanders taking refuge in a massive castle, the size of a small town. How would they manage with the whole of the island population forced into the building? How would they all be fed? Where would they all sleep and was there a good water supply? They would need food, ammunition, blankets and fuel for the fires. She would invent a secret passage that ran under the castle from the cellars and down to the sea. One of the Young Men would bring boats in under darkness with all the equipment and it would be carried up through the long dark tunnels with the sea booming in the background, threatening to flood the passageways and drown the men. Emily's mind was working so hard that she missed the polite enquiry from one of the curates.

'So, Miss Emily, and how do you intend to celebrate Christmas? Have read your Bible today about the birth of our Lord?' Mr Truscott beamed at the girl sitting opposite him and was a little shocked to be met by silence.

'Emily,' Papa called across the table, 'Emily, you are being spoken to, please answer the gentleman.' Their father was smiling but obviously a little concerned and when Emily still failed to answer he shouted rather loudly and all the children jumped from their reveries.

'Emily! Where are your manners?' Papa cried. Then realising that he was drawing unwelcomed glances from his guests modified his voice.

'Emily dear, are you unwell?' he asked quietly, but his eyes blazed at his daughter and his look was one of deep displeasure.

Emily had no idea how to regain her composure or cover the fact that she had been so lost in her thoughts that she had heard none of the previous conversation. She was aware that Papa had made an enquiry after her health and she knew from the silence around the table that she had made some awful social error. Looking around for help, she caught Charlotte's eye and her sister, jumping to her rescue, obliged by announcing.

'Emily said she felt a little sick earlier, , Papa. I think she has a headache.'

'Is this true, Emily?' Papa's voice softened, 'Are you ill, now, in the middle of our festivities?'

Emily looked at her plate, the lovely slice of goose, the potatoes and parsnips roasted in the goose fat, the Yorkshire puddings made with the batter that she had earlier helped to beat in a bowl for Tabby. She looked at the spoonful of forcemeat stuffing and the rich gravy and knew that she had only one choice. She could not let Papa down or make the visitors think that his children were lacking in good manners. Looking at her Papa and with tears brimming in her eyes, Emily replied.

'Yes, Papa, I am sorry but I do feel quite unwell. My head is aching and so are my teeth. I wonder if I could be excused from the table. I think that I had better retire to bed for the rest of the afternoon. Please excuse me everyone, I do apologise and hope I have not spoilt your special meal. Please forgive me.'

Aunt, too, was a little torn between the lovely pile of food on her plate and her retreating niece.

'Go straight up and get into bed Emily, I shall be up to see you before long with some herbs and some oil of cloves. Close the shutters and try and get some sleep. You will feel better tomorrow.'

The remaining children stared at Emily's plate, each one knowing that any one of them could have met the same fate. Poor Emily, no dinner, and probably no supper and Christmas Day in bed pretending to be ill. This was awful. They must concentrate and please Papa and his guests. They must eat their meals and make polite conversation when spoken to. They must each try to save a little food to smuggle up to their sister later in the day. Most of all, they must push all thoughts of the Islanders out of their heads for the next few hours. That would be the most difficult part.

Chapter Forty-Five
April 1829

April 21st dawned bright and breezy. It was a clear and sunny day and Charlotte's thirteenth birthday. Most birthdays were not noted particularly at this time, but passage from childhood to teenage years was seen by Papa and Aunt as a cause for celebration. Charlotte had survived all the dangers and diseases of childhood and was growing up into an intelligent, demure, neat and rather tiny, young woman.

For some weeks, Papa and Aunt had discussed between them a suitable gift to mark this important anniversary.

'The child is very clever,' acknowledged Mr Brontë, 'possibly gifted. She works hard at her lessons, reads and writes very well and is altogether a good and intelligent girl. She has done well in taking on the role of the eldest child and she is capable and protective over her younger brother and sisters.'

'She loves reading and writing, as you must have noticed Patrick,' Aunt answered, 'they all do. Do you think that we could afford to purchase some new pens and writing paper for her? I have already purchased a new pocket Bible to replace the one her Godmother gave her when she was little. It is beautifully bound and I have written a nice inscription inside the cover.'

'A wonderful gift, Elizabeth,' replied Mr Brontë, 'I know that she will treasure it always. I must think of something appropriate that I can perhaps repeat when the others reach this age.' He wandered off into his study for a while and then the slamming of the front door, half an hour later, signalled his leaving on an errand.

Mr Brontë was gone for the rest of that day and returned late in the evening on a drover's cart from Keighley, having made the long journey to Leeds and back. Under his arm was a large parcel and he had gone straight to his study on arrival. He emerged a while later, smiling and rubbing his hands together and calling for Tabby to produce some supper for a very hungry parson!

The birthday had now arrived and at the breakfast table Aunt produced her gift and kissed her niece, who was overcome with Aunt's kindness.

'It is beautiful Aunt, thank you so much,' Charlotte murmured as she turned the book over in her hands and felt the leather binding and read the personal inscription. 'I shall treasure it for my whole life, Aunt. Thank you. Look, everyone, look at this beautiful Bible that Aunt has given to me.'

The others each examined the book, holding it reverently in their hands, marvelling at the quality of it.

'We have gifts for you to,' whispered Anne, producing a wooden quill and a set of three new nibs. 'Look, Charlotte, these will help you write the second half of your Young Men's...em, these will help you to write your lessons,' Anne quickly corrected as Branwell and Emily glared at her. 'We all saved our pennies and walked all the way to Keighley with Aunt and chose them ourselves. Didn't we, Aunt?'

'You certainly did and now children, let us clear this table and start lessons. It may be Charlotte's birthday, but you must do your studies and your needlework. Emily, you have a piano lesson today and Branwell, you must copy some Greek verses. You will begin further Greek studies next month and you need to be preparing yourself. Come now girls, clear these pots away and let us get started.'

The girls groaned, but Branwell gave a shout of delight. He had been longing to begin studying the Greek poets and philosophers and felt that it would, again, put him before the girls in his studies and be the next step towards him becoming a true scholar. His sisters ignored his joy and Charlotte gathered together her gifts and carried them carefully away upstairs where she laid them on the large chest of drawers, in which most of the children's clothes were kept.

'I am thirteen today,' she thought, 'I shall be a young woman soon. I wonder if I shall start to grow taller, I am so small.'

Charlotte was already aware that she did not in her, or anyone else's opinion, have a pretty face or a tall, shapely figure. The loss of a few of her second teeth had made her reluctant to smile, especially amongst strangers. Branwell was often quite rude about his sisters' appearances, but he picked on Charlotte especially, as being "little, ugly and plain."

Although this hurt Charlotte deeply, she was realistic enough to realise that this was, in fact, an apt description of her. She knew that she would never be beautiful, that she would never be attractive and sophisticated in company, or witty and flirtatious. This knowledge of her physical unattractiveness saddened Charlotte more than she would care to admit but she tried to console herself with the conviction that she had other qualities that were almost as important.

Charlotte knew that she was intelligent, quick-thinking and had a good imagination. She was loyal and trustworthy and stood up for what she believed in. She cared about other people, especially those as plain and small as herself, and she felt that she understood how and why people behaved in the ways that they did. She already had a fierce independence and a willingness to learn and go out into the world in her thirst for knowledge. She also realised from her family, her reading and local events, that it was a male-dominated world into which she had been born and that to succeed in anything she would have to be as least twice as clever as the average man; twice as strong and twice as determined.

Descending the stairs, Charlotte turned her thoughts to her birthday and the set of pens the others had bought her. She had recently completed her tales of "The Twelve Adventurers" and "The Adventurous Island". She had also completed her

"History of the Year" and was half way through the "Tale of the Islanders". She and Branwell were writing more between themselves and had begun to drift from the stories and ideas of Emily and Anne. Charlotte could imagine a time when she and Branwell would create their own kingdoms and they would write and illustrate their own stories. Branwell was bright and enthusiastic about their writing and seemed a natural writing partner to Charlotte's more sophisticated and thoughtful stories.

Charlotte had mixed feelings about her brother. Branwell was irritating, arrogant and rude, at times, but there were moments when she felt an extraordinary need to almost mother and protect him. He was vulnerable beneath his childish flamboyance and Charlotte felt that his overconfidence and noisiness hid a much quieter, almost frightened little boy. To Charlotte, Branwell appeared rather overwhelmed at times and perhaps unable to bear all the responsibility and praise that, as the prized only son, he naturally received. Charlotte knew that she loved him and would defend him against anyone outside of the family who tried to hurt him, but, at times, he pleased and annoyed her in equal measure.

Sitting back down in the parlour Charlotte drew her chair to the table and extricated her writing and text book from the pile in the centre. Beside her Anne was copying her nine times table and repeating it softly as she wrote. Branwell was also copying some Greek verses from one of Papa's books. Emily was reading her geography text book and Aunt was doing some complicated tatting with her cottons and silks spilling over from her sewing cushion. The room was still and quiet as they all attended to their work.

The church clock struck the hours, the half hours and the quarters as they all continued with their labours. Emily sighed occasionally and Branwell grimaced and shuffled in his chair. Anne rose and as she softly chanted her tables she began to circulate the room, each step in rhythm to the numbers she repeated. Charlotte smiled and after a while got up to join her. Emily too, laid down her book and began to follow. Only

Branwell stayed with his head down and tongue out, copying the ancient words.

Aunt allowed this chanting and measured stepping around the table for a few minutes before insisting that they all sat down and got on.

'Oh Aunt,' complained Anne 'I can learn things so much easier when I walk at the same time.'

'I do too,' Emily joined in. 'Especially when we are reading and learning poetry. It is almost like dancing, it has a rhythm to it like music.'

'Aunt,' wailed Branwell, 'They are so noisy and I am trying to do my Greek lessons. Can you make them stop?'

'You are only copying a few letters' barked Emily at her brother, 'Anyone can copy Branwell you don't need silence, not unless you are stupid'

'Enough, Emily, stop that at once,' cried Aunt, 'Right girls, all of you out of here. It is nearly twelve o' clock and as it is Charlotte's birthday we will stop lessons for the day. You girls can go down into the village and buy some sugar and post a letter for me and then help Tabby prepare luncheon. This afternoon you can all go out for a walk on to the moors. Branwell you can stay in if you wish and study some more Greek and try to read some of your father's book.'

Branwell looked horrified. 'Oh no, Aunt, It's alright. I will work until lunch time, whilst the girls are out and then I will go for a walk with them this afternoon. I don't mind. You can have some peace and quiet Aunt and I will make sure that they don't go too far or come to any danger whilst we are out.'

The girls fled the room before one of them was tempted to strangle their brother.

Aunt beamed at her nephew. 'If you are sure Branwell, you are such a good boy. I hope the girls are grateful for all that you do for them. You are becoming a very charming young man. Your Papa and I are so proud of you, and here you are studying Greek. My, my you are such a clever young fellow.'

Chapter Forty-Six
Charlotte's Birthday

Luckily the girls missed this part of the exchange as they were busy fetching their cloaks, but when Emily went back in to the parlour for some money from Aunt, she was most annoyed to be reminded how clever Branwell was and that he would be coming out with them that afternoon as their protector.

'You are all old enough to go on your own these days and Tabby does not walk as well as she did,' explained Aunt, to Branwell and Emily, 'She says that you tire her out. But if you have no adult present you must not go too far and you are all safer when your brother is with you. It is a lovely day, if a little breezy. The fresh air will do you all good. Your Papa should be back by five o'clock and we shall be having a treat for tea in celebration or our birthday girl. Now off you go Emily and don't you girls talk to any strangers in the village or be getting involved in any games. You may also post this letter for me and please ask the postmaster about my parcel from Penzance, I have still not received it.'

Emily glared at the grinning Branwell and left to join Anne and Charlotte waiting by the garden gate.

'The boy is coming with us this afternoon, Aunt's orders,' complained Emily, 'He is such a snide, creeping round Aunt and making her think that he is so special.'

Anne and Charlotte slipped their arms through Emily's. 'Sorry Emily,' chided Charlotte. 'I know he can be a pain, but you know, we all know, that boys are held in much higher regard than us girls. It's not really his fault. Branwell will be expected to take over as head of the family if and when anything happens to Papa. We may be grateful one day for his help and protection. In the mean time we just have to put up with his deviousness. He is a bright boy and he will no doubt do very well in life. He is talented.'

'He irritates me beyond measure,' complained Emily.

'He irritates all of us, Emily,' murmured Anne. 'I think that Papa should perhaps send him to school where he would have to survive amongst other boys and would not be the centre of attention. I wonder that Papa does not send him to Woodhouse Grove School.

'I think it might be too costly,' replied Charlotte, 'or perhaps Papa has had enough of sending his children to boarding school. Look what happened last time!'

The girls walked on in silence before Anne remarked.

'Perhaps it is because Papa is so clever that he can teach Branwell everything he needs to know and he can thus save the expense of sending him off to be educated.'

'Do you want to know what I think?' asked Emily. 'I think Papa will keep him at home for as long as possible. He and Aunt dote on their precious boy. It is us that will be sent away to be educated as teachers or governesses and Branwell will be kept pampered at home, just because he is a boy. It is so unfair.'

Emily wrenched her arms from her sisters' hold and marched off back up the street, with them staring after her. Anne made to follow but Charlotte held her back.

'Leave her, Anne, when she is cross like this there is no reasoning with her. Unfortunately, she sees all of Branwell's bad points and none of the good.'

'What good bits are there?' enquired Anne innocently. 'I think Emily is right, he is spoilt and pampered and he should jolly well treat us girls with more respect.' With that, she too pulled away from Charlotte and ran back up the street to follow Emily.

Charlotte stood alone at the top of the main street staring after her sisters. Well, charming! She thought and on my birthday too! Now none of her siblings were happy and no-one wanted to talk to her. She carried on to the post office and then the grocers and it wasn't until the sugar was weighed out and wrapped that she realised that Emily was still carrying the money.

The children all gathered in the parlour for a very subdued lunch and hardly spoke to one another. Aunt was cheerful and appeared quite oblivious to the cool atmosphere.

'Now children, wrap up warm this afternoon. You can leave at two o'clock but be back for five, in time for tea with your Papa. Are you having a good birthday Charlotte?

Charlotte looked at Aunt and sudden tears began to well up. She was feeling quite distressed and saddened by her brother and sisters' moods. They were spoiling her day and she knew that they would all argue on their walk and it would be extremely unpleasant.

'Yes, thank you Aunt,' she whispered. 'I am having a wonderful day.'

The silent meal finally ended and Aunt rose and left them with a reminder to clear the table and help Tabby wash the pots. Emily and Anne immediately began to argue with Branwell and the three of them swopped insults until Charlotte could stand no more and fled from the room in tears.

The warring children stopped and looked at each other in dismay. Anne was the first to comment.

'What are we doing? It is Charlotte's birthday and here we are fighting amongst ourselves. Oh Emily, do you think we have upset her? We shouldn't have left her in the village and we shouldn't be arguing on her birthday. Branwell, you go and bring her back. Let's stop quarrelling and all go out for a nice walk together.'

Branwell stood up, as quick to peace and harmony as he was to anger and discord. He left the room calling Charlotte's name.

Emily sat stern-faced at the table for another minute before saying softly to her sister.

'You are right, Anne, as always. We have been horrid to Charlotte, today of all days. We must make it up to her. I am quite ashamed of myself and Charlotte is so good to us. I will finish clearing the table and you and Branwell meet me outside with her in ten minutes.'

Fifteen minutes later, Aunt stood in one of the back bedrooms watching her four charges setting out over the fields at the back of the house. Branwell and Charlotte were arm in arm and behind them ran Emily and Anne with their arms around each other's waists. The four were laughing and calling to each other, frequently stopping to tie a shoe lace or wrap their cloaks around them against the wind.

So, thought Aunt Branwell, another crisis over. Whatever it was that had upset them all and caused their silent meal time had vanished and peace was restored. What strange little creatures they were. Their capacity to laugh and cry was like sunshine and rain, and just as unpredictable.

By half past five that afternoon, four laughing and happy children were lined up in the hallway outside of the parlour. The door was firmly shut and instructions not to enter were issued by Tabby.

'Mr Brontë and Miss Branwell, sez as you mun wait outside 'til they is ready for thi,' announced Tabby beaming at some secret that she knew and they did not.

This had never happened before and the children were excited and thrilled by the prospect of what was happening inside the room. At last the door was flung open by Papa with a great flourish and a bow, as he stood back to allow the children to enter. Inside the table was set with the best tea service and little bunches of spring flowers stood in fancy pots. A warm loaf of bread, muffins and scones were piled on to plates and little pots of jam, a dish of boiled eggs and a bowl of clotted cream completed the meal. However, as well as the food and fancy tableware, laid in front of Charlotte's place and with her name standing out in large letters was a square package carefully wrapped and with a note attached. Charlotte shook as she sat down and gazed at the parcel. Papa's beaming smile let her know that this was a special gift from him to his eldest child.

As usual, everyone bowed their heads whilst Papa said Grace, his loud Irish tones ringing out over their heads. Charlotte opened one eye and stared at the paper in front of her overwhelmed with delight and anticipation. There was a sudden silence as Papa's voice stopped and all eyes turned to Charlotte. With trembling hands she lifted the note; a beautifully decorated card with a simple message in her father's neat handwriting. Bringing it up close to her weak eyes Charlotte read 'To my beautiful daughter Charlotte on her special day, a gift that will last for ever, from your loving Papa.'

The tears that so easily sprang to Charlotte's eyes once again blurred her vision and she felt a huge lump begin to form in her throat.

'Open it, Charlotte, Open it at once!' shouted Branwell from across the table. 'Yes, Charlotte open it quickly, we must know what it is,' cried Anne.

With tears and smiles Charlotte carefully unwrapped the heavy object and suddenly, as the paper fell away there, laid before her, was the most beautiful, the most exquisite and the most wonderful gift Charlotte had ever seen or could ever have wished for.

There before her was the one thing she wanted in all the world, the gift that was hers and hers alone; the means by which she could write, could really write as she had never written before and would continue to do so for the rest of her life. Before her was a beautiful wooden writing desk.

For a minute Charlotte just sat and stared at this gift, too overcome to speak. The box measured about fourteen inches wide and nine inches high at its highest edge. It was veneered in mahogany inlaid with a thin line of brass. The desk was lacquered and polished until it shone. It had a brass lock with a tiny key and on the lid, for all to see was a brass plate with the legend, C Brontë, engraved into the metal.

'Look inside, Charlotte, what is inside!' shouted Branwell excitedly.

Charlotte carefully turned the key and lifted back the lid which revealed a beautiful purple, velvet surface on which she could rest her paper and write her letters and stories. The writing desk was designed so that the inside could be lifted out to reveal a series of divided compartments. Only one was filled and it held a glass inkwell containing black, Indian ink. There were various grooves for storing pens and quills and little spaces for keeping wafers and sealing wax, envelopes and papers.

Charlotte was completely overwhelmed and her eyes glistened as she gazed at her proud father, her smiling Aunt and her grinning siblings. This was the happiest she had ever felt and for once all the sadness and worries of the last few years disappeared.

'Over time, you will be able to fill it with various writing materials, my dear and perhaps a little seal and a letter opener. It should last you your whole life time.' Papa smiled across the table at his eldest daughter. Even he had not realised the effect this beautiful gift would have. Charlotte looked happier than he had ever seen her.

'Thank you, Papa, thank you so much,' Charlotte breathed. 'It is the most beautiful thing that I have ever seen. I cannot believe that it belongs to me.'

'It has your name on it,' laughed Emily. 'What a shame, now we won't be able to borrow it.'

'I don't think that I will ever be able to let it out of my sight,' murmured Charlotte in reply.

'I am hungry,' came Branwell's voice, 'can we start tea now Papa?'

'Yes, of course, my boy. Come now children, let us devour this wonderful meal that Tabby and Aunt have organised.'

Throughout the meal, Papa kept looking across at Charlotte and noted that she ate nothing. Her eyes remained fixed on her writing desk. He was pleased, very pleased, that he had chosen well and had brought her so much happiness. If he had the money, he might repeat this idea for each of his children in turn on their birthday. It would encourage their studies and reward them for all their hard work. He was proud of them all and he beamed around the table at his fine, young family.

At that moment, Charlotte felt that the future would be a much better time for them all and that a lot of it would be spent in creating and writing, using her beautiful desk. She would treasure it forever and hoped that writing would become a major part of her life, not as work or as a chore but as a life-long pleasure. She would write because it was the most natural thing for her to do; her greatest pleasure and her deepest enjoyment. She would write throughout her life and in her writing all her ideas, thoughts and feelings would have free expression. She would write because she had to, because she could not stop herself and as she beamed at her family seated around the table, Charlotte felt that nothing in the future could spoil this moment; that the past, her childhood, was behind her and from now on, surely, all would be well?

Haworth parsonage from the Graveyard.

The church of St Michael and All Angels as it is today.

Ponden Hall.

Haworth moors near Penistone Crags.

Haworth Moor.

The Parlour in Haworth Parsonage showing the original dining table used by the Brontë family and on which the sisters later wrote their novels.

The children's study.

Charlotte's writing desk.

Haworth Main Street.

Path above the ruins of Top Withins.

Rev. Patrick Brontë in old age.

The font from the Bell Chapel Church at Thornton where the youngest five Brontë children where baptised.

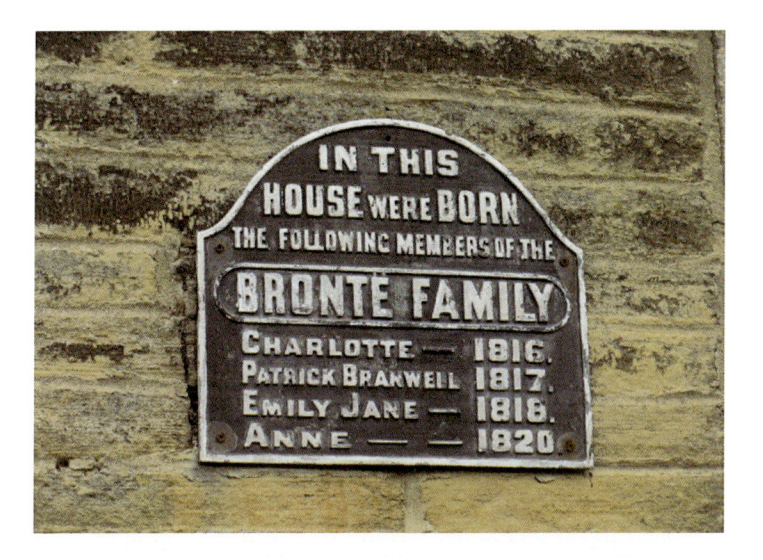

The plaque on the wall of the house in Thornton where
Charlotte, Branwell, Emily and Anne were each born.

View from one of the stone windows in Top Withins Farm.

The Hallway of Haworth Parsonage.

Haworth Parsonage.

Church Street, Haworth.

One of the miniature books written and constructed by the Brontë children.

The ruin of Top Withins as it is today.

Haworth Graveyard in the Autumn.

Haworth Moor with the ruin of Top Withins in the distance.